THE McGRAW-HILL INTERNATIONAL SERIES IN SOFTWARE ENGINEERING

Consulting Editor

Professor D. Ince
The Open University

Titles in this Series

Further titles in this Series are listed at the back of the book

SAFER C:
Developing Software for High-integrity and Safety-critical Systems

Les Hatton

Programming Research Ltd

McGRAW-HILL BOOK COMPANY

London · New York · St Louis · San Francisco · Auckland
Bogotá · Caracas · Lisbon · Madrid · Mexico · Milan
Montreal · New Delhi · Panama · Paris · San Juan · São Paulo
Singapore · Sydney · Tokyo · Toronto

Published by
McGRAW-HILL Book Company Europe
Shoppenhangers Road, Maidenhead, Berkshire, SL6 2QL, England
Telephone 01628 23432
Fax 01628 770224

British Library Cataloguing in Publication Data
Hatton, L.
  Safer C: Developing Software for
  High-integrity and Safety-critical
  Systems.—(McGraw-Hill International
  Series in Software Engineering)
  I. Title II. Series
  005.133

  ISBN 0-07-707640-0

Library of Congress Cataloging-in-Publication Data
Hatton, Les,
    Safer C: developing software for high-integrity and safety-critical
  systems / Les Hatton.
      p. cm.—(The McGraw-Hill international series in software
  engineering)
      Includes bibliographical references and index.
      ISBN 0-07-707640-0
      1. Computer software—Reliability. 2. Computer software—
  Development. 3. C (Computer program language). 4. System safety.
  I. Title. II. Series.
  QA76.76.R44H38   1994
  005.13′3—dc20   94-23202
                                                              CIP

Reprinted 1997
Typeset by Alden Multimedia, Northampton, England
and printed and bound in Great Britain at the University Press, Cambridge

Printed on permanent paper in compliance with ISO Standard 9706

This book is dedicated to all those people who start hyperventilating when told their plane is being controlled by software.

CONTENTS

PREFACE

If this book has any theme, it is this:

> The use of C in safety-related or high-integrity systems is not recommended without severe and automatically enforceable constraints. However, if these are present using the formidable tool support for C, the best available evidence suggests that it is then possible to write software of *at least* as high intrinsic quality and consistency as with other commonly used languages.

This book attempts to distil these constraints from the vast body of existing experience with this language into a concise and consistent form of immediate applicability to the C developer, and thus attempts to define good working practice. In this regard, no distinction is made between developers working in safety-related areas and those working in non-safety-related areas. For a developer working in a safety-related area, following known good defensive practice should be mandatory; for his or her counterpart in non-safety-related development, it is merely prudent. Ignoring good defensive practice is always wrong, always expensive and frequently dangerous. In common with current practice, high-integrity systems, as included in the title of the book, are treated here as requiring the same duty of care as the lower levels of safety-related systems, as discussed in Chapter 1, and are implicitly treated as such throughout the book.

The origins of this book lie in my experience in leading a million line FORTRAN 77 development project in seismic data processing in the early 1980s (Hatton, 1988). Throughout this project, the same problems would re-occur with monotonous regularity. Furthermore, exchanging views with developers in other companies at conferences and seminars confirmed that everybody else was experiencing them as well. It became obvious that the fundamental principle of learning from the mistakes of others was not terribly well established in the software world and indeed was a symptom of an immature profession. My colleagues and I tried everything to ensure the success of the project, including judicious use of formal methods, 4GLs and a number of other somewhat tarnished silver bullets. The project ultimately succeeded, but could have been done considerably more cheaply and more reliably if the techniques and accumulated experience now collected in this book had been available in a more easily accessible form.

In that application area, although the language concerned was FORTRAN 77, the essence of good practice was and remains essentially language independent:

Identify dangerous practice and ruthlessly eliminate it.

If the development language is comparatively more unreliable in use, there is simply more to eliminate before the situation becomes tolerable. From a safety point of view, this book is not really concerned with how safe the standard language is, *but how safe it can be made.*

All of this has become particularly relevant at the time of writing of this book, as many well-intentioned software quality initiatives are in progress. These include ISO 9001 in Europe and the Carnegie-Mellon Capability Maturity Model in the USA. There are also moves afoot to develop these two paradigms for software process maturity. Unfortunately, such initiatives suffer from one of the central failings of software development in its quest to become a branch of engineering, in that they can become an end in themselves. They are therefore all too frequently viewed as an end rather than a beginning. If I had a dollar or an ECU for every time I have heard the word 'quality' in the last twelve months, this would be a book of entirely altruistic origin. In this regard, the quality revolution is in great danger of becoming yet another failed silver bullet. As we are reminded by the admirable Fred Brooks, there aren't any. When all the dross is cleared to one side, the fundamental principles are very simple, just as they are in more mature branches of engineering. They just have to be followed, but with the best will in the world, perfection will always elude us.

The main contributing factors to the appearance of this book were:

- A large and growing body of evidence gleaned by the author from auditing millions of lines of C code from numerous different industries around the world which shows that there is currently little relationship between the quality of the software process and the *intrinsic* quality of the resulting code.
- The widespread trend of adopting C or even C++ for safety-critical systems for a variety of reasons which were seen as compelling by the prospective users but which, on their own, do not constitute a satisfactory justification.

The background behind the above two statements appears in the body of this book, but one thing at least is very clear. Taken together, these two points suggest that using C with conventional quality control is simply unsuitable for any safety-related development. Only by identifying and eliminating potential problems can any language be taken seriously in critical, or to be frank, any other, situations. C has one massive advantage over all languages in this regard. There is a huge amount of experience with C development spread over quite spectacularly diverse application areas. This has led to certainly the best tool support of any language, and this in turn enables so many of the pitfalls to be avoided, provided the tools are used in a systematic and verifiable manner, of course.

At this stage, I must in all fairness declare a commercial interest in one such tool, QA C, as one of its designers and implementors. However, this is irrelevant to the contents of the book, in so far as no one tool solves all the problems there are, but the judicious use of the tools described in this book or their equivalent will go a long way towards it. Use of QA C on many packages around the world did contribute most of the measurements reported in this book, however. The tools described here are by no means all that are available, but I have had direct or close indirect experience with these and they are capable of implementing all of the techniques described in this book. If you don't have access to any or all of them, the techniques can still be used, but will require either manual application or configuration of other tools, which I didn't have space for. *Either way, the important thing is that C is full of holes, but we know where just about all of them are and we know how to plug most of them, and that's one of the primary functions of this book.* It is most emphatically not an academic text in the sense of presenting merely ideas, however good. It is about the application of good engineering practice by standing on the shoulders of all those people who found the problems in the first place and had the foresight to document them.

The book also attempts to put intrinsic product quality into the context of quality systems generally. I have been going quietly crazy at many conferences listening to the word 'quality' being rapidly devalued to the extent that at one stage I was considering offering an award for the most gratuitous use of the word 'quality' in a software engineering presentation. There is no sign that this trend will stop and 'quality' may well go the way of 'database' in the 1970s and 'CASE' in the 1980s unless we are very, very careful about our claims.

Many people in many companies contributed to the experience related in this book. I can't list them all, but I should like to single out particularly my colleagues at Programming Research, Sean Corfield, Norman Clancy, Grant Elliott, Robert Consoli, Charles Robinson, Andrew Ritchie and Paul Blundell (who isn't a programmer but believes in software quality enough to try and make a living out of it). I owe a particularly large debt to Sean, who has an encyclopaedic knowledge of C (and C++) and came up with many examples, suggestions, insights and horror stories as well as critically reading this book from top to tail. As the lead author of the British Standards Institute Model C Implementation and with years of experiencing, writing and suffering from compilers, he is in a better position than just about anybody to know. An impromptu chat on C with Sean usually leads to an hour with a copy of the standard and an ice-pack. If it's C++, make that two hours, an ice-pack and a large gin and tonic. On the legal side, Anthony Garrod, a partner at Clyde & Co. and specialist in legal matters, kindly agreed to write the last chapter and shared many valuable insights, not to mention guitar music.

Lastly, I should also like to acknowledge many conversations over the years with a number of other people who share the same kinds of concerns. In alphabetical order these include Tom Anderson, David Blyth, Norman Fenton, Michiel van Genuchten, John Harrowven, Tony Hoare, Tim Hopkins, Darrell Ince, Derek Jones (of Knowledge Systems and one of the other contributors to the Model C implementation), Bev Littlewood, Ian Nussbaum, Dave Sayers, Ian Shannon, John Shore, John Souter, Dave Wilkins and Nicholas Zvegintzov. David Blyth and Ian Nussbaum in particular provided much valuable feedback on some sections of this book, whilst Derek Jones kindly provided numerous preprints of his own work in standardization which contributed significantly to my understanding of some of the more abstract problem areas, and I have freely quoted him. Two anonymous reviewers also provided further valuable feedback and caught quite a few things I had missed. Tony Hoare put my longstanding unease with software into a more formal context in many conversations over Wolfson College lunches, and Tim Hopkins proved to me repeatedly, that there is no software in the world, in any language, on any computer, that he can't break in about 30 seconds, often by simply sitting down at the machine. I don't know how he does it, but I'm convinced that software is actually terrified of him. He is also an absolute goldmine of information about numerical computation and its rather erratic implementation. If I've forgotten anybody, my sincere apologies. Finally, books such as *C Traps and Pitfalls* by Andrew Koenig remain a constant reminder of programmer fallibility, as well as an inspirational example of clear writing. If only language designers would think more of reliability than features and ... whoops, there goes another flying pig.

I must justify one perhaps eccentric act. The references to the standard document for the C programming language made in this book refer to the ISO version, but I have numbered any such references as they originally appeared in the ANSI standard, (in general, you add 3 to the first number of the ANSI document item to get the equivalent ISO item so $4.9.4.4^{ANSI} = 7.9.4.4^{ISO}$, although the wording is sometimes slightly different). The reason for this was that at the time of writing, those people who had a copy of the standard invariably had the ANSI document but not the ISO document, so I attempted to match the book to current practice! Another very good reason for using the ANSI document where possible, is that the excellent Rationale (more later) was inexplicably removed from the ISO version. Note that in case I have inadvertently misquoted or misspelt items through error, the original ISO C standard document should be taken as the correct source.

Finally, I would like to acknowledge the deep debt I owe to Gillian, Leo, Felix and Isabelle who inevitably have to pay for the literary aspirations of their husband/ daddy. This isn't the first time those aspirations have spilled over into their lives but if their and everybody else's safety is improved by just a tiny bit as a result of experience culled from this book, it would have repaid itself a thousand times over. If you think this sounds evangelical, you're right. Each and every one of us involved in any kind of safety-related or high-integrity software development must do our absolute very best as software becomes more pervasive and the effects of its failure more traumatic. Nothing else is acceptable, and even that isn't good enough.

Les Hatton
les_hatton@prqa.co.uk

TRADEMARKS

DC-9 is a trademark of McDonnell Douglas.

Fender is a trademark of Fender Ltd.

MS-DOS is a trademark of Microsoft Corporation.

PC/AT is a trademark of International Business Machines Corporation.

PDP-11 is a trademark of DEC.

Smalltalk is a trademark of Xerox.

Sparcstation is a trademark of Sun Microsystems, Inc.

Stratocaster is a trademark of Fender Ltd.

Sun is a trademark of Sun Microsystems, Inc.

UNIX is a trademark of American Telephone and Telegraph Corporation.

VMS is a trademark of Digital Equipment Corporation.

Word is a trademark of Microsoft Corporation.

X-Windows is a trademark of Massachusetts Institute of Technology.

SAFETY AND STANDARDIZATION IN SOFTWARE-CONTROLLED SYSTEMS

The last few years has seen intense efforts at standardization throughout the world as open systems have naturally assumed a more important role than the proprietary systems they replaced. The most important vehicle for standardization generally has been the UNIX operating system. Prior to that, the only form of standardization of which users were aware was either language standardization through the medium of ANSI (American National Standards Institute) or ISO (International Organization for Standardization), or *de facto* standards whereby a manufacturer's product would become so widespread as to be as effective as a formal standard. Such *de facto* standards were particularly effective when the specifications were placed in the public domain, for example, as was the case with Sun Microsystems and NFS (Network File System). Numerous other important *de facto* standards exist, such as X-Windows for graphical user interfaces.

Since 1983, when AT&T were at last allowed to market the UNIX operating system, commercial users around the world became aware of the then unique ability of UNIX to render the target hardware effectively irrelevant. This was truly revolutionary and effectively created the environment whereby other ambitious efforts at standardization could flourish. Another result of the rapid growth of this portable operating system, of particular importance to this book, was the intimate relationship between the C language and the UNIX operating system. The most natural language to use with UNIX is C. It is usually free, is accompanied by highly reliable compilers and is fashionable. The resulting temptation is simply too much, and is one of the contributing factors to the increasing use of C in safety-related systems: a trend not welcomed by the safety-related community in general, but in the author's experience widely considered to be unavoidable by the developers concerned. Other reasons most frequently given to the author in support of this will be discussed later.

The problem with the explosive growth in standardization efforts in the 1980s and 1990s is that there are now a bewildering number with which to contend. As at least one famous computer scientist has said, '... the nice thing about standards is that there is such a wide variety to choose from'. In contrast, for safety-related development, there is unusually little guidance. In consequence, this book, as a prelude to its real aim of discussing C in a safety-related context, will attempt to cover those standardization efforts of relevance, although this will be a rather generalized discussion as there are currently no formal standards for safety-related work. It is to be hoped that this extraordinary situation will be corrected as soon as possible.

There are several areas in which such standardization efforts are of interest to safety-related development, notably:

- General efforts in process and product standardization.
- Specifically safety-related standardization initiatives.
- Measurement standardization initiatives.

Before focusing on specifically safety-related or measurement initiatives, it will be useful to review generally relevant standardization efforts in areas as apparently intangible as the software development process itself (the distinction between process and product will be made shortly). All current draft safety-related standards explicitly discuss the importance of the *software process* at some length and it is of considerable importance to understand the implications of this. Following this, those standardization initiatives specifically related to safety will be discussed, and also measurement standardization initiatives. It will become apparent in this discussion that of all standardization efforts, *product* standardization is in its infancy and one of the main aims of this book will be to show first of all how variable software product quality is and second, what can be done about it. From this, suggested standards for C development in a safety-related context will be presented in Chapter 5. The author would emphasize, however, that everything presented in this book is measurement driven, this being one of the great advantages of working directly with source code, and so the discussion of a measurement methodology standard is also highly relevant.

Before finally diving into process, product and the rest, it is important to distinguish here between software quality and safety. When discussing software process the word quality appears everywhere, even more frequently than commas. The reader should understand that software quality is driving a great sub-culture within software engineering, and, like all new technologies, hides a lot of cracks and even more unfulfilled promises. It is certainly true that software process control and software quality are incorrectly seen by many people as synonymous. It is also true, as has been said already, that all current draft safety standards emphasize the importance of a well-defined software process, but the reader should be aware that it is perfectly possible to define a complete, consistent and hopelessly unsafe process for the development of software. Software safety, like safety in other engineering disciplines, is about the enforced avoidance of known problems, the avoidance of needless complexity and the adherence to simple and well-established engineering principles which are observed to behave safely. It should not be assumed that having a well-defined and certified software process will be sufficient to produce the safest software possible, but it helps.

1.1 INTRODUCTION

Computer safety and reliability is a big topic in the 1990s. It makes headlines varying from billion dollar telephone outages, to misdirected space craft, to rogue financial transactions. As the years pass, it will get bigger still as software plays an ever more intrusive role in people's lives and affairs, through areas such as braking and ignition systems in cars, control systems in household appliances and communications to name but a few. The scope of these systems is extraordinarily wide, as some of the following problem areas show.

1.1.1 Just a few little problems

Some aerospace bugs of note

- Gemini V splashed down 100 miles off course because the programmers forgot that the Earth moved.
- A moonshot was forced way off course by a FORTRAN format error.
- A CMOS memory chip on the DC-9 aircraft was discovered to be sending erroneous messages to the Digital Flight Guidance Computer.
- On 9 December 1991, the Hubble Space Telescope shut itself down because the computer control system issued a command to redirect the antenna more quickly than a software imposed limit allowed.
- The launch of the first space shuttle was delayed by a software error.

It is very educational to follow NASA's heroic battle against software errors in the last 20 years. That their efforts are slowly paying dividends is well illustrated by a study reported by the University of Maryland's Software Engineering Laboratory when studying 80 software projects used for ground-based tracking of space missions at NASA's Goddard Space Center, as shown in Fig. 1.1.

This diagram should amply prepare the reader for the awful static fault rates in modern commercially available software reported in Chapter 4. *The striking thing about Fig. 1.1 is that most of the improvement has come by improving the really bad ones rather than the quite good ones.* If the above rate of improvement continues, errors should be pretty rare by about 2050. It is a sobering thought that progress is so slow, even with NASA's resources and experience. The reader is referred to Keller (1993) for an excellent account of the extraordinary ends to which NASA shuttle engineers now go to eliminate error and risk.

Some defence bugs of note

- NORAD (North American Defence Command), 5 October 1960. Went to 99.9% alert when programmers forgot about the rising Moon and it triggered the defence radars.

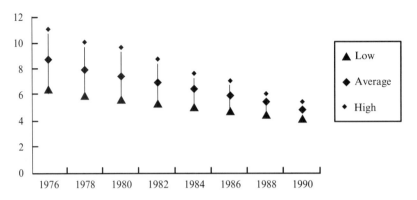

Figure 1.1 Errors per 1000 lines at NASA Goddard 1978–1990 (graph published in the December 1991 special issue of *Business Week*, showing the drop in software errors at NASA Goddard).

- NORAD, 3 June 1980. Put all systems at full alert and threatened to launch everything.
- NORAD, 6 June 1980. Did it again. The problem was traced to a software fault in a communications integrated circuit.
- The Royal Signals and Radar Establishment (RSRE), now the Defence Research Agency (DRA), a part of the UK Ministry of Defence (MOD), performed a study of NATO software in the early 1980s using static analysis techniques (see later). Of the modules sampled, 1 in 10 were found to contain errors and of those 1 in 20 (i.e. 1 in 200 overall), had errors serious enough to result in loss of a vehicle or plant! (This is the accountant's definition of plant, not the green leafy things.) The same findings were made whether the code came from Britain, the USA or Germany. What really roused the MOD, however, were several 'near-miss' accidents, including one involving 'general ordnance' which might have resulted in hundreds of deaths. Further studies determined that incidents were associated, with approximately equal frequency, with three kinds of problem: incorrect or incomplete specifications, errors in programs and 'unexpected functionality' from microprocessors. This latter category is one of the author's favourite euphemisms and means that the microprocessor did not behave in the same way as its assembly language reference implied. (There are notorious errors in the microprocessors used in everyday PCs.)

Before the American SDI (Strategic Defense Initiative) was finally cancelled, it is amusing to compare its estimated requirement of 30 million lines of error-free software with the above. This requirement is at least three orders of magnitude better than has ever been achieved.

Miscellaneous problems

- An estimated 200 people have been killed or maimed so far in industrial control environments by bugs in microprocessor or application software (RSRE, 1988). At the time of writing, the author had been told of an incident whereby as a result of having its control software 'enhanced', an industrial robot on a rugged vehicle production line had thrown a vehicle on top of the safety inspector's hut, who had seconds earlier vacated it. A number of lessons were learnt here, not the least of which that a four-wheel drive vehicle is not a creature of the air.

- Severe flooding killed six people in 1983 when a dam stored too much water as a result of an error in snow-melting calculation software.
- A London Docklands automatic train was left hanging over a roadway with its doors open after system bugs were encountered. This was the so-called *fail-safe* mode. This occurred just one week before it was due to be opened by the Queen. The opening went ahead under manual control (*Guardian*, 29 July 1987). The author has since been on this train, and confesses to a state of mild panic throughout the journey, although no problems were encountered.
- A bug in the Digital VMS security module allowed the 'Chaos Computer Club' to wreak havoc in the NASA space physics analysis network (*Digital Review*, 23 November 1987).
- The Bank of America abandoned its $100 million trust department software system as being untenable in April 1988. In early 1993, the London Stock Exchange abandoned its Taurus automatic trading system for similar reasons (*plus ça change, plus c'est la même chose . . .*).
- The Australian Commonwealth Bank doubled all debits and credits during the night of 25 February 1988. This particular incident prompted the bank computer manager to make the now famous quote 'the effects of software errors are limited only by the imagination . . .'.
- In December 1988, a bug in an automatic bank teller of two of the largest banks in the UK created chaos among the many customers making use of these services, refusing service, halting the system for hours on end and so on.
- On 24 November 1991, the UK newspaper *The Independent* reported that a computer error at the Sellafield nuclear reprocessing plant caused radiation safety doors to be opened accidentally (fortunately affecting no one).
- In July 1991, a software error led to long distance telephone bills ten times too large being issued by US West. Three days passed before this was caught.

Concerning limits of the imagination, the next category of errors waiting to happen includes a number of ones relating to date and time:

- Some experts suggest that people should withdraw all their money from banks on 31 December 1999 as COBOL, the principle and ancient programming language used to implement many existing systems, only has a two-character year field.
- The Ada time-of-year field will return an error after the year 2099.
- MS-DOS may have problems after 31 December 2048.
- A central factor in the great financial crash of October 1987 was the huge volume of automatic trading which could be generated (even a single venerable IBM PC/ AT can trade up to three million shares a minute). No feedback control appears to have been built into these systems. This is in stark contrast to some systems which only had a two-character field for points change during a day and consequently failed to register that anything amiss was happening.

While on the subject of October 1987, the following fascinating quotation appeared on British television:

Of course there won't be a hurricane in England
(Michael Fish, London Weather Centre, 15 October 1987)

Just a few hours later, the worst storm since 1703 uprooted over 30 per cent of the trees in southern England with peak wind speeds of around $160 \, \text{km} \, \text{h}^{-1}$. One of the author's local parks lost 15 000 out of 22 000 trees and presented a scene of indescribable devastation, leaving the park's maintenance staff in tears. The author happened to be in New Orleans at a conference at the time, sipping a Margarita in $34 \, ^\circ\text{C}$, blissfully unaware that his fence was taking to the air like a startled condor and an immense 250-year-old oak tree at the bottom of his garden was bending like a sapling. A spokesperson for the UK Meteorological Office said, 'The Cyber 205 is not an easy machine to work with but all computers are fallible. ... Control Data did not comment.' (*Computer News*, 22 October 1987). This last exchange reveals an endemic problem with computer users: *the spokesperson blamed the machine, and not its software*. It is interesting to note that from the same input data, the French forecasting service predicted the storm track with an accuracy of about 16 km, and, along with other European forecasting services, were warning people not to visit Britain under any circumstances at about the same time as the now justifiably famous quote above was made. (The UK Meteorological Office's prediction was over 160 km from the correct storm track.)

The author had some experience of the intractability of weather prediction software while working as a numerical weather prediction scientist in 1973–74 at the UK Meteorological Office, his first real job. While rewriting a forecasting model in a new coordinate system, he discovered a gross error in the existing model whereby the non-linear terms in the governing fluid equations of motion, the Navier–Stokes equations, shown in their compact majesty as Fig. 1.2, were zeroed every other time step. This error is indeed gross, in that the non-linear terms are entirely responsible for the weather: without them, the atmosphere would essentially degenerate to hydrostatic equilibrium. Amidst expectations of immediate fame and fortune, the correction (an accidental transposition of two assembler statements), was duly made and a 72 hour forecast rerun. The differences were almost undetectable. To this day, the author does not fully understand why and has an abiding distrust of weather forecasting software, not to mention most other software. A suitable ending to this story is that 20 years later, a full appreciation of chaos and the so-called 'butterfly effect', whereby the beat of a butterfly's wings on one side of the world can lead to a major environmental catastrophe on the other side, suggests that the atmosphere may not be very predictable anyway, although it is expected to lead to a major growth industry in insurance for winged insects.

One of the author's favourite software problems is the following which led to a warehouse being lost. In 1985, an input error in the master inventory program of Montgomery Ward caused an entire distribution warehouse in Redding, California, to go missing. No trucks arrived to deliver or take goods away for *three*

$$\frac{\partial \boldsymbol{u}}{\partial t} + (\boldsymbol{u} \cdot \nabla)\boldsymbol{u} = -\frac{1}{\rho}\nabla p + \nu \nabla^2 \boldsymbol{u}$$

Figure 1.2 The Navier–Stokes equations of fluid dynamics. This formidably intractable set of equations is responsible for making weather forecasting somewhat hit and miss. They describe the dynamical relationship between $\boldsymbol{u}$, the velocity vector, p, the pressure, ρ, the density and ν, the kinematic viscosity of a fluid. In essence, the second term on the left is responsible for generating the weather.

years. The staff of the warehouse didn't complain as they were still getting paid and all assumed they were about to be made redundant. Given that software issues rarely occur in isolation, it is amusing to contemplate whether a similar situation exists elsewhere at the present time.

And finally, to close this section on a somewhat frivolous note: 'Computer program drives Arab to sexual exhaustion' (*Computer Talk,* 1 February 1988). The problem here was an error in the gentleman's harem organization program which led to his downfall. Happily, he recovered, and like all great software engineers was completely unrepentant and had a few new updates up his sleeve.

For an appreciation of the real scale of current failure of computer-based systems, the reader should study the excellent and pioneering regular review by Neumann (1993). Here, each quarter, a sample of the world's recent software failures, including some of the above, is presented with analysis. Such reviews as this are extremely valuable in spreading awareness that there is a problem and that it is not diminishing,[1] and in disseminating causal analysis so that lessons can be learned and similar problems avoided in future.

Of course, the above high-visibility failures are not the only kinds of failure. As an example of the more mundane, the author encounters a bug about every two weeks from use of his wordprocessor, spreadsheet and presentation graphics combination, which admittedly he uses quite heavily. A recent purchase of a very widely used piece of route-planning software (over 20 000 users claimed) led to a different bug being encountered on each of the first four times it was used, one of which would have had the author setting off in the opposite direction! When discussing the word processing failures with Glen Myers, author of a seminal work on testing (Myers, 1979), at Eurostar '93, Glen suggested that the author should complain by returning the product. The author explained that such works as this book would not then appear, to which he responded along the lines that the author shouldn't then expect the software to get any better. Glen Myers is quite right, but there will need to be an overwhelming response from the public to make things improve in practice. (I returned the route planner.)

---

[1] It certainly isn't. To illustrate how an apparently innocuous problem can entail hours of soul-destroying work, the author suddenly found during printing of the final text of this book (on a Mac IIvx running System 7.1 with Microsoft Word 5.1a) that every paragraph went off the right-hand side of the page. Somewhat inconvenienced, his detective notes read:

- Try from Powerbook. OK, so can't be printer.
- Copy book text from Powerbook. Now not OK. So can't be book text.
- Copy Laserwriter driver from Powerbook. Still not OK, so driver not damaged.
- Copy Word executable from Powerbook. Still not OK, so Word not damaged. Damn, damn, damn.
- Restart printer. Still not OK. So printer behaving.
- Restarted IIvx. Still not OK. So it's not that.
- Rebuilt desktop on IIvx. Still not OK. (Definitely grasping at straws here.)
- Bite chair and bang head on wall.
- Reload Word 5.1a in entirety. Still not OK. Feels sorry for himself and whimpers a little.
- Reload System 7.1. Still not OK. Now filled with righteous indignation. All author wants is to print book.
- Realizes while standing on the birdbath in the garden screaming, that he loaded a narrow Helvetica font last week. Hmmm. Wonder if Word 5.1a gets number of characters per line from narrow font by mistake and applies it to wide font (in which book was written). Argh!!
- Remove narrow Helvetica. All well again. That's four hours down the pan.

Of course, the above issues show real failures, but the scale of potential failure is far more worrying. At the time of writing this section (November 1993), there is considerable debate going on about the software systems built into the Sizewell B nuclear power station in Suffolk, England, and operated by Nuclear Electric. It is worth describing this debate in a little more detail, as it will give the reader some insight into the nature and scale of concern.

The software system under debate is the PPS (Primary Protection System). The idea of this system is that, if the nuclear plant develops a major fault, the reactor will be shut down in a controlled way without human intervention, although such intervention is possible if necessary. The aim is not to be reliant on human operators in the event of an emergency, as they may not be able to react quickly enough. The main criticism of the Sizewell software is not so much that it is used to control safety measures, but that *it is too complex to be verified*. This appears to contravene the requirements of such draft or interim safety standards as 00-55 (discussed later) and IEC 880, which specifically addresses the safety of reactor software. The problems of over-complexity will be dealt with later on in this book. Much of the debate has been spawned by the fact that the UK Government's Nuclear Installations Inspectorate (NII) had indicated that it is ready to approve this software *in spite of the fact that 52 per cent of the 49 694 independent tests on the software failed*. The idea of these tests was to subject each of 11 fault scenarios to 5000 tests. In the event, one scenario was subjected to only 69 tests, all of which failed. Some 90 per cent of the other failed tests were said to be due to faulty test equipment. This is compounded by the fact that some critical areas of responsibility, for example in the event of a decrease in reactor coolant, are the sole responsibility of the computer-controlled part of the system and have no automatic secondary backup system apart from operator action. This does not support well the layered 'defence in depth' strategy described by the designers. The NII then described the software as 'adequate' and stated that it would be unreasonable to force Nuclear Electric to repeat the tests. The use of the word 'adequate' is interesting here and will be enlarged upon in a later chapter covering legal issues. In the author's opinion, the word 'adequate' is not enough for a safety-related application of such criticality. It is also interesting to note the comments made by David Parnas, an internationally renowned expert in this area, to the BBC's *Nine O'clock News* in October 1993. He described the NII report as 'alarming'—and he doesn't live here!

The author holds a rather cynical view on such issues, in that in the absence of any history of accident, politics and economics will always override safety arguments. This is a direct result of the fact that safety-related software systems are a recent phenomenon in engineering. In other areas of engineering, it has taken a really serious disaster or series of disasters to catch the public eye and thus impose the appropriate degree of care. For example, prior to the Tay Bridge disaster in December 1879, when a bridge carrying the 5.20 p.m. passenger train from Burntisland collapsed into the Tay in Scotland during a gale, safety standards were very inadequate in railway engineering. This single accident, which killed 75 people, changed the face of the practice of safety in railway work. This lesson was further enhanced by the Clapham Junction signalling disaster in 1988, just outside London. As was commented in the BBC programme *Locomotion*, broadcast on 7 November 1993, 'Disasters are the motivator of progress and innovation'. Unfortunately, in software engineering our appreciation of fallibility does not inhibit us from using software to control systems with a far greater potential for disastrous consequence than the collapse of a bridge, and it is to be hoped that the inevitable price to be paid for progress in safety-related software development isn't too high. It is interesting to note that software has, by some accounts, already killed more people than the railways in about one-fifth of the time (excluding the wanton slaughter of the navvies (workmen) who built the railways in the first place (Coleman, 1968)).

On this somewhat sombre note, the scope of the present book will now be discussed. Its aim is to provide guidelines to the widespread existing practice of coding safety-related systems in C and to prove that if such guidelines are strictly and verifiably followed, the resulting code is comparable to current best practice anywhere. Consequently, when programmers are put into the position of having to use C in an application with safety implications, they can feel reassured that there is a defensible supporting methodology. Of course, they still have to design it correctly!

1.1.2 A road map of this book

This book is divided into eight chapters. Chapter 1 is introductory and is meant to give an overview of standardization initiatives of relevance to the safety-related software developer. The distinction between process and product is presented along with key standards and progress in measurement is described. Surprisingly, there are no formally defined standards which cover safety-related development yet, but a few relevant draft or interim standards are discussed with particular reference to the production of the code itself.

Chapter 2 specifically discusses the C language from a safety-related viewpoint. Rather than being yet another treatise on C programming, this chapter focuses on the weak links of the language with a view to their automatic detection and exclusion from safety-related development. The aim of any safer programming exercise must be to maximize the number of problems that can be detected. In addition, the earlier they can be detected, the cheaper they are to repair. This is also important in safety-related systems, as economics ultimately decides when testing must cease. Hopefully, this would be based on an assessment of achieving a required level of maximum failure rate, as opposed to the more common 'testing shall take N weeks'. The importance of statically-detectable issues as contrasted with run-time detectable issues is obvious and will be discussed in depth.

Chapter 3 specifically addresses an area of concern expressed in the Sizewell B debate described above: that of complexity. A great deal is known about this, but the experience has yet to make its impact in most software development. The measurement of complexity and the results of making sample measurements among large C populations (and FORTRAN populations also, as some measures are language-independent) will be presented. A central and hard-earned engineering principle in older engineering areas such as mechanical and civil engineering is that *simplicity rules*. This experience has been gained from the observed high failure rate of complex components compared with simpler components. Some branches of computing have begun to learn this already. This accounts for the widespread dominance of RISC (reduced instruction set computers) technology in CPU design.

RISC technology is easier to design, build, and, for compiler writers, to reason about. In this sense, it is interesting to speculate whether on average a compiler for a RISC-based design would be more reliable than the same compiler for a CISC (complex instruction set computer) design. The author has no figures for this, but would be interested to hear of any. Unfortunately, the lesson of simplicity has not diffused into general software development and programmers all too often meet it head on rather than avoiding it at the critical design stage. Chapter 3 gives some useful guidelines for thresholds of complexity, which can be enforced before code is even compiled, while it is still soft.

Chapter 4 summarizes the results of the author's measurements of populations of C code in the last few years to assess the frequency of occurrence of statically-detectable faults, standards non-conformances, non-portable constructs and many other features. The results of this chapter above all else show that there is a serious problem of inconsistency, that it is detectable, and, most importantly, that it is avoidable. Later chapters use this information to lay down guidelines of what should be required for safety-related applications.

Chapter 5 discusses stratagems and solutions for safety-related development. These include such things as the content of those parts of a safety argument which justify the use of the language, the features which must necessarily be inhibited and the consequent standards for coding and testing. A major part of this chapter then covers process issues and describes how and where software product quality can be built into the software process control. This discussion of process is closely knitted in with the contents of Chapter 1, which covers process standardization issues, among other things.

Chapter 6, after discussing the safety of computer languages in general, gives a balanced critique for the use of C compared with other languages, which although intrinsically more sound, may not be so in practice, due to inferior tool support and other factors. Other critiques that have been published have not perhaps been as even-handed as they should, so this chapter seeks to redress the balance. As it currently stands, the use of C has, in one draft standard, been deprecated in safety-related development on narrow and sometimes incorrect grounds and yet many engineers are forced to use it. This is clearly an intolerable situation which this book hopes to resolve satisfactorily.

In Chapter 7, practical guidelines are given for a safer use of C. Strict adherence to the suggestions of this chapter will guarantee the absence of a large number of reliability, and therefore safety-reducing, features. Of course, truly safe use of any language cannot be guaranteed, but the essence of this chapter is to assess what would constitute best practice and how to achieve it. The chapter covers written standards, what should be avoided, and how to embed this knowledge in a software process.

Chapter 8 discusses the relationship between software engineering and the law specifically. Although there is very little case law yet, it is widely believed that the first 'juicy' case will have profound effects on software development owing to the power and role of legal precedent. It seems possible that software engineers' insistence on being called engineers rather than programmers, and the industry's aspirations to be treated as a branch of engineering, will lead to the legal profession and the public at large requiring them to assume the responsibilities of those other engineering professions. This will almost certainly accelerate the impact of safety issues in software engineering, and not before time. This chapter can be read separately from the others as it is more general in extent and was prepared with the close cooperation of, and largely written by, a legal expert. Its structure is, however, woven into the arguments presented in the preceding seven chapters. As a result, it places more emphasis on liability than on contract. Even if the reader is not terribly interested in the law, the insights into how laws evolve will be of value to all. Note that this book was written in the UK, and legal issues as they are relevant in Europe are presented, although parallels are drawn with corresponding law in the USA. It was unfortunately not possible to spread the net wider than this.

1.1.3 Safety and reliability

As this is a book on safety, one important distinction should be made immediately. Safety and reliability, although frequently treated synonymously, are not the same, and the difference will be discussed in a little more detail now. According to the *Concise Oxford Dictionary*, they have the following meaning:

reliability: 'Of sound and consistent character or quality'
safety: 'Freedom from danger or risks'

So a program could be unreliable but safe, in that its unreliability did not lead to risk, or it could be reliable but unsafe, in that it did something consistently but incorrectly, leading to a hazard. Nancy Leveson, an author with an international reputation for her work in software safety, distinguished these two particular cases with memorable examples (Leveson, 1993). The two examples both covered torpedoes. The first torpedo was designed to self-destruct if it turned 180°. Unfortunately, it got stuck in the tube, and the Captain then turned his boat round.... The second, a shy sort of torpedo, immediately dived down to the sea bottom on release and lay there: safe, but useless.

By their very nature, computer programs are inherently reliable in the sense of consistency, as they will, in the overwhelming majority of cases, do the same thing when given the same data. Note, of course, that the data could include deterministic values which the programmer has supplied and non-deterministic values, which would be obtained by dependence on an uninitialized heap variable, for example. In this case, the program would behave reliably, but not in its view to the programmer, who has no control over such uninitialization and actively seeks to avoid it. In this book, the production of programs which rely entirely on programmer-supplied information is the central topic, along with the supporting tools necessary to guarantee that the programmer has no inadvertent dependence on other features. In this restricted case, computer programs behave consistently and are not subject to fatigue, as are other engineering constructions. The closest analogy would be a bridge which fell down because castings had faults which had been disguised by filling in holes and cracks with putty. In other words, it was built incorrectly from the beginning. This was, in fact, one of the main contributors to the Tay Bridge disaster mentioned earlier. The findings of Chapter 4 show that programs are released to users all the time with statically-detectable 'cracks' in them. The author overwhelmingly believes that this is done without knowledge, but if a bridge falls over as a result, the effect is the same.

In the author's experience, it is usual for software developers to deny that their software is safety-related at first, perhaps reluctantly acknowledging it later. In a way, this is quite reasonable given the current state of standards guidance; however the author can recall being dumbstruck on several occasions, as evidenced by the following conversation, held with a commercial aerospace software development manager, quoted verbatim from the author's notes:

Author: Do you use C in any safety-related system?
Manager: Oh definitely not.
Author: What do you use C for then?
Manager: Things.[2]
Author: What things?
Manager: It appears in a module.
Author: What module?
Manager: It monitors undercarriage tyre pressures.
Author: [Stricken silence at first] Er..., and it's not safety-related?
Manager: No, no, we have manual backup.
Author: In the air?!

In a subsequent conversation, it transpired that the same developers were also using substantial amounts of C to simulate test results for safety-related systems written in Ada and Pascal, and yes, the reader has guessed it, that wasn't considered safety-related either.[3] To cap the interview, the developers also appeared unaware of any of the reliability issues reported in this book, and were utterly disinterested in them. The author finds interviews like this very depressing sometimes. That particular one took around half an hour on his Fender Stratocaster guitar with all the amplifier knobs on 10 to purge from his system. He also decided never to fly on that particular aircraft, having once before landed with the undercarriage in flames.[4]

In the next and subsequent sections, various standardization efforts aimed at redeeming the above situation will be presented.

1.2 PROCESS AND PRODUCT STANDARDIZATION

It is necessary first to distinguish between the *process* and the *product*. The distinction is very simple, but often confused. A product is a tangible commodity which is the result of a process. Although at least one aspect of software is intangible, a software product is nevertheless a commodity and consists of the medium on which the software is stored along with any accompanying documents.[5] It

---

[2] It was at this point, that the author began to get a horrible feeling.

[3] This directly contravenes sections 36.1, 36.2 and possibly other parts of Def Stan 00-55 (see Section 1.3.2).

[4] When the captain says 'There is no cause for alarm ...' instead of rambling on about how the plane is doing 643.25 km h^{-1} on course 043° at 8426 m over Heligoland, it is a sure sign of trouble.

[5] The law currently takes a different view in that software is *not* usually a product in the sense of coming under the umbrella of product liability, unless expressly embedded in a system. This is discussed in Chapter 8.

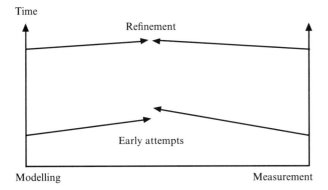

Figure 1.3 How modelling and measurement converge with time.

follows then that *process standardization* is attempting to define the way software products should be manufactured and *product standardization* defines the properties which the resulting software product must satisfy. Some software strategems for implementing this are described in more detail in Chapter 5, but here the discussion will be restricted to an overview and an assessment of recent initiatives.

The relationship between the process and the product is the classic one between modelling and measurement in scientific progress over the ages. Science makes progress by first measurement and then modelling. There is a long and distinguished history of measurement. The first reliable linear unit of measurement was the cubit, several thousand years ago. Used by the Egyptians, Sumerians, Babylonians and Hebrews as a prime unit, its origin is uncertain. It was defined as the distance from the elbow to the tip of the middle finger, but because this distance varied from person to person (from about 0.45 m (17.7 in) to about 0.52 m (20.6 in)), so did the cubits used among various civilizations. There was therefore a natural variation of around ±8 per cent. The ancient Egyptians, a race of natural architects, avoided this by standardizing on two cubits, a short one of 0.45 m and a royal cubit of 0.524 m. Variable as it was, the cubit is still a far more reliable measure of length than is any known metric of software quality, as will be seen later!

When measurements have been made, patterns emerge and models result. Measurement and models proceed side by side, systematically improving, as shown in Fig. 1.3.

Software is at a very early stage of maturity in comparison with other scientific and engineering disciplines. Although there has been much measurement in recent years, only a few apparently worthwhile metrics have emerged, and even they have drawbacks when considered from a rigorous point of view, such as establishing even something as basic as monotonicity. The situation is further exacerbated by the fact that so few software systems have a reliable and consistent maintenance history from which correlations can be extracted. The reader is encouraged to consult the text of Fenton (1991) for more detail. In addition, the discourse by Hoare (1982) is also worth reading by any aspiring software engineer and the subject will be discussed in more detail in Section 3.1.

1.2.1 Process standardization

One of the principal reasons for discussing this well-worked subject in this book at least more than just superficially is the fact that all draft or interim software standards of which the author has knowledge explicitly refer to the need for such standardization. Furthermore, each of these standards has something explicit to say about code quality, one of the central topics of this book. Unfortunately, the standards differ somewhat over what is said, so at the end of this chapter an effort will be made to combine what each of the various standards covers with regard to code quality into a 'lowest common denominator' of best practice to guide developers of safety-related software.

There has been a massive growth in awareness of quality systems and process control generally in the last few years, largely driven by the initiative shown by Japan and the manufacturing successes it has achieved. Japan's introduction to quality systems came just after the Second World War, when the American statistical process control expert W. Edwards Deming was employed as a consultant by the Japanese government to help rebuild the economy. Using the sampling techniques pioneered by Fisher and re-tooled for manufacturing by Shewhart, Deming helped Japan become the dominant manufacturing force it is today.

It is worth providing a little background here. The entire quality movement, and the field of statistics in general, spring from agricultural research, and most notably from the pioneering work of the statistician R. A. Fisher. In essence, Fisher devised short cuts for analysing the mountains of data collected in order to spot key causal relationships to allow crop growing methods to be speeded up. This is vital in agricultural research because the experiments take so long to complete. This work was taken up by Walter A. Shewhart, a physicist at Bell Laboratories, and by the 1930s he had transformed Fisher's work into a quality-control discipline for manufacturing industry. This in turn inspired Deming and Juran in the USA and Taguchi in Japan. Regrettably for the USA, its manufacturing industry turned its back on Fisher and Shewhart in the post-war boom, while Japan painstakingly built a quality culture based on statistical methods following Deming and Taguchi. Today, statistical methods such as just-in-time[6] technology and other powerful second-generation techniques are becoming the norm. For a general reference to the quality initiative in all industries including software, the special issue devoted to the Quality Imperative published by the American journal *Business Week* at the end of 1991 (*Business Week*, 1992) is strongly recommended. Perhaps the most striking impression that a software engineer would get from reading this magazine is how far behind they are compared with other branches of engineering, although the magazine contains some striking examples of software quality, particularly that of the Hitachi software factory. For an excellent discussion of the software factory, including the economics of software development such as case histories of over-runs, see Genuchten (1991).

Statistical process control (SPC) is fundamentally simple. A good reference is Shinskey (1988). The key premise of SPC is that product quality can be improved by sampling the output of a manufacturing process, using the sample to estimate

---

[6] Also known as just-too-late technology by companies who have not quite grasped this concept.

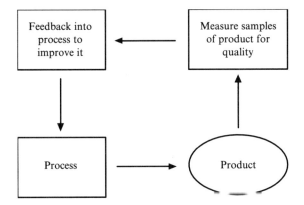

Figure 1.4 A process-control loop whereby measurements of product are fed back into the process to improve its quality. In software this is complicated by not knowing what to measure and by the fact that it is not clear that a subset is representative of software, owing to its chaotic nature.

the product failure rate of the process and then adjusting the process accordingly to reduce this failure rate to some desired degree. This is achieved by a process control loop. Such a loop comprises measurement—evaluation—adjustment. SPC merely states that a subset of the output of the process is sufficient to do this rather than having to inspect all the output. This subset can be dramatically smaller than the whole. The fundamental basis for improvement using this technique is the adjustment or feedback into the process, as shown in Fig. 1.4. The theory can be extended to any manufacturing process, provided that satisfactory relevant measurements can be made of the quality of the product. This has been the problem historically with applying the method to software development.

In the last five years or so, there has been considerable pressure to apply the techniques of process control to software development. This has occurred even to the extent of neglecting the measurement feedback, simply because it has been recognized that the state of the software development process in most organizations is so immature that merely the existence of a recognizable process without the benefit of feedback would be a considerable step forward. This pressure brings with it some danger of considering process control as yet another answer to all the problems of software development. Lehman (1993) counsels against this most eloquently as '...to expect process models of themselves to improve the quality of software or the cost-effectiveness and responsiveness of the software development and evolution process, permitting, for example, total mechanisation of the process, is as futile as the search over the last three decades for automatic programming; is in fact, part of the same mirage'. The author would go further and say that this is merely an extension of the medieval alchemist's goal of the transmutation of other elements into gold by chemical means alone. The absence of a process model and any dependable measurement is filled by wish fulfillment.

Given that all recent draft or interim safety standards explicitly refer to the need for a defined software process, the next few sections will discuss some of the primary software process initiatives in some detail. The relevance of this to the safety-related software developer is that it is impossible to make use of the principles outlined in this book without the pre-existence of a recognizable software development process, just as the effectiveness of the development process is fatally impaired without measurement feedback.

ISO 9001

ISO 9001 is that part of a family of quality systems ISO 9000–9004 which is relevant to software engineering projects. Its scope is defined by the following statement:

> For use when conformance to specified requirements is to be assured by the supplier during several stages which may include design/development, production, installation and servicing.

ISO 9001 is, of course, an international standard, and each country will generally have its own equivalent standard differing only in language. For reference, the equivalent standard for a number of countries is shown in Table 1.1. The bold print indicates a range of numbers. Readers are left to their own devices to contemplate why arguably the most advanced manufacturing nation in the world, Japan, is alone among the manufacturing nations in not having an equivalent. In the UK, ISO 9001 corresponds to BS 5750 part 1. At first glance, this document is thin and difficult to interpret in terms of software engineering, and in the late 1980s such interpretations could (and did) vary widely. Problems of interpretation of

Table 1.1 ISO 9001 standards equivalents

Standards Body	Standard reference
ISO	ISO 9000–**4: 1987**
European Union	EN 29000–**4**
Australia	AS 3900–**4**
Austria	OE NORM-PREM 29000–**4**
Belgium	NEN X 50–002-**1–2**, 50–003–**5**
China	GB/T 10300.**1–5**-88
Denmark	DS/EN 29000–**4**
Finland	SPS-ISO 9000–**4**
France	NF X 50–121–**2**, 50–131–**3**
Germany	DIN ISO 9000–**4**
Hungary	MI 18990–**4**-1988
India	IS: 10201 PT **2–6**
Ireland	IS 300 PT **0–4**/ISO 9000–**4**
Italy	UNI/EN 29000–**4**-1987
Netherlands	NEN-ISO 9000–**4**
New Zealand	NZ S 5600–**4**-1987
Norway	NS-EN 29000–**1**-1988, ISO 9002–**3**
Russia	40.9001–**2**-88 (partial coverage)
Singapore	SS 308 PT **0–4**: 1988
Spain	UNE 66900–**4**
Sweden	SS-ISO 9000–**4**: 1988
Switzerland	SH-ISO 9000–**4**
Tunisia	NT 110.**18–22**-1987
UK	BS 5750 PT **0–3** (+ sections)
USA	ANSI/ASQC Q 9**0–4**
USA (Defense)	MIL-Q 9858A, MIL-I 45208A, SF-32 (partial coverage)
NATO	AQAP **1–3** (partial coverage)

ISO 9001 are discussed by Ince *et al.* (1993), among others. A relatively recent initiative in the UK, however, is to interpret ISO 9001 using the international guidelines for ISO 9001 embodied in ISO 9000–3. This is at the heart of the UK Department of Trade and Industry TickIT initiative, which has also received considerable overseas support.

In essence, ISO 9001 covers two issues:

- The definition of and supporting principles necessary for a *quality system* to ensure that *products* meet their requirements during each stage of their production.
- The appropriate management responsibilities and authorities for its effective use.

It is most important to note that ISO 9001 does not define what a quality system is and does not enforce any particular model. Instead, it requires that an organization define and document its own quality system and adhere to it verifiably. The standard explicitly requires that the quality system must cover the following areas:

- All stages of product development, including contractual agreements, design, production, inspection and testing, delivery and servicing, and *must cover third-party supplied components*.
- The product development must be supported by appropriate document control, internal auditing, training of staff, quality records, statistical techniques, subcontractor selection and control, and fault identification procedures.
- The management of development by a defined and documented quality policy, defined and documented quality responsibilities, and a quality management function which has an *independent* reporting channel from the development function.

ISO 9001 has a number of strengths, but also has some points of concern including:

- Some companies see it as a badge to get for the sole purposes of bidding rather than as a permanent commitment to quality improvement. ISO 9001 is supposed to be a beginning and not an end.
- It is not incremental. A company is certified or not.
- Because it merely codifies a process, it is perfectly possible to formalize an ineffective and inefficient process and achieve compliance, and a significant number of companies have admitted as much to the author.

The above points are worthy of a little expansion, particularly with regard to the lack of an incremental approach. The author gained an unexpected insight into this quite recently, when reading an excellent book on sales techniques in which detailed psychological verification experiments had been carried out (Rackham, 1988). Prior to reading this, he had always believed that the sales process was random and personality-driven rather than the analytical and highly developed process it can be. Rackham's book offers much practical advice, but the particular item that caught this author's eye concerned quality and increment. In a final chapter turning theory into practice, several rules are laid down by Rackham. The first rule states that to improve a complex phenomenon, the best advice is to *tackle one thing at a time*. A later rule is entitled 'Quantity rather than Quality'. It observes that in language training, the traditional techniques of concentrating on quality which set the author back years in his early efforts to speak French (e.g. use the pluperfect subjunctive in this situation on Mondays, Wednesdays and Fridays), have given way to an emphasis on just speaking as much as possible. It is observed that progress is much faster this way and ultimately quality is also much higher (the author can personally vouch for the accuracy of this). So the way to improvement seems to be to master one thing at a time by doing a lot of it until quality naturally emerges. (The author can hear the word 'prototyping' going through the reader's mind.) Numerous examples are quoted in Rackham (1988) to support this important learning concept. The reason for raising this subject is that these lessons are the antithesis of the way ISO 9001 is currently administered and may account for some of the considerable dissatisfaction which the author has heard voiced at quality conferences recently. For a constructive discussion of some of these problems, the paper by Flynn (1993) is highly recommended.

It is worthwhile summarizing some of Flynn's observations, as they relate to code quality, the main theme of this book. First of all she notes the following observations on the current norm, which is entirely in agreement with the author's experience:

- *Code inspection.* Often not done or done only by inexperienced staff. Standards usually layout-related and not 'good programming practice'-related; results not usually recorded.
- *Testing.* Unit testing carried out by programmer not to any particular standard. Test coverage unknown; results perhaps recorded but not evaluated.

Flynn then makes the point that the amount of code verification which is done is related to the 'fit-for-purpose' aspect of price of delivered product. For example, nuclear power station control software should reasonably be subjected to far more verification than a PC game. (On this topic, Leveson (1993) quotes the staggering figure of $15 million to inspect and verify a 1200 line program for a nuclear reactor application on the Darlington Nuclear Reactor Control Project in Canada. This is in stark contrast to the Sizewell B experience quoted earlier.) Flynn finally makes the point that TickIT assessment of code verification procedures is very variable and suggests ways that this could be improved. The relevance of this is that assessment to TickIT or its local ISO 9001 equivalent would be expected for any safety-related developer (cf. Def Stan 00-55 (Section 1.3.2) for example). However, the object of safety-related development is to make something as safe and well as it can be made within the given budget—TickIT cannot currently be relied upon to provide reassurance that code verification is adequate.

The position so far with ISO 9001 is that it has gained ground very rapidly in the UK and Europe and legislation requiring subcontractors to the European Community to be ISO 9001-registered is expected. Quite apart from such pressures, ISO 9001, like DNA, contains the property of self-replication in that Section 4.6-7 relates specifically to the fact that third-party code must be considered in the same manner as internal code if it forms part of the delivered product. Many companies are handling this by simply passing on the requirement of ISO 9001 to their own subcontractors thus replicating the requirement for certification down through the system to the smallest suppliers. Unfortunately, the leaves at the ends of the branches are frequently traders too small to cope with the substantial overheads of the ISO process, but to whom quality is second nature because without it they cannot survive. The whole process is expected to take 12–18 months to complete, although some have done it rather quicker.

Until relatively recently, ISO 9001 had made little impact in the USA owing to the existence of the Carnegie-Mellon Capability Maturity Model (CMM), which is discussed next, but the requirement to trade successfully in Europe has led to considerable interest among US companies currently.

Before moving on, it is interesting to note the customer's perspective of the goals of an ISO 9001-registered company as gleaned from brainstorming sessions at seminars in the UK. These include:

- To get the certificate
- To increase profitability through improvements in management procedures
- To pass on the quality message to both internal and external customers
- To pressurize customers to improve their own inputs, such as better requirements capture
- To force suppliers to conform more closely to their own standards
- To improve internal communications
- To shorten the learning curve for staff starting new projects

The simple pleasure of a job well done was regrettably absent.

Carnegie-Mellon CMM

The Carnegie-Mellon CMM originated at the Software Engineering Institute (SEI) at Carnegie-Mellon University in the USA. It was originally known as Software Process Maturity (SPM) and in essence is the embodiment of Deming's principles into a software context. Its founding father was Watts S. Humphrey and the scope of the project, which is supported by the US Department of Defense, is described in detail in Humphrey (1990). The most current incarnation of this work which the author had seen at the time of writing was dated August 1991. The original document, which created widespread interest, was Humphrey and Sweet (1987). In common with seemingly everything to do with software, the latest incarnation is some 10 times bigger than the original, perhaps obscuring the real object of process improvement, which is to make the software better.

The CMM is a five-level model with level 1 representing the lowest level of process maturity ('initial') and level 5 ('optimizing') the highest. It is shown in some detail in Table 1.2. The model is incremental, so that in order to move from one level to the next higher level the deficiencies at that level *must* be removed. For example, the priorities for a level 1 company to address before it can move to level 2 are project management, project planning, configuration management and software quality assurance. These are expanded upon and re-ordered in Table 1.3. These can be compared with the equivalent challenges facing the level 2 company wishing to move to level 3, shown in Table 1.4.

The CMM initially takes the form of a questionnaire. This should be completed independently by both programming staff *and* management because in the author's

Table 1.2 The basic structure of the Carnegie-Mellon CCM for software

Level	Characteristic	Key challenges
5 Optimizing	Improvement fed back into the process	• Still human intensive • Maintenance of optimization
4 Managed	(Quantitative) Measured process	• Changing technology • Problem analysis • Problem prevention
3 Defined	(Qualitative) Process defined and institutionalized	• Process measurement • Process analysis • Quantitative quality plans
2 Repeatable	(Intuitive) Process dependent on individuals	• Training • Technical practices • Process Focus
1 Initial	(*Ad hoc*/chaotic)	• Project management • Project planning • Configuration management • Software quality assurance

experience, there are frequently dramatic variations.[7] These are due essentially to over optimism as to what can be achieved by programming management, and undue pessimism by programming staff, who are frequently ignorant or dismissive of what has been achieved within the organization. The results must therefore be analysed carefully. When inconsistencies have been resolved, the results give a good idea of the level and key deficiencies remaining. The author has carried out this exercise frequently, although mostly on level 1 companies which are generally easy to improve.

The CMM has many intuitively attractive features, which is perhaps not surprising given its strong empirical lineage. Perhaps its most intuitively appealing aspect is its incremental nature. This in stark contrast to ISO 9001, which an organization satisfies or not, and after which there is no real guidance as to what the next quality steps should be. In the CMM, there is a clear set of objectives with well-defined problem areas to be solved at each stage. In particular, it illustrates that *balance* is crucial to an organization's performance. There is no point trying to optimize a deficient process. Of the safety-related companies with which the author has dealt, configuration management was often a problem. This has led to extreme situations when an automated code audit against standards had to be carried out on site because the company concerned were unable to deliver all the required source code components after several attempts. Furthermore, more than half of the safety-related companies with which the author has dealt were deficient in project management. This is a very dangerous deficiency, as it invariably leads to a rush at the end of a development project in order to meet a deadline which has

---

[7] In one company that the author encountered, 80 per cent of the questions received a *yes* from a software manager, in contrast to about 20 per cent from a programmer working in the same group, when completing the questionnaire independently.

Table 1.3 The priorities which must be addressed in a level 1 company wishing to get to level 2 of the CMM

Standards and procedures	Formal project management system to cover planning, estimation, scheduling and tracking
	Formal information strategy planning
	Formal data, process and interaction modelling
	Data administration
	Prototyping
	Regression testing
Organization	Software quality assurance function
	Staff training programme to support standards and procedures.
Tools and technology	Systems planning, analysis and design support
	Project management support
	Source code configuration management system
	Data dictionary if applicable
	Regression testing support
Process metrics	Collection and analysis of code error and test efficiency measurements

always been unrealistic. Quality cannot help but suffer, usually terminally, in such circumstances.

As an emphatic example of organizational imbalance, another safety-related systems company with which the author has had contact had a requirement to use formal methods, in this case SSADM, imposed on its development group by external influences. The result was considered to be a huge leap backwards by the development staff and their management. Why should this be the case? Further discussion revealed that the main reason why it was considered to have had such a negative effect was in severe delays to product delivery and, like most safety-related organizations, there was a marketing window of opportunity for the products. *The reason why there were severe delays was that the company had no formal project planning*, and attempted to meet management- and marketing-driven deadlines. The moral is this. *Like all other technology, the introduction of formal methods should take account of the existing software process.* Project planning is a fundamental problem area at the

Table 1.4 The priorities which must be addressed in a level 2 company wishing to get to level 3 of the CMM

Standards and procedures	Defined software development process
	Risk management
	Inspections and walkthroughs
	Testing standards
	Design level maintenance
	Quality management
Organization	Software engineering process group
Tools and technology	CASE strategy
	Requirements traceability
Process metrics	Collection and analysis of life-cycle metrics

first level of the CMM. To attempt to introduce a high-level design concept, such as tool-supported formalism, when the underlying software process is undefined is extremely foolhardy and invariably damaging. The simple problems should be solved first. Goodness knows that there are enough of them.

Although the strengths of the CMM are considerable, it also has areas of concern. In particular, the questionnaire is heavily biased to larger companies and to run-time systems. Several attempts have been made to address this, including the assessment techniques used by the Institute of Software Engineering in Belfast, Northern Ireland (Thompson, 1991). In addition, a number of initiatives are in progress with a similar goal of extending its relevance, for example the Quantum Project, sponsored by the UK DTI (Department of Trade and Industry) as well as the EC (European Commission) funded SPICE project. A special issue on process modelling in practice appeared in Ince and Tully (1993), and is recommended as an up-to-date review.

Humphrey (1990) found that perhaps 81 per cent of all companies audited were at level 1, with around 12 per cent at level 2 and around 7 per cent at level 3. At the time of writing, there were no companies known at level 5 although one or two software groups are believed to operate at this level. This highlights a further deficiency of the CMM: there is so little data at levels 4 and 5 that it is difficult to define them adequately. It is important to note that Humphrey, after extensive research, believes that 1–2 years is necessary to graduate between each level, so climbing the CMM ladder represents a major commitment in resources and could be expected to take 10 years. The problem of so many companies being at level 1 has been resolved in a somewhat tongue-in-cheek manner by Finkelstein (1992), who proposed a software process *immaturity* extension of the CMM model to include level 0 (foolish), level − 1 (stupid) and level − 2 (lunatic). Although the descriptions are highly amusing, the author has seen examples of each level in real life.

ISO 9001 vs. CMM In comparing ISO 9001 and the CMM, the general consensus of opinion at quality conferences suggests that an ISO 9001 company could be at levels 1, 2 or 3, depending on who you ask. Perhaps not surprisingly, representatives of ISO 9001 certifying bodies usually state that it corresponds to level 3 when asked. On the other hand, the author has been told on a number of occasions during interviews with ISO 9001 companies that they are categorically level 1. The key deficiencies stated confirmed this. As a result, there is a reasonable body of opinion which suggests that ISO 9001 should be ignored until important deficiencies at CMM levels 1 and 2 are satisfactorily resolved. This does not imply that ISO 9001 is equivalent to level 3, just that ISO 9001 may actually be harmful to organizations lower than level 3. A level 3 company doesn't need ISO 9001, but would be very likely to get it. A level 1 company could get ISO 9001, but would probably self-destruct in the process by formalizing a chronically deficient software process. The author finds it disturbing when draft and interim standards specify process certification to ISO 9001 as a requirement, when the above suggests that such companies may very well have some dangerous process deficiencies. Perhaps these could be resolved eventually by requiring dual certification, such that a company have ISO 9001 and as a minimum be at level 3 of the ISO-CMM when it appears. At least this guarantees that the company has been able to formalize a reasonable process. Alternatively, ISO 9001 could be strengthened along the lines of the CMM.

There is a tolerable correspondence between the Carnegie Mellon model and ISO 9001 as can be seen in Table 1.5. The numbering in the case of the CMM refers to the original questionnaire. The author has not yet attempted this with the latest version of the CMM, and in order to carry out even this comparison he was forced to resort to typing both documents into his Sparcstation and then used `grep` extensively to compare words in the two documents. The 'Quality of fit' column was an attempt to estimate how good the conceptual match was. When the CMM section number is in italics, this indicates that it is a level 3 issue. When not, it is a level 2 issue.

There is inevitably a degree of subjectivity in this comparison in spite of the process used to carry it out, but the result is useful.

On a final note, there is a considerable impetus to adopt the SEI model in the USA, and it is being made a requirement in some quarters. For example, as Yourdon (1992) reports, internal software centres within the US Department of Defense have been told that they must reach level 2 in order to bid for DoD contracts. In addition, some external sites have been told that they must reach level 2 by 1991 and level 3 by 1992 in order to bid on US government contracts. This confirms the move to mandatory process qualification on both sides of the Atlantic with the European Union's requirement for its subcontractors to be ISO 9001 certified.

It is interesting to note, earlier in this section, yet another manifestation of one of the biggest contributors to software failure of all—management ignorance and unrealistic time goals. As was stated above, Humphrey recommends that 1–2 years should be required as a minimum to move sensibly between the CMM levels. All of the author's experience suggests that this is reasonable. If then ISO 9001 is equivalent to level 3, it ought to take a company 3–4 years to achieve, and yet it takes 12–18 months in practice. How can this be? In addition, for the US government to require level 2 by 1991 and level 3 by 1992 also flies in the face of Humphrey's excellent practical advice. At least one chairman of a giant multinational company has beat his chest and stated that his company will be at level 3 in about one third of the time it could reasonably be expected to take. Such people are not really serious about quality or they would understand better how hard it is to achieve. By making ridiculous statements, they immediately break Deming's rules, as laid out below, and demean the object of quality in the eyes of their employees. Quality is not about a flag in the company car park; it is about a studied commitment to its internal or external customers to provide the very best service or product that the employees of the company are capable of producing, and never to stop trying to improve it. The next section repeats this last sentence in quality-speak.

TQM

TQM, or Total Quality Management, is one of those acronyms which is frequently bandied around with very little understanding or even agreement as to what it actually means. In the West, there is therefore a real danger that quality initiatives

Table 1.5 A cross-reference between the CMM and ISO 9000-3 (*Continues*)

CMM section	Item	ISO 9000-3 section	Quality of fit
1.1.1	Designated project manager	5.4.2.2	Poor
1.1.2	Chain of command	5.4.2.2	Poor
1.1.3	Separate quality assurance function	4.1.1.2.2	Good
1.1.6	Configuration management function	6.1	Good
1.2.2	Develop training program	6.9	Medium
1.3.1	Maintain up-to-date awareness	6.9	Poor
2.1.3	Formal management review	5.2.1	Good
2.1.4	Progress control	5.4.3	Good
2.1.5	Included software product	6.7.2, 6.7.2, 6.8	Good
2.1.7	Independent audits	5.4.6, 5.6.4	Good
2.1.9	Coding standards	5.6.3	Good
2.1.14	Project sizing	5.4.1	Poor
2.1.15	Project schedules	5.4.1	Good
2.1.16	Project costs	5.4.1	Good
2.1.17	Verifying requirements	5.4.6, 5.6.4	Good
2.2.1	Tracking staffing profiles	5.4.3	Medium
2.2.2	Tracking item size	6.1.1	Poor
2.2.4	Tracking code and test errors	5.7.3	Medium
2.2.7	Designed units profiles	5.6.2	Poor
2.2.8	Tested units profiles	5.7	Poor
2.2.9	Integrated units profiles	5.7	Poor
2.2.10	Memory utilization profiles	—	Absent
2.2.11	Throughput utilization profiles	—	Absent
2.2.12	I/O utilization profiles	—	Absent
2.2.16	Tracking problems to closure	5.7.3	Good
2.2.18	Test progress by component	5.7.2	Poor
2.2.19	Software build profiles	5.4.2.2	Poor
2.4.1	Senior management reviews	5.4.3, 5.6.4	Poor
2.4.5	Regular technical interchanges	4.1.3, 5.3.2	Good
2.4.7	Sign-off on schedules and costs	5.4.2.2	Poor
2.4.9	Requirements changes	5.2.2	Good
2.4.17	Control of changes	6.1.3.2	Good
2.4.20	Routine regression testing	5.7.2, 5.7.3	Medium
1.1.4	Control of software interfaces	6.1.3.1	Medium
1.1.5	System engineering in design	5.6.2	Poor
1.1.7	Software engineering process group	4.1.1.3, 6.4.2	Good
1.2.1	Workstation per developer	—	Absent
1.2.3	Required developer training	6.9	Poor
1.2.4	Required supervisor training	6.9	Poor
1.2.5	Required code review training	6.9	Poor
1.3.2	Evaluate external technologies	—	Absent
2.1.1	Defined development process	5.4.2.1	Good
2.1.2	Process defined tools	5.4.2.3, 5.6.3	Good
2.1.6	Use of standards	5.4.2.3, 5.4.5, 5.6.3	Good
2.1.8	Assessment of reuse	5.4.6, 5.6.3	Poor
2.1.10	Preparation of unit tests	5.7.2	Good
2.1.11	Code maintainability standards	5.9	Poor
2.1.18	Human interface standards	—	Absent
2.2.3	Software design error statistics	5.6.2, 6.4.2	Poor
2.2.15	Design review items tracked	5.6.4	Poor
2.2.17	Code review items tracked	5.6.4	Poor
2.4.3	Engineering issues affecting software	6.1.3.1	Poor

Table 1.5 A cross-reference between the CMM and ISO 9000-3 (*Concluded*)

CMM section	Item	ISO 9000-3 section	Quality of fit
2.4.4	Manage integration and test issues	5.7.3	Good
2.4.6	Enforcement of software standards	5.6.4, 5.6.5	Good
2.4.8	Requirement design traceability	5.4.6	Good
2.4.11, 14	Software design traceability	4.1.3	Good
2.4.12	Design reviews	5.6.4	Good
2.4.13	Controlling design change	5.2.2, 5.3.2	Good
2.4.15	Unit development progress	5.4.15	Medium
2.4.16	Software code reviews	5.6.4	Good
2.4.18	Configuration control of tools used	6.1.3.1	Good
2.4.19	Representativeness of reviews	5.6.4	Poor
2.4.21	Adequacy of regression testing	5.7	Poor
2.4.22	Formal review of test cases	5.7.2	Medium

will simply disappear in hype, while the Pacific Rim nations simply get on with it.[8] Put very simply, TQM focuses on customer satisfaction and emphasizes employee teamwork to remove expensive inefficiencies and bottlenecks. It was invented by Americans and among its most famous practitioners are Deming, Crosby, Ishikawa, Taguchi and Juran. Deming's work dates back to the Second World War, following which he was invited to Japan to help rebuild its economic infrastructure. As a result, it was the Japanese in the 1950s and 1960s who really practised its doctrine and it was not until the late 1970s that it became popular in the USA. For reference, Deming's work can be summed up in his 14-point plan as shown in Table 1.6.

On first reading, Deming's advice seems to represent simple common sense although it is worth noting that items 9, 10, 11 and 12 are at best highly unpopular and item 4 alone would cause heart failure in the average Western manager. In fact, it formalizes a very simple concept: if suppliers are continually played off against each other on price, ultimately their collective quality will suffer and hence that of the purchaser who depends on them. Explaining this with patience and imperturbability to the average Western purchasing manager is one of the author's least favourite pastimes. Unfortunately, it makes sense only if the medium and long term are important, and Western companies do not generally think in such terms.

In theory, TQM sounds promising, but as Hewson (1993) points out, while very little advice given by the experts is bad advice, equally little of it is specific and

---

[8] This was brought home most forcibly to the author by the first Pacific Rim client to purchase a software tool from the author's company. The client simply sent a cheque *immediately* after receiving the appropriate brochures and list of references. It transpired that the client had simply checked the literature to confirm the product solved the relevant problem and checked the customer references to make sure the product was OK. The whole process took three days. When questioned by an admittedly incredulous sales person punch drunk with normal Western purchasing procedures, the client simply said, '... after these checks, there was a very small risk and *it is then cheaper to buy it as soon as possible rather than either continuing to suffer the problem or spending months analysing it internally...*'. Amongst Western companies, the same cycle can take months, to the extent that the product costs much less than even the purchasing effort, let alone the lost opportunity in development.

Table 1.6 Deming's 14-point plan

1. Constancy of purpose
2. Adopt the new thinking
3. Cease dependence on mass inspection
4. Cease doing business on price tag alone
5. Continual improvement of process
6. Institute training on the job
7. Institute leadership
8. Drive out fear
9. Break down barriers between departments
10. Eliminate slogans, exhortations and targets
11. Eliminate numerical quotas
12. Allow pride in workmanship
13. Institute a program of self improvement
14. Do it

much of the advice is conflicting. After considerable study of the TQM market-place, he comes to the conclusion that there are indeed four laws to TQM:

1. Lasting success for a business is achieved by delivering products and services that are recognized for their quality.
2. Quality can be achieved only by building it in, using the right tools and the right process.
3. Quality can only be built in by people who are provided with the means and environment to channel their creativity to building in quality.
4. Improvement must be continuous.

Hands up anybody who thinks the above isn't obvious! However, in spite of its intuitive appeal, there have been notable disasters, such as that of McDonnell-Douglas, who had embraced TQM in 1989 (Mathews, 1993). This latter article bore the splendid title 'Totaled Quality Management' and hit hard at some of the excessive claims which have been made and at the many TQM consultants which it has spawned.

Perhaps the author is a hard-bitten case, but he feels an overwhelming desire to take a bite out of the nearest piece of furniture every time he hears the phrase TQM spoken in tones oozing with sincerity. TQM simply seems to be about rediscovering the lost virtues of pride in one's work and the sheer pleasure of satisfying a customer by a job well done and being praised for doing so. Why on earth must the quality industry invent an entirely new nomenclature and priesthood for something so basic? The author attempted to explain this to his father, a craftsmen carpenter, who was unable to understand what all the fuss was about. How could people work any other way? Why would anybody make something knowingly inadequate? The only difference the author could discern was that to the old-fashioned craftsmen, the discipline of doing something so well that any customer would be satisfied was the *only* thing that mattered, and frequently transcended even short-term profitability. The epithet TQM merely cheapens a once treasured ideal. It is rather like the famous Groucho Marx quote that he would not join any club that would have him as a member; if readers believe that TQM will solve all their problems, they don't understand what the problems are.

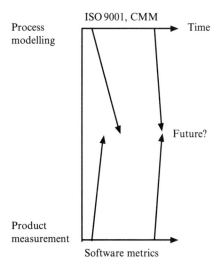

Figure 1.5 The evolution of process modelling and product measurement.

If the reader would like to follow up on some of the references for TQM, Crosby (1979) is recommended, as is the *Business Week* issue of January 1992, which was devoted entirely to the Quality Initiative in the USA (*Business Week*, 1992).

Turning round Fig. 1.3 into the traditional software engineering top-down/bottom-up viewpoint gives Fig. 1.5, which shows the relationship between software process initiatives and product measurement. The next section discusses the latter.

1.2.2 Product measurement and standardization

The most important aspect of product standardization is that there is currently almost none at all. Surprisingly, there is an international standard, ISO 9126, covering software quality and measurement, which was published in December 1991. The development of this standard was led by the Japanese and it identifies six aspects of software quality: functionality, reliability, usability, efficiency, maintainability and portability. For each of these aspects or attributes, it provides a definition and a set of suggested sub-attributes. In the case of functionality, for example, these are suitability, accuracy, interoperability, compliance and security. Unfortunately, the promise of this standard is considerably reduced by its admission that 'the state of the art at present does not permit standardization in this area'. In other words, for the purposes of actual measurement it is largely useless.

Nevertheless, the need for good measurement is very quickly being recognized. For example, the British Standards Institute, at a Continuous Improvement Seminar held in the form of a debate on 2 November 1992, moved the following motion:

> [ISO 9001] Registered IT Software businesses should not release programme code that contains statically determinable errors

Although such issues as to what exactly constitutes a statically-determinable error are obvious areas for debate, the motion was passed with a more than 2:1 majority. This rather surprised the author, but the audience, which consisted of representatives of a large number of ISO 9001-certified companies, were certainly aware of some of the results described in Chapter 4, as they were supplied at the request of the BSI and presented during the debate.[9] At the same debate, the important potential role of the *programming standard* as a quality instrument was also recognized. This is also an important step forward. As any software developer knows, the history of programming standards enforcement within a company is too often a tale of woe, with the following identifiable stages:

1. Boundless enthusiasm.
2. Endless acrimonious discussions over indentation standards and how to name the identifiers.
3. The production of vast documents.
4. An agreement to tacitly ignore the results and not to discuss it ever again.

It seems quite clear that the notion of a programming standard will become an important and quantifiable aspect of software product quality in the near future. As a result, this book devotes some time in a later chapter to a discussion of some of the issues, including aspects of good programming standards and successful strategies for their introduction and enforcement.

It is useful to consider what might constitute evidence of software product quality. This book will argue forcibly that there is a property of software which experienced programmers can identify with quality *without knowing the function of the software*. This will be referred to as *intrinsic product quality* here. There are many analogies in conventional engineering and manufacturing. An electrical engineer can look at a circuit board and decide on the basis of layout and quality of wire-wrap or soldering as to whether the product is well constructed, without knowing what the board does. This is precisely what occurs in magazine reviews of microcomputers, where the reviewer will inevitably take it apart just to look at the quality of build. A carpenter can look at a piece of furniture to see if it is constructed well or poorly. A builder can decide whether the overall layout of the drainage system of a house is sensible. In all walks of life, products are imbued with a notion of intrinsic quality. If they are really good products, they will suit their intended function equally well, but the point is that *if they do not have intrinsic quality, they are intrinsically poor*. The essential feature of all of these examples is that there is a self-evident measure of intrinsic quality which is instantly recognizable and has built up with experience over the years. Unfortunately, it is only recently that some such measures have become obvious for software, and it is one of the prime objectives of this book to define them and demonstrate their reasonableness. They are not complete, but will serve as a suitable base on which to build.

Other workers discuss the relevance of the quality of internal structure. For example, Fenton (1991) said that 'Good internal structure implies good external quality' and goes on to say that if this is wrong, twenty years of software research have been wasted. This book wholeheartedly endorses this view and adds the following:

Poor internal consistency and dependence on weak linguistic features implies poor external quality

[9] Such statistics seem hard to come by, and at the time of writing the author was unaware of any other large-scale population studies of them, which was another reason for publishing them in this book.

The property of good intrinsic product quality is here defined to comprise the following features:

1. Zero statically-detectable faults. These concern inconsistencies which are determinable without running a program, by simply inspecting its source code, and are discussed in Chapter 2.
2. Zero transgressions of internal programming standards. This involves transgressions of an organization's or project's definition of good practice. These will typically involve further restrictions on the use of language and are discussed further in Chapter 5.
3. Zero dependence on relevant unspecified features or *any* undefined linguistic features. These refer specifically to parts of the language which are deemed questionable *by the programming language standard definition itself.*
4. Limitation of component complexity. This involves limiting the values of certain measurements of complexity to lie within prescribed bounds because of the known relationship between increased maintenance costs and the breaking of those bounds.

Software product compliance is further defined to be adherence to the above. Note that although the above definition was formulated with source code in mind, the concepts are applicable to other written forms of text, including designs and documentation.

For software, the key to the application of statistical process control (SPC) and the achievement of verifiable compliance lies in automation of the process and the integration of product quality measurement and control. This will be discussed in detail in Chapter 5.

So far, the discussion has covered generic quality initiatives which affect all software developers. At this stage of the discourse, therefore, it will be useful to review progress in the definition of software safety and some corresponding safety initiatives.

1.3 SAFETY STANDARDS

There are unfortunately very few safety standards which explicitly refer to software. Indeed, such safety standards as there are frequently explicitly exclude software. For example, as reported in Littlewood and Strigini (1992a) the US Federal Aviation Administration Advisory Circular 25.1309–1A, which describes 'acceptable' means for showing compliance with some federal aviation regulations, explicitly excludes software on the grounds that 'it is not feasible to assess the number of kinds of software errors, if any, that may remain after the completion of system design, development and test'. Similarly, the Radio Technical Commission for Aeronautics, RTCA/DO 178A, avoids all software measures and refuses to mandate quantitative terms for evaluating software reliability. This document gives guidelines for manufacturers seeking certification by aviation authorities, but relies on engineers taking a disciplined approach to software involving requirements definition, design, development, testing, configuration management and documentation. This sounds very similar to the requirements

Table 1.7 Five levels of safety integrity defined in draft safety standard SC 65A

Level	Description of software safety integrity
4	Very high
3	High
2	Medium
1	Low
0	Non safety-related

for compliance to ISO 9001 or level 2 or 3 of the CMM; however, as discussed in Chapter 4, such a level of process maturity is not yet affecting the statically-detectable fault rate beneficially. Jackson (1993) provides a good up-to-date review of current safety initiatives and their evolution.

The two standards discussed in more detail here *are both draft standards at the time of writing*; however, they do attempt to set restrictions on software development in safety-related systems and are therefore worthy of elaboration.

1.3.1 ISO/IEC SC65A (65A (Secretariat) 122)

This draft standard is a product of the International Electrotechnical Commission and has the title 'Software for computers in the application of industrial safety-related systems'. At the time of writing, the document was still under study and therefore subject to change, although very comprehensive in its scope and running to almost 100 pages, an unusually long document for its subject material. *Owing to this state of flux, it specifically states that it should not be used for reference purposes.* Unfortunately, as the draft has been in circulation for some 18 months with at least two extensions to its commentary period, most companies that the author has encountered in safety-related work have started to refer to it and use it for guidance. Indeed, as Jackson (1993) notes, at least one sector-specific standard, RIA (1991), has already emerged under the aegis of IEC (1991). An attempt will therefore be made here to cover the scope and intent of the draft standard to give the reader a flavour of what is likely to follow, as the author believes it would be negligent not to discuss it. The situation, however, was very fluid at the time of writing and it is quite conceivable that this discussion will be disjoint with the eventual form of the standard, which is yet to be published, and little attention should therefore be given to specific wording and section numbers.

This draft standard (referred to as the 122 Standard from now on in this section) is intended to be read in conjunction with International Standard 65A (Secretariat) 123—'Functional Safety of Programmable Electronic Systems: Generic Aspects' (referred to as the 123 Standard from now on in this section). Its key concept is that it splits up software safety into five levels, as in Table 1.7. The scope of the five levels of safety themselves is defined in the accompanying 123 Standard. The function of the 122 Standard is to specify those measures necessary to achieve these requirements. As a matter of general usage, levels 1 and 2 are being referred to as *high-integrity* and levels 3 and 4 as *safety-critical* at the time of writing.

Safety integrity levels for software are decided on the basis of the level of risk associated with the software, where risk includes at least the following categories:

(a) Loss of human life
(b) Injury to or illness of persons
(c) Environmental pollution
(d) Loss of or damage to property
(e) Economic loss

A glance at this list reveals that safety relationship has a far wider scope than many might have thought, to the point that it is hard to think of a piece of commercial software which is not thus related. For example, a spreadsheet undoubtedly incorporates the possibility of (e). Even an apparently innocuous scientific calculation in a general purpose statistical package could, in the right environment, affect any member of the list. This is particularly relevant to the developers of a scientific subroutine library for general distribution, as it is more than likely that it will be used in safety-related environments. Such use, however, will not have been foremost in the numerical analyst's mind when developing algorithms for the library. It might even be useful to mark such packages as unsuitable for such use if reliability was compromised too much for market considerations, and it is certainly the author's experience that the intrinsic quality of some general purpose scientific libraries is definitely no better than the average. As legal implications of software failure develop, it may well be inevitable that packages contain a health warning rather more specific than the traditional clause of software contracts which states something to the effect that the user is terminally insane to consider using this package for anything other than keeping the door open. Even so, the user of such a package may well be better off than if the needed functionality was developed from scratch.

The breadth of coverage of safety relationship should not come as a surprise. In essence *safety relationship is only about doing the very best job that can be done within a certain budget, given the limitations of the technology, while specifically recognizing the risks of failure.* As the reader will immediately observe, this is no different from the development goals for non safety-related software. There is never any excuse for not doing the best job that can be done. There is obviously a need to impress upon software developers by use of the epithet 'safety' that something special is at risk, namely life and limb, but at the same time there is a trap in that developers working in non-safety-related areas might come to the conclusion that they don't have to do 'all that stuff'. They do. The only difference is that they might not spend as much on it, but this should nevertheless devolve naturally from a formal assessment of risk.

Another key aspect of the draft standard is that it formally recognizes that the development of perfect software in a complex application is unrealistic and therefore damage limitation and risk assessment should be built into the development itself.

The draft standard covers all aspects of the software life-cycle, but it is linguistic issues that are of the greatest relevance here. The following are particularly relevant and encapsulate best engineering practice:

* The software shall be limited in size and complexity and each functional component should be readable, understandable and testable.

- The programming language should have a compiler or translator which is internationally certified to a recognized standard or defended for its suitability. This former ensures that the compiler obeys a comprehensive validation suite. This author at least is unhappy about the use of any language which is not internationally certified, however attractive, as one of the purposes of international certification is to expose the language to the greatest possible audience before its use becomes too ingrained.
- The programming language shall be complete and unambiguously defined or *subsetted* until it can satisfy this criterion. This incidentally, is one of the key aims of a programming standard, which also *must* be in existence and *must* be adhered to.
- The programming language must encourage the discovery of error. In this regard, raw C certainly fails in comparison with Pascal and Ada for example, although, as will be described later, tools exist which can perform the necessary detection.
- Coding standards and style guides should be distinct entities.

With the above in mind, the draft standard goes on to make recommendations about the use of various languages for different integrity levels making four levels of recommendation, Highly Recommended, Recommended, Not Recommended and No Comment. If something is Highly Recommended and is not done *or* is Not Recommended and is done, an argument must be presented to an independent assessor as to the reasons why. It is to be hoped that this draft standard proceeds speedily to a formal release, as in spite of the inevitable deficiencies it represents the most comprehensive assessment of the requirements for safety-related software that the author has seen.

Not surprisingly, the draft standard requires that C must be subjected to careful and major subsetting before its use is Recommended at the higher integrity levels. These even include the use of features considered fundamental to C (and indeed other languages), such as the use of pointers, dynamic objects and recursion. In this regard, the draft standard is somewhat Draconian, given the existence of the tool support necessary to render use of these features safe and predictable. However, on the subject of subsetting in general, this author would go so far as to say that *no* programming language in regular use today should *ever* be used without subsetting, even if it is only to be used for a home cataloguing scheme for a CD collection. After all, do people really want to plunge down the same holes that so many before them have done, or do they actually want to be able to use their CD catalogue? The author believes fervently that the time has come to constrain linguistic use as a general programming paradigm in the interests of good engineering practice. Programmers wanting to experiment with linguistic foibles should do so only in a carefully controlled experimental environment designed to illuminate such problems and should studiously report all the new holes they have fallen into. Unfortunately, this is not yet the norm.

This seems an appropriate point to end this particular diatribe and continue with another draft standard which, although it will never become an international standard, has been particularly influential and from which safety insights can be gained.

1.3.2 Def Stan 00-55

This particular UK Ministry of Defence standard (MOD, 1991), is also currently in draft form, the MOD parlance for this being that it is an *interim* standard. The title of the standard is 'The procurement of safety critical software in defence equipment'. It is freely circulated on request and the latest version is dated 5 April 1991. The standard is very detailed and comprehensive and covers all aspects of the life-cycle, including verification and validation as well as provision for formal proof methods.

Perhaps most relevant to this book are the requirements it mandates for the programming language, which although far less detailed than IEC SC65A nevertheless include the following:

(a) A formally defined syntax.
(b) A means of enforcing the use of any subset employed.
(c) A well-understood semantics and a formal means of relating code to the formal design.
(d) Block structured.
(e) Strongly typed.

Using the techniques described in this book, (a), (b), (d) and (e) can be satisfied and to a certain extent (c), in that use of features of well-defined semantics can be enforced. It is useful to compare these requirements with those defined for IEC SC65A.

The standard goes on to define extremely severe requirements for testing, which in the author's experience would be very difficult to achieve in practice. These are that testing shall continue until at least the following have been exercised:

(a) All statements.
(b) All branches for both true and false conditions, and case statements for each possibility including 'otherwise'.
(c) All loops for zero, one and many iterations, covering initialization, typical running and termination conditions. (Note that the meaning of 'many' in this context is not clear to the author.)

Over the next few years, it is hoped that both draft standards described above will become full standards, as standardization in this area is long overdue and eagerly awaited.[10] It is certainly comforting to see the same threads in both standards, indicating consensus on what needs to be done to make software as safe as possible.

1.4 MEASUREMENT STANDARDS

In any attempt to improve the safety of software, measurement must play an important role. However, as will be expanded further later in this book, there is

---

[10] Another safety initiative worthy of comment is the British Computer Society's policy statement on safety-related computer systems (SRCS) dated 8 June 1993. This 10-point policy statement includes the importance of professional qualifications such as Chartered Engineering Status for engineers responsible for quality in SRCS, the need for best engineering principles, the need for registration of such systems, the balance of cost against safety, and above all, the urgent need for standardization.

little in the way of calibrated measurement for software, although both of the process standards discussed in Section 1.2 specifically mention the acquisition of relevant measurements. Fenton (1991), is a very good comprehensive reference for such metrics research as there is, but in view of the intimate relationship between the restrictions necessary for safety-related development and the software quality measurement process, it seems appropriate to bring to the reader's attention such standardization initiatives as there currently are.

1.4.1 IEEE 1061

IEEE 1061 is the first IEEE-issued standard that deals with quality metrics, and was released in December 1992 (IEEE, 1992). Its most significant features are that it is a process standard and that it does *not* mandate any specific metrics which should be used. Instead, its philosophy is that an organization can use whatever metrics it thinks are appropriate, so long as the methodology is followed and the metrics are validated (Schneidewind, 1993). In terms of IEEE 1061, *validation* is a key concept. The author had used the word calibration for this concept for some years before he became aware of IEEE 1061, as calibration is more closely related to the fundamental basis of measurement. In support of standards adherence generally, however, the word validation will be used for this concept here. In essence, the validation of metrics involves:

• The accumulation of data relating to specific metrics and their relationship with certain factors associated with software quality such as reliability, followed by:
• verification that the metrics are indeed associated with such factors in a predictive context.

The standard itself has a wide scope and is equally relevant to project managers and users. The methodology for metrics proposed by this standard is in five stages:

(a) *Establish software quality requirements.* Basic parameters are defined against which the quality of the system can be assessed.
(b) *Identify software quality metrics.* Appropriate metrics related to quality parameters are identified.
(c) *Implement the software quality metrics.* Metrics are extracted manually or using tools.
(d) *Analyse the software quality metric data.* The metrics data are analysed and used to control the quality parameters.
(e) *Validate the metrics.* The metrics data are used on other projects in a predictive mode and their success assessed.

Validation of the metrics is described by the standard as being done using the following criteria:

• *Correlation.* Metrics and their associated parameters must correlate beyond a specified threshold.
• *Tracking.* The derivatives of the metric and the associated parameters must be of the same sign.

- *Consistency*. An ordering of the metrics must imply the same ordering of the associated parameters.
- *Predictability*. The metric must have specified predictive power.
- *Discriminative power*. The metric must be able to distinguish between high- and low-quality products and processes.
- *Reliability*. The metric must reliably exhibit the above properties for some specified percentage of use.

The standard also includes a bibliography and some well-known metrics, but the reader could be excused for being a little disappointed at how little guidance there is so far. The *only* metrics of which the author is aware which possess the above properties are static fault occurrence rates, which are described in detail in Chapter 4.

1.5 STANDARDS AND CODE QUALITY

This section brings together selected relevant elements of the various standards initiatives described above to attempt to provide a reasonable definition of best practice as it relates to the *intrinsic* quality of the code. Each feature will be followed by the appropriate references. The versions of the various draft, interim and full standards used to compile Table 1.8 were TickIT (1992) for TickIT, IEC (1991) for IEC 65A and MOD (1991) for Def Stan 00-55. The components of Table 1.8 and other appropriate issues will form an important part of the practical advice given later on in this book as to how C might be developed in a safety-related environment.

1.6 SAFETY-ENHANCING DESIGN PROCEDURES

The purpose of this book was not to address design issues, but to recognize that many safety-related systems are already being developed or have been developed in C, and to provide guidance as to how this language can be used safely. It would be remiss, however, not to mention some of the techniques which impinge on the design of safety-related systems, however they are implemented, before returning to the core subject of this book in Chapter 2.

1.6.1 Fault-tree analysis

A graphical technique normally used for hardware systems in which an undesired event is tracked back to its causes, where the analysis terminates (Vesely, 1981).

1.6.2 Event-tree analysis

This is a superset of fault-tree analysis in that it uses graphical techniques to move events logically through a system to determine the consequences of these events (Connolly, 1993). It is possible to estimate probabilities of the occurrence of events from these diagrams.

Table 1.8 A summary of various code quality issues and the relevant portions of various standards

Code quality feature	Category	Standard reference(s)
Code walkthroughs/reviews	Static	ISO 9000-3 (4.1.1.2, 5.5.2, 5.6.4) TickIT supplier's guide (4.5.7) TickIT Auditor's course (15.2, 15.7) ISO 9001 (4.4, 4.10) CMM (level 3) Def Stan 00-55 (31.3.4) IEC 65A (Table D.9)
Code walkthroughs/reviews using coding standards	Static	ISO 9000-3 (maximum) (4.1.1.2.1, 5.6.4, poss. 6.4) TickIT Auditor's course (15.2) CMM (level 3) Def Stan 00-55 (31.1.1, 31.2.2) IEC 65A (12.2.13)
Coding Standards	Static	ISO 9000-3 (5.4.2.3, 5.4.5c, 5.6.3) TickIT supplier's guide (4.5.7) CMM (level 2) Def Stan 00-55 (31.1.1) IEC 65A (11.2.18, 19, 20)
Enforcement of safe subsets employed	Static	Def Stan 00-55 (31.2.2) IEC 65A (11.2.15)
Formally defined syntax and approved international or national validation certificate for compiler	Static	Def Stan 00-55 (36.3) IEC 65A (11.2.14)
Guaranteed interface consistency	Static	ISO 9000-3 (5.3.1, 5.6.2) European IT Quality System Auditor's guide (4.4.5) CMM (level 3) Def Stan 00-55 (30.1.5) IEC 65A Table D.10/5
Complexity/size limit or monitoring of components	Static	CMM (level 2) Def Stan 00-55 (30.1.3) IEC 65A Table D.10/1
Strongly typed language	Static	Def Stan 00-55 (31.1.2) IEC 65A (Clause table 11/7)
Statement coverage	Dynamic	Def Stan 00-55 (33.2)
Branch coverage including default clauses	Dynamic	Def Stan 00-55 (33.2)
Loop coverage	Dynamic	Def Stan 00-55 (33.2)
Coverage of boundary values, singularities, special values, out of range and erroneous values	Dynamic	ISO 9000-3 (5.7.2) Def Stan 00-55 (35.3) IEC 65A (Table D.2)
All path coverage	Dynamic	TickIT Auditor's course (15.5)
Use of regression testing	Dynamic	TickIT supplier's guide (4.5.15) CMM (level 2)
Recommendation for ISO 9001	—	Def Stan 00-55 IEC 65A

1.6.3 Check-lists

The idea of check-lists is to promote a critical appraisal of all aspects of the system rather than tracing through individual requirements, a sort of brainstorming. It supplements, not replaces, other techniques. See Myers (1979) and IEC (1986) for more details.

1.6.4 Common-cause failure analysis

The aim of this is to identify potential failures in redundant systems which could appear in redundant parts at the same time. In software terms, for example, the detection of software *clones* is of vital importance. This is a common problem when programmers hurry. An existing component is cloned and modified slightly, faithfully reproducing any errors in the original. In a safety-related system, any component in which a fault occurs should immediately lead to a search for any clones of that component within the system. Ideally, there should be no clones, only true reuse where a common component is used in more than one place.

1.6.5 Decision (truth) tables

A decision or truth table describes logical relationships between the states of program variables and associated actions. It is a very successful technique and is described in more detail in Chapter 5 in relation to the propositional calculus.

1.6.6 Failure modes, effects and criticality analysis (FMECA)

In essence, this decomposes a system into functional components and ranks them in terms of their effect on the safety of the overall system. Components with the highest such effect should then be treated with more exacting procedures. In software, this is not easy, although one such avenue is to count fan-in/fan-out of components to measure how tightly they are woven into the design. This is discussed in more detail in Section 3.2.1. For more details of FMECA, see SAE (1967).

To conclude this section, probably the biggest weapon available in improving the safety of a system is diversity. Littlewood (1993) notes for example, that there is undue reliance on the idea that having the right people and methods will lead to a dependable system. He then goes on to note that there is no empirical evidence to confirm that specific recommended techniques, such as formal methods or fault tolerance, can ensure an adequate level of safety and argues convincingly that only by integrating quantitative assessments of system safety from various sources can believable statements be made about such safety.

In the next chapter, the C language will be analysed in depth for its suitability as a candidate language for safety-related development.

2

THE C PROGRAMMING LANGUAGE:
A SAFETY CRITIQUE

2.1 OVERVIEW

The history of the C programming language is one of those stories that gets told again and again. The reader is referred to some of the many excellent textbooks such as the definitive reference, Kernighan and Ritchie (1988).

The growth in the use of C, and more recently C++, is phenomenal, with the latter language apparently attracting a doubling in its user base every seven months at the time of writing. To get some idea of the popularity of C-based languages and to introduce the idea of metrics early, Fig. 2.1 illustrates a relevant metric, the number of books recently published on mainstream programming languages by a major book distributor.

The aspect of particular importance here, however, is the fundamental safety of the standard language definition.

2.1.1 History of the C language

The C language was created at Bell Laboratories by Dennis Ritchie in 1972. One of its first uses was to rewrite the UNIX operating system, which had previously been written in PDP-11 assembly language. This link provides many clues to the essence of C programming. In its early years, it was used to write other systems programs, including text formatters, compiler generation tools, editors and the multifarious applications familiar to users of the standard UNIX toolset. Using a high-level language for such tools at the time was considered radical because the standard wisdom was to write them in assembly language for efficiency. In spite of this, C programs frequently outperformed their assembly counterparts.

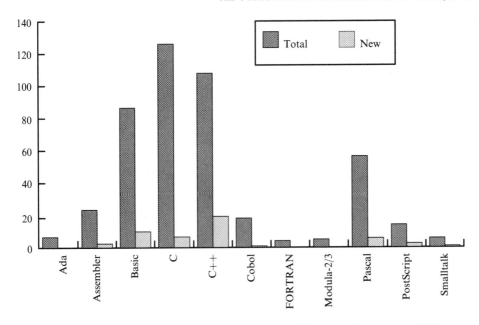

Figure 2.1 New and existing books available from one major publisher in the first quarter of 1993 split by language.

In order to understand language design it is necessary to understand the underlying model for the problems to be solved. Languages such as Smalltalk manipulate objects, whereas assembly language is much closer to the physical machine, although not as close as programming in machine code directly. C is highly unusual in that it provides a low-level model allowing overlap with applications formerly programmed in assembly language *and* a high-level model allowing programmers to build their own models with considerable powers of abstraction.

It is this low-level model aspect of C which frequently attracts vilification from the safety-related software development community,[1] although it has been the author's experience that the greatest abuse tends to come from people who are not familiar with the language. It is one of the central points of this book that if the weak points of a language are known as well as they are for C, then they can be controlled, yielding a simple and considerably safer language of great familiarity. Of course, if they are not controlled, then *big* problems can and will arise.

The author will avoid the temptation of describing some of the history of the C language and instead refer the reader to the evergreen Kernighan and Ritchie (1988). The language was finally standardized by ANSI in December 1989, after some 50 person years of work, with the reference number ANSI X3.159-1989. The standard took some six elapsed years to produce, which is actually an excellent sign of the quality of the standard in comparison with other languages, such as

---

[1] Interestingly enough, the supporters of other higher-level languages such as Ada in safety-related systems have a considerable self-acknowledged problem in proving the equivalence of the original source code and the generated object code. The closer relationship of C to the machine model inherently implies that this is much easier. This is discussed in more detail in Chapter 6. Engineers call this 'small steps first . . .'.

FORTRAN 90, which took 13 years. The amount of time taken to produce a standard is of course inversely proportional to the amount of natural agreement, which the author (at least) believes to be a useful quality metric for a programming standard. A year later, the standard was adopted by the ISO and the ANSI standard was dropped, although it is still known almost universally, but incorrectly, as the ANSI C standard. It is now formally known by its ISO standards reference number ISO/IEC 9899:1990. From now on this book will refer to the standard as Standard C to avoid perpetuating incorrect terminology while re-asserting the following:

> The ISO C standard has now replaced the ANSI C standard but is functionally identical apart from section numbering.[2]

Note that where references to Standard C occur in the text, they use the ANSI section number, rather than the ISO one. The reasons for this were described in the preface and attempt to match the observed availability of the respective standards in organizations. Before continuing, the author would like to lament the disappearance of the Rationale which appeared in the original ANSI C document but which was removed from the ISO document which replaces it. This is most unfortunate, as not only did it give invaluable insight as to why the committee came to the decisions it did, it is also the only source of the so-called *quiet changes*, which were those areas leading to different semantics between the original *de facto* Kernighan and Ritchie C and Standard C. This is discussed again shortly.

2.1.2 Some useful definitions

An excellent dictionary of all the various nomenclature used in the C language can be found in Jaeschke (1991), but the author has found that a knowledge of the following definitions is particularly useful when discussing and programming in the C language:

- Casting
  The act of explicitly converting one type to another, for example,

```
int        i = 0;
double     d = 1.;


i = (int)  d;    /* Explicit cast to convert types   */
```

This can be distinguished from implicitly converting types according to well-defined rules in Standard C:

```
int        i = 0;
double     d = 1.;


i =        d;    /*  Implicit cast to convert types   */
```

In a safety-related system, implicit casting should not be allowed because there is always the chance that either the program author or the program maintainer does

---

[2] The wording differs slightly in a few places, but there is no functional difference.

not understand the rules for implicit conversion. In contrast, explicit casting shows that the programmer is at least aware that something is going on, and this also makes it more amenable to inspection. In the higher levels of safety integrity, it may be that explicit casting also is expressly forbidden without appropriate sign-off confirming that there is no other practical way of implementing the algorithm.[3]

- Constraint
  A constraint is a syntactic or semantic restriction in the language which a compiler implementation must diagnose to be conformant with the standard. An example is 'Each of the operands of the division, multiplication and remainder operators shall have arithmetic type'.

- Conversions
  This is the word used to describe when an operand changes from one type to another. It is intimately associated with casting. Many kinds of conversion go on in C, including the (almost)[4] universal implicit converting of an array expression to a 'pointer to the first element' and the implicit converting of a function expression to a 'pointer to function'; the conversions between integer types; and the conversions between function arguments, formal and actual. The author has frequently been tripped up by these last two, the first because there were *quiet changes* between K&R C and Standard C,[5] and the second because the rules are different depending on whether old-style or new-style declarations and definitions are used.[6] Note that the act of widening a narrower version of an integral type is also known as a *promotion*.

---

[3] In general, all casting can be avoided by appropriate design when starting with a clean sheet, as it is not essential to the implementation of algorithms. However, in practice, the requirements to interface to a third-party software package or to implement communications links, for example, could lead to unavoidable use of casting. This has frequently been quoted to the author as a justification in both C and Ada safety-related systems. In Ada, these appear as use of the generic function `Unchecked_Conversion`.

[4] The exceptions are when the array or function is the operand of `sizeof` or the unary & operator. In fact, applying `sizeof` to a function type is a constraint violation. For an array, an additional exception occurs when it is a string used as an initializer of an array of characters or wide characters.

[5] There were a number of such quiet changes between the *de facto* K&R standard and Standard C. They are all documented in the Rationale in the original ANSI C document, but this conversion issue is considered by far the most important. In essence, if conversions between different widths of integer arise (i.e. char, short, int and long), K&R C would preserve *unsigned* values by casting an unsigned char to an unsigned int, for example (Unsigned Preserving Rule). In contrast, Standard C tries to fit them into a signed version of the wider integer first, and if it won't fit, it then uses an unsigned version (Value Preserving Rule). It is possible to distinguish statically the circumstances under which each rule would be used and the tool QA C, for example, can do this.

[6] This is most interesting. If old-style declarations and definitions are used, the functions referenced always expect and get widened types (integer or floating point, e.g. float to double). In contrast, if new-style function prototype declarations and definitions are used and specify narrow types, the implementation has the option to widen some, all or none. This is a terrible own goal, placing programmers in the predicament of either using old-style declarations and definitions for a superficially better-defined behaviour, but which is not normally checked for consistency, or new-style equivalents giving consistency checking but implementation-defined behaviour. Life gets even more complicated by the fact that the K&R C compilers were not terribly reliable with this, and that old-style behaviour is likely to disappear from future C standards. Given that function prototypes are mandatory in C++, they are universally recommended here. Note finally that, if declarations are inadvertently not visible at the same time as the definition, it is possible to get potentially worse behaviour than using the old-style versions. This however can be statically prevented.

- Order of evaluation and precedence
  These two concepts are mentioned together for the very important reason that they are most often confused in the many programming standards which the author has reviewed. This confusion commonly takes the form that 'order of evaluation should be guaranteed by parenthesizing the expression ...', or some such words. In fact, order of evaluation is unaffected by precedence. Precedence refers to the order in which *operators* are evaluated, whereas order of evaluation refers to the order in which the *operands* are fetched and evaluated. Precedence is fully defined by the C standard, whereas order of evaluation is formally unspecified. Consider the following examples:

```
x = 2 + 3 * 2;          /* x = 8 (* done before +)    */
x = 2 + (3 * 2);        /* x = 8, order explicit       */
x = (2 + 3) * 2;        /* x = 10, order overridden    */

x = i++ + a[i];         /* Order in which operands     */
                        /* evaluated is undefined      */
x = (i++) + a[i];       /* Still unspecified           */
```

These topics will be covered in more detail in Section 2.8.2.
- Scope and linkage
  Scope governs the region of a program in which an object is visible. There are four types of scope: block, file, function and function prototype. File scope is related to linkage. Objects of file scope which are not declared static are visible outside the file and are said to have *external linkage*. File scope objects declared using static are said to have *internal linkage*.
- Strictly conforming program
  A program that uses only the defined features of Standard C. Its output must not depend on unspecified, undefined or implementation-defined features.
- Translation unit
  This is that set of source lines resulting from complete pre-processing of the user's original source file, i.e. all referenced include files have been expanded, macros expanded and so on.

2.1.3 The current position

Language standardization efforts do not stop when a standard appears. It will be useful here then to summarize the position with C at the time of writing. An excellent review with approximately the same vintage can be found in Jones (1993b). The following paraphrases this paper, but the original is recommended for details.

As the C standard is now international, it is no longer the responsibility of the ANSI C Committee but has passed to the ISO C Committee who are active in three main areas.

The ISO Addendum

In essence, this covers certain 'insecurities' in the text of the Standard C document itself. However, the greater part of the work is involved in processing the Danish proposal and the Japanese proposal, both of which are related to characters which cannot be represented by the Standard C standard character set, which is based on ASCII. Of these, the Japanese proposal for Multi-byte Support Extensions to cover a character set of potentially thousands of characters has the greatest chance of success, with no nations currently voting No on the proposals.

The contents of this Addendum have the same weight as the C Standard itself, and as such it is known as a Normative Addendum.

Defect Report processing

These are concerned with queries regarding the semantics of the C Standard itself. Formally known as Interpretation Requests, they are now being treated under the ISO banner of Defect Reports. The questions take several forms:

- An item in the Standard is not understood.
- An item in the Standard is understood, but the questioner does not like the wording.
- The Standard does not say anything.
- The Standard is not consistent.

There are currently just over 50 such requests outstanding, which is remarkably good for a document as complex as a programming language definition. This compares very favourably with other languages (as Chapter 6 verifies), and is a strong argument in favour of its use in safety-related systems.

Numerical extensions to C

This work is being carried out by a subcommittee of the original ANSI committee X3J11, called the NCEG, the Numerical C Extensions Group. It has no relationship to the ISO and is being driven mainly by the needs of supercomputing users. It is very likely to be an extremely influential document in the future of C (and also C++), however. A number of items are under discussion by the committee and the following are at an advanced stage:

- *Variable length arrays* In C, such arrays are implicitly handled by pointers which remove most of the clues regarding data dependency whereby an optimizing compiler could vectorize the code. This feature will restore such clues, such that arrays can be handled as in FORTRAN.
- *Compound literals and initialization* This will allow entire arrays, structures and unions to be initialized in one assignment other than in an initializer statement.

2.1.4 A safety-related view

All computer languages used in safety-related systems should be subject to very serious soul-searching indeed, because weak links are built into them in a number of different ways. These include, but are not limited to, the following:

(a) Features whose definition the language standards committee cannot agree on for some reason and for which some kind of caveat is issued with the standard.

(b) Features which the language standards committee inadvertently leave out or incompletely define.

(c) Features which seem entirely well-defined but cause problems in practice, either directly or indirectly.

Items (b) and (c) will be dealt with shortly, but in the case of (a), perhaps one of the C standard's most significant features was the explicit recognition that there remain issues which the standards committee could not resolve or specify, and which have been itemized. This is by no means common in programming language standards. Now, as has already been seen, the notion of specifiability is a key concept in any safety-related area. For example, the IEC SC65A draft safety standard previously discussed in Chapter 1 requires that a candidate language be completely and unambiguously defined. It is quite likely with the current state of knowledge that no such language exists, so the next best alternative is to delineate, as far as is possible, precisely those areas which are ambiguous or undefined. For the C language, issues for both the language and the run-time library are grouped together and appear as Appendix F of the Standard under the following four categories:

- *Unspecified behaviour*   These concern those features of the language whose behaviour gives the implementor some latitude in translating the program, although this does not extend so far as failing to translate the program. Put a little more simply, it concerns correct program constructs and correct data for which the C Standard imposes no requirements. An example is the evaluation order of certain expressions (those not involving '&&', '||', '?:' or ','), as described earlier.

    In all there are 22 such items, grouped together as Section F.1 of Appendix F of the C Standard.

- *Undefined behaviour*   In essence, this allows the implementor licence *not to catch* certain program errors which may be difficult to diagnose. Put another way, it concerns illegal program constructs for which the C Standard imposes no requirements. From a safety-related point of view, these very definitely represent dangerous areas. In addition, this category allows the implementor licence to enhance the language by providing a definition of the officially unlicensed behaviour. An example is the behaviour resulting when an actual argument of incorrect type is passed to a function call.

    In all there are 97 such items, grouped together as Section F.2 of Appendix F of the C Standard.

- *Implementation-defined behaviour*   This category allows the implementor freedom to choose an appropriate approach, *providing that the approach is explained to the user*. From the safety-related viewpoint, these are well-defined and therefore capable of proof, but would not in general be acceptable in an application designed for multiple platforms without special steps to prove that the system did not depend on them. It should be noted that, in practice, the degree of implementation definition varies wildly from those features implemented the same way in all practical compilers to those which seem to differ in every implementation. There are a large number of these and a view must be taken on many of them in order not to bring development to a complete halt.

    In all there are 76 such items, grouped together in 14 categories as Section F.3 of Appendix F of the C Standard.

• *Locale-specific behaviour* The set of features that are allowed to vary according to international requirements such as the character set.

In all there are 6 such items, grouped together as Section F.4 of Appendix F of the C Standard.

The most natural way of subdividing each of these categories is into those that can be detected at the *compilation* stage, and those that can only be detected at *run-time*.

2.1.5 Static vs. dynamic detectability

This subdivision into *compilation detectable* and *run-time detectable* features is of immense importance in safety-related systems, and is a feature of the Ada language definition, for example, which carefully distinguishes between the two (Ghezzi and Jazayeri, 1982). The reason for this is quite simple. By definition, all code is subject to the 'quality test' of being compilable, otherwise it is guaranteed not to form part of the target system as no object code will have been generated. From a safety-related point of view, the notion of being compilable is further strengthened by using a compiler which is formally validated, as, in the case of C, this mandates that some form of diagnostic message shall be output for any program containing a syntax error or a *constraint violation*.

In contrast, as is very well known, run-time testing is always incomplete, except perhaps for the most trivial of programs. This important topic is discussed in more detail in Sections 5.1.2 and 5.3.3.

The conclusions are simple. All compilation detectable problems will be detected, *and must be corrected,* whereas run-time problems are relatively unlikely to be detected during testing and could first manifest themselves as a system failure. This concept is well illustrated by the notion of *strongly typed languages.* By definition, a strongly typed language is one for which all type mismatches can be detected at compile-time, and therefore all will be, provided the compiler does its job properly. A language which does not have this property automatically implies that some type mismatches can only be detected at run-time and may therefore not be detected at all. Type mismatches are a rich source of error in computer programs and in recognition of this IEC SC65A, as discussed in Chapter 1, currently recommends that only strongly typed languages be used for Integrity Levels 1 to 4, i.e. anything which is safety-related.

It is immensely desirable to extend the notion of strong typing to other features of a programming language, such that other potential sources of unreliable behaviour can be detected by or before compilation. The more that can be detected before or at compilation, the better. It has already been seen in Chapter 1 that there is a strong initiative towards the production of systems in which there are no statically-detectable faults. The following sections of this chapter will therefore discuss all items of C covered by parts (a), (b) and (c) in the list at the beginning of Section 2.1.4, and attempt to list those that are detectable statically, i.e. before compilation. The rest will be assumed to be detectable dynamically and will be treated as immensely desirable but impossible to mandate from the point of view of safety-related systems. Note that, at this stage, the existence of tools to detect them is irrelevant; we are simply interested in the property of being detectable.

It is assumed therefore that *all* statically-detectable features could in principle be found, given appropriate tools, whereas dynamically-detectable features will only be found if the testing is sufficiently comprehensive, even assuming the presence of appropriate tools. From this analysis can spring tools to support the concept. It will be seen that although the Standard C notion of a strictly conforming program defined to contain *no* unspecified, undefined or implementation-defined features would be very difficult to achieve in practice, nearly all such features are either detectable by existing tools or avoidable. Note, finally, that for each of the following lists discussing the unspecified, undefined and implementation-defined features, a reference number is added which corresponds to the order in which the feature appears within Appendix F, although this number is not present in the Standard C document itself. This reference number will be used later when constructing lists of things which it is reasonable to exclude from safety-related applications.

2.2 UNSPECIFIED BEHAVIOUR

This section refers directly to Appendix F.1 of the C standard, categorizing each unspecified feature appropriately, and enlarging upon them where the standard itself is rather terse. The potential severity of any of these items is also judged, based on the experience of their occurrence rate in the field as is discussed in Chapter 4, although not all features are covered. The reader is reminded that unspecified behaviour refers to the behaviour when certain *legal* features are encountered but about which the standard declines to comment.

Each feature is classified (see Table 2.1) according as to its potential severity, its detectability, its potential for automation, and its recommended treatment, using the nomenclature:

Potential severity	*Detectability*	*Automation*	*Treatment*
severe | medium | mild | nil	static | dynamic	automatic | semi | manual	avoid | wrap it | benchmark | ban it

If an item is flagged as automatic, it means that there is existing tool support to detect it among those discussed in Chapter 5. The severity is influenced by whether or not the author had come across it in practice or by discussing with others. Note that when a feature is stated to be statically detectable, this is meant to imply that *dependence* on the feature is statically detectable.

As can be seen, there are various treatments as summarized below:

- *Static*
  If a feature is statically detectable, it can therefore be avoided. Its avoidance can be guaranteed if the static detectability is tool-supported. Wherever the third column states Semi or Automatic, the author is aware of a tool which can detect it.
- *Wrap for consistency*
  In this case, a format of a returned entity is not defined by the standard. The simple solution is to define a set of returned values and a wrapper function for the standard function. For example, a wrapper function `std_time()` could be used to hide the standard `time(...)` function, while also mapping its output to a

Table 2.1 A list of all unspecified items in Standard C (*Continues*)

1. The manner and timing of static initialization.

Nil	—	—	—

2. The behaviour if a printable character is written when the active position is at the final position of a line.

Mild	—	—	—

3. The behaviour if a backspace character is written when the active position is at the initial position of a line.

Mild	—	—	—

4. The behaviour if a horizontal tab character is written when the active position is at or past the last defined horizontal tabulation position.

Mild	—	—	—

5. The behaviour if a vertical tab character is written when the active position is at or past the last defined vertical tabulation position.

Mild	—	—	—

6. The representations of floating types.

Medium	Dynamic	Semi	Benchmark

7. The order in which expressions are evaluated.

Severe	Static	Automatic	Avoid

8. The order in which side-effects take place.

Severe	Static	Automatic	Avoid

9. The order in which the function designator and the arguments in a function call are evaluated.

Severe	Static	Automatic	Avoid

10. The alignment of the addressable storage unit allocated to hold a bit-field.

Mild	Static	Automatic	Ban bit-fields

11. The layout of storage for parameters.

Nil	—	—	—

12. The order in which # and ## operators are evaluated during macro substitution.

Medium	Static	Automatic	Ban them

13. Whether `errno` is a macro or an external identifier.

Mild	—	—	—

14. Whether `setjmp` is a macro or an external identifier.

Mild	Static	Automatic	Ban `setjmp`

15. Whether `va_end` is a macro or an external identifier.

Mild	Static	Automatic	Ban va_end

Table 2.1 A list of all unspecified items in Standard C (*Concluded*)

16. The value of the file position indicator after a successful call to the `ungetc` function for a text stream, until all pushed-back characters are read or discarded.

Mild	Static	Automatic	Wrap for consistency

17. The details of the value stored by the `fgetpos` function on success.

Medium	—	—	Wrap for consistency

18. The details of the value returned by the `ftell` function for a text stream on success.

Medium	—	—	Wrap for consistency

19. The order and contiguity of storage allocated by the `calloc`, `malloc` and `realloc` functions.

Mild (in practice)	Dynamic	Automatic	Detect abuse

20. Which of two elements that compare as equal is returned by the `bsearch` function.

Mild	Static	Automatic	Wrap for consistency

21. The order in an array sorted by the `qsort` function of two elements that compare as equal.

Mild	Static	Automatic	Wrap for consistency

22. The encoding of the calendar time returned by the `time` function.

Medium	Static	Automatic	Wrap for consistency

standard format. The new function `std_time()` in general would need to be modified for each system, but mandating its use and forbidding the standard `time(...)` function using a simple screening tool, such as the UNIX filter `grep`, solves the problem.

- *Benchmark*
  In this list, this only covers item 6 on the representation of floating-point types. It is recommended here that the floating-point implementation is benchmarked using an application such as `paranoia`, as described later. In addition, the usual precautions about forbidding the casting of doubles to narrower types should hold as discussed later.

2.3 UNDEFINED BEHAVIOUR

This section refers directly to Appendix F.2 of the C Standard, categorizing each feature appropriately as was done for the unspecified features tabulated above (Table 2.2). The reader is reminded that undefined behaviour refers to the behaviour when certain *illegal* constructs are encountered.

2.4 IMPLEMENTATION-DEFINED BEHAVIOUR

This section refers directly to Appendix F.3 of the C standard categorizing each feature appropriately (see Table 2.3), as was done for the unspecified and undefined

Table 2.2 **Complete list of explicitly undefined items in Standard C** (*Continues*)

1. A non-empty source file does not end in a new-line character, ends in a new-line character immediately preceded by a backslash character, or ends in a partial preprocessing token or comment.

Nil	Static	Automatic	Avoid

2. A character not in the required character set is encountered in a source file, except in a preprocessing token that is never converted to a token, a character constant, a string literal, a header name or a comment.

Mild	Static	Automatic	Avoid

3. A comment, string literal, character constant, or header name contains an invalid multibyte character or does not begin and end in the initial shift state.

Mild	Static	Semi	Ban multibyte

4. An unmatched ' or " character is encountered on a logical source line during tokenization.

Mild	Static	Automatic	Avoid

5. The same identifier is used more than once as a label in the same function.

Severe	Static	Automatic	Avoid

6. An identifier is used that is not visible in the current scope.

Severe	Static	Automatic	Avoid

7. Identifiers intended to denote the same entity differ in a character beyond the minimal significant characters.

Medium	Static	Automatic	Avoid

8. The same identifier has both internal and external linkage in the same translation unit.

Severe	Static	Automatic	Avoid

9. The value stored in a pointer that referred to an object with automatic storage duration is used.

Severe	Static	Automatic	Avoid

10. Two declarations of the same object or function specify types that are not compatible.

Severe	Static	Automatic	Avoid

11. An unspecified escape sequence is encountered in a character constant or a string literal.

Severe	Static	Automatic	Avoid

12. An attempt is made to modify a string literal of either form.

Severe	Dynamic	Semi	Avoid

13. A character string literal token is adjacent to a wide string literal token.

Mild	Static	Automatic	Avoid

14. The characters ', \, ", or /* are encountered between the < and > delimiters or the characters ', \, or /* are encountered between the " delimiters in the two forms of a header name preprocessing token.

Mild	Static	Automatic	Avoid

Table 2.2 Complete list of explicitly undefined items in Standard C (*Continues*)

15. An arithmetic conversion produces a result that cannot be represented in the space provided.

Severe	Static/Dynamic	Semi	Avoid

16. An `lvalue` with an incomplete type is used in a context that requires the value of the designated object.

Mild	Static	Automatic	Avoid

17. The value of a void expression is used or an implicit conversion (except to `void`) is applied to a void expression.

Mild	Static	Automatic	Avoid

18. An object is modified more than once, or is modified and accessed other than to determine the new value, between two sequence points.

Severe	Static[7]	Automatic	Avoid

19. An arithmetic operation is invalid (such as division or modulus by 0) or produces a result that cannot be represented in the space provided (such as overflow or underflow).

Severe	Dynamic	Automatic	Avoid

20. An object has its stored value accessed by an `lvalue` that does not have one of the following types: the declared type of the object, a qualified version of the declared type of the object, the signed or unsigned type corresponding to the declared type of the object, the signed or unsigned type corresponding to a qualified version of the declared type of the object, an aggregate or union type that (recursively) includes one of the aforementioned types among its members, or a character type.

Severe	Dynamic	Semi	Avoid

21. An argument to a function is a void expression.

Mild	Static	Automatic	Avoid

22. For a function call without a function prototype, the number of arguments does not agree with the number of parameters.

Severe	Static	Automatic	Avoid

23. For a function call without a function prototype, if the function is defined without a function prototype, and the types of the arguments after promotion do not agree with those of the parameters after promotion.

Severe	Static	Automatic	Avoid

24. If a function is called with a function prototype and the function is not defined with a compatible type.

Severe	Static	Automatic	Avoid

25. A function that accepts a variable number of arguments is called without a function prototype that ends with an ellipsis.

Severe	Static	Automatic	Avoid

26. An invalid array reference, null pointer reference, or reference to an object declared with automatic storage duration in a terminated block occurs.

Severe	Dynamic	Automatic	Avoid

---

[7] For full static avoidance of this, functions would have to be forbidden to alter internal statics, globals or actual arguments. This prevents expressions such as f() + g() causing problems.

Table 2.2 Complete list of explicitly undefined items in Standard C (*Continues*)

27. A pointer to a function is converted to point to a function of a different type and used to call a function of a type not compatible with the original type.

Severe	Dynamic	Automatic	Avoid

28. A pointer to a function is converted to a pointer to an object or a pointer to an object is converted to a pointer to a function.

Severe	Static	Automatic	Avoid

29. A pointer is converted to other than an integral or pointer type.

Severe	Static	Automatic	Avoid

30. A pointer that does not behave like a pointer to an element of an array object is added to or subtracted from.

Severe	Dynamic	Automatic	Avoid

31. Pointers that do not behave as if they point to the same array object are subtracted.

Severe	Dynamic	Automatic	Avoid

32. An expression is shifted by a negative number or by an amount greater than or equal to the width in bits of the expression being shifted.

Severe	Static/Dynamic	Automatic	Avoid

33. Pointers are compared, using a relational operator, that do not point to the same aggregate or union.

Severe	Dynamic	Automatic	Avoid

34. An object is assigned to an overlapping object.

Severe	Dynamic	Semi	Avoid

35. An identifier for an object is declared with no linkage and the type of the object is incomplete after its declarator, or after its init-declarator if it has an initializer.

Severe	Static	Automatic	Avoid

36. A function is declared at block scope with a storage-class specifier other than `extern`.

Severe	Static	Automatic	Avoid

37. A structure or union is defined as containing only unnamed members.

Nil	—	—	Ban bit-fields

38. A bit-field is declared with a type other than `int`, `signed int` or `unsigned int`.

Severe	Static	Automatic	Ban bit-fields

39. An attempt is made to modify an object with const-qualified type by means of an `lvalue` with non-const-qualified type.

Severe	Dynamic	Semi	Avoid

40. An attempt is made to refer to an object with volatile-qualified type by means of an `lvalue` with non-volatile-qualified type.

Severe	Dynamic	Semi	Avoid

Table 2.2 Complete list of explicitly undefined items in Standard C (*Continues*)

41. The value of an uninitialized object that has automatic storage duration is used before a value is assigned.

Fatal	Static/Dynamic	Semi	Avoid

42. An object with aggregate or union type with static storage duration has a non-brace-enclosed initializer, or an object with aggregate or union type with automatic storage duration has either a single expression initializer with a type other than that of the object or a non-brace-enclosed initializer.

Severe	Static	Semi	Avoid

43. The value of a function is used, but no value was returned.

Fatal	Static	Automatic	Force in function

44. An identifier with external linkage is used but there does not exist exactly one external definition in the program for the identifier.

Severe	Static	Automatic	Avoid

45. A function that accepts a variable number of arguments is defined without a parameter type list that ends with the ellipsis notation.

Severe	Static	Automatic	Avoid

46. An identifier for an object with internal linkage and an incomplete type is declared with a tentative definition.

Severe	Static	Automatic	Avoid

47. The token `defined` is generated during the expansion of a `#if` or `#elif` preprocessing directive.

Medium	Static	Automatic	Avoid

48. The `#include` preprocessing directive that results after expansion does not match one of the two header name forms.

Mild	Static	Automatic	Avoid

49. A macro argument consists of no preprocessing tokens.

Mild	Static	Automatic	Avoid

50. There are sequences of preprocessing tokens within the list of macro arguments that would otherwise act as preprocessing directive lines.

Medium	Static	Automatic	Avoid

51. The result of the preprocessing operator `#` is not a valid character string literal.

Mild	Static	Automatic	Avoid

52. The result of the preprocessing concatenation operator `# #` is not a valid preprocessing token.

Mild	Static	Automatic	Avoid

53. The `#line` preprocessing directive that results after expansion does not match one of the two well-defined forms.

Mild	Static	Automatic	Avoid

Table 2.2 Complete list of explicitly undefined items in Standard C (*Continues*)

54. One of the following identifiers is the subject of a #define or #undef preprocessing directive: defined, _LINE_, _FILE_, _DATE_, _TIME_ or _STDC_.

Mild	Static	Automatic	Avoid

55. An attempt is made to copy an object to an overlapping object by use of a library function other than memmove.

Severe	Dynamic	Manual/Semi	Avoid

56. The effect if the program redefines a reserved external identifier.

Severe	Static	Automatic	Avoid

57. The effect if a standard header is included within an external definition, is included for the first time after the first reference to any of the functions or objects it declares, or to any of the types or macros it defines; or is included while a macro is defined with a name the same as a keyword.

Medium	Static	Automatic	Avoid

58. A macro definition of errno is suppressed to obtain access to an actual object.

Medium	Static	Automatic	No #undef errno

59. The parameter member-designator of an offsetof macro is an invalid right operand of the operator for the type parameter or designates bit-field member of a structure.

Medium	Static	Automatic	Ban offsetof

60. A library function argument has an invalid value, unless the behaviour is specified explicitly.

Severe	Dynamic	Automatic	Avoid

61. A library function that accepts a variable number of arguments is not declared.

Severe	Static	Automatic	No implicit decls.

62. The macro definition of assert is suppressed to obtain access to an actual function.

Medium	Static	Automatic	Avoid

63. The argument to a character-handling function is out of the domain.

Severe	Dynamic	Automatic	Avoid

64. A macro definition of setjmp is suppressed to obtain access to an actual function.

Medium	Static	Automatic	Ban setjmp

65. An invocation of the setjmp macro occurs in a context other than as the controlling expression in a selection or iteration statement, or in a comparison with an integral constant expression (possibly as implied by the unary ! operator) as the controlling expression of a selection or iteration statement, or as an expression statement (possibly cast to void).

Severe	Static	Automatic	Ban setjmp

66. An object of automatic storage class that does not have volatile-qualified type has been changed between a setjmp invocation and a longjmp call and then has its value accessed.

Severe	Static	Automatic	Ban setjmp/longjmp

67. The longjmp function is invoked from a nested signal routine.

Severe	Static	Automatic	Ban longjmp

Table 2.2 **Complete list of explicitly undefined items in Standard C** (*Continues*)

68. A signal occurs other than as the result of calling the `abort` or `raise` function, and the signal handler calls any function in the standard library other than the `signal` function itself or refers to any object with static storage duration other than by assigning a value to a static storage duration variable of type `volatile sig_atomic_t`.

Severe	Static	Automatic	Ban signal

69. The value of `errno` is referred to after a signal occurs other than as a result of calling the `abort` or `raise` function and the corresponding signal handler calls the `signal` function such that it returns the value `SIG_ERR`.

Severe	Static	Automatic	Ban signal

70. The macro `va_arg` is invoked with the parameter `ap` that was passed to a function that invoked the macro `va_arg` with the same parameter.

Medium?	Static	Automatic	Ban va_arg

71. A macro definition of `va_start`, `va_arg` or `va_end` or a combination thereof is suppressed to obtain access to an actual function.

Medium	Static	Automatic	Ban them

72. The parameter *parmN* of a `va_start` macro is declared with the register storage class, or with a function or array type, or with a type that is not compatible with the type that results after application of the default argument promotions.

Medium	Static	Automatic	Ban va_start

73. There is no actual next argument for a `va_arg` macro invocation.

Medium	Static	Automatic	Ban va_arg

74. The type of the actual next argument in a variable argument list disagrees with the type specified by the `va_arg` macro.

Medium	Static	Automatic	Ban va_arg

75. The `va_end` macro is invoked without a corresponding invocation of the `va_start` macro.

Medium	Static	Automatic	Ban them

76. A return occurs from a function with a variable argument list initialized by the `va_start` macro before the `va_end` macro is invoked.

Medium	Static	Automatic	Ban them

77. The stream for the `fflush` function points to an input stream or to an update stream in which the most recent operation was input.

Medium	Dynamic	Automatic	Avoid

78. An output operation on an update stream is followed by an input operation without an intervening call to the `fflush` function or a file positioning function, or an input operation on an update stream is followed by an output operation without an intervening call to a file positioning function.

Medium	Dynamic	Automatic	Avoid

79. The format for the `fprintf` or `fscanf` functions does not match the argument list.

Severe	Static/Dynamic	Automatic	Avoid

Table 2.2 Complete list of explicitly undefined items in Standard C (*Continues*)

80. An invalid conversion specification is found in the format for the `fprintf` or `fscanf` functions.

Severe	Static/Dynamic	Automatic	Avoid

81. A `%%` conversion specification for the `fprintf` or `fscanf` functions contains characters between the pair of `%` characters.

Mild	Static/Dynamic	Automatic	Avoid

82. A conversion specification for the `fprintf` function contains an h or l with a conversion specifier other than d, i, n, o, u, x or X, or an L with a conversion specifier other than e, E, f, g or G.

Mild	Static/Dynamic	Automatic	Avoid

83. A conversion specification for the `fprintf` function contains a # flag with a conversion specifier other than o, x, X, e, E, f, g or G.

Mild	Static/Dynamic	Automatic	Avoid

84. A conversion specification for the `fprintf` function contains an 0 flag with a conversion specifier other than d, i, o, u, x, X, e, E, f, g or G.

Mild	Static/Dynamic	Automatic	Avoid

85. An aggregate or union, or a pointer to an aggregate or union, is an argument to the `fprintf` function, except for the conversion specifiers `%s` (for an array of character type) or `%p` (for a pointer to `void`).

Mild	Dynamic	Automatic	Avoid

86. A single conversion by the `fprintf` function produces more than 509 characters of output.

Mild	Dynamic	Automatic	Avoid

87. A conversion specification for the `fscanf` function contains an h or l with a conversion specifier other than d, i, n, o, u or x, or an L with a conversion specifier other than e, f or g.

Mild	Dynamic	Automatic	Avoid

88. A pointer value printed by `%p` conversion by the `fprintf` function during a previous program execution is the argument for `%p` conversion by the `fscanf` function.

Mild	Dynamic	Automatic	Avoid

89. The result of a conversion by the `fscanf` function cannot be represented in the space provided, or the receiving object does not have an appropriate type.

Severe	Dynamic	Automatic	Avoid

90. The result of converting a string to a number by the `atof`, `atoi` or `atol` functions cannot be represented.

Medium	Dynamic	Automatic	Avoid

91. The value of a pointer that refers to space deallocated by a call to the `free` or `realloc` function is referred to.

Severe	Dynamic	Automatic	Avoid

92. The pointer argument to the `free` or `realloc` function does not match a pointer earlier returned by `calloc`, `malloc` or `realloc`, or the object pointed to has been deallocated by a call to `free` or `realloc`.

Severe	Dynamic	Automatic	Avoid

Table 2.2 Complete list of explicitly undefined items in Standard C (*Concluded*)

93. A program executes more than one call to the `exit` function.

Severe	Dynamic	Automatic	Wrap for consistency

94. The result of an integer arithmetic function (`abs`, `div`, `labs` or `ldiv`) cannot be represented.

Severe	Dynamic	Automatic	Avoid

95. The shift states for the `mblen`, `mbtowc` and `wctomb` functions are not explicitly reset to the initial state when the `LC_CTYPE` category of the current locale is changed.

Mild	Static	Automatic	Allow ASCII only

96. An array written to by a copying or concatenation function is too small.

Severe	Dynamic	Automatic	Avoid

97. An invalid conversion specification is found in the format for the `strftime` function.

Severe	Dynamic	Automatic	Avoid

features tabulated above. The reader is reminded that implementation-defined behaviour has to be defined, but is allowed to vary from implementation to implementation. In other words, it is in principle suitable for formal argument,[8] but the formal argument would have to be different for each implementation. In other words, in a safety-related application, given the cost of a typical formal argument, *it makes far more sense simply to ban the offending items*. Given its nature, it is probably reasonable to claim that all implementation-defined characteristics of an implementation can be determined by suitably constructed test programs, although there will always remain obscure issues that cannot be addressed. One such nasty area concerns the requirements for explicit timing of some safety-related applications and its relationship with optimization. It is probably best to ban optimization of any safety-related code on the grounds that it is responsible for the bulk of compiler errors reported in most languages and also because it effectively alters the defined characteristics of the program (hopefully without changing the end-product).[9] It is good practice, however, to test a program with and without optimization turned on. If the results are the same, this lends further confidence in the implementation.

The implementation-defined features are split into 14 categories in the standard itself and these are repeated in Table 2.3, although individual items are numbered sequentially.

In this section, it is suggested that a number of functions are wrapped for consistency, as was described in Section 2.2.

---

[8] Assuming it is deterministic, as pointed out by David Blyth in a personal communication. Defining non-deterministic behaviour would be excessively perverse, however.

[9] Section 2.1.2.3 of Standard C states, among other things, that 'An actual implementation need not evaluate part of an expression if it can deduce that its value is not used and that no needed side effects are produced (including any caused by calling a function or accessing a volatile object)'. So in theory, it is possible for changes to take place even if optimization is not turned on, although traditionally compiler writers tend to 'go for it' only when given *carte blanche* by the supply of an appropriate compiler flag. This perhaps unlikely but potentially dangerous loophole is present in other languages also.

Table 2.3 Complete list of implementation-defined features of Standard C (*Continues*)

Translation

1. How a diagnostic is identified.

Nil (in practice)	—	—	—

Environment

2. The semantics of the arguments to `main`.

Mild	Static/Dynamic	Semi	—

3. What constitutes an interactive device.

Nil	—	—	—

Identifiers

4. The number of significant initial characters (beyond 31) in an identifier without external linkage.

Mild	Static	Automatic	Avoid

5. The number of significant initial characters (beyond 6) in an identifier with external linkage.

Mild (in practice)	Static	Automatic	Can get away with

6. Whether case distinctions are significant in an identifier with external linkage.

Mild (in practice)	Static	Automatic	Can get away with

Characters

7. The members of the source and execution character sets, except as explicitly specified in the standard.

Mild	Static	Semi/Auto	Enforce character set

8. The shift states used for the encoding of multibyte characters.

Nil	Static	Automatic	Ban multibyte

9. The number of bits in a character in the execution character set.

Mild (in practice)	?	—	Can be determined

10. The mapping of members of the source character set (in character constants and string literals) to members of the execution character set.

Mild (in practice)	—	—	—

11. The value of an integer character constant that contains a character or escape sequence not represented in the basic execution character set or the extended character set for a wide character constant.

Medium	Static	Automatic	Avoid

12. The value of an integer character constant that contains more than one character or a wide character constant that contains more than one multibyte character.

Medium	Static	Automatic	Ban multibyte

13. The current locale used to convert multibyte characters into corresponding wide characters (codes) for a wide character constant.

Mild	—	—	Ban multibyte

14. Whether a 'plain' char has the same range of values as `signed char` or `unsigned char`.

Medium	Static	Automatic	Easily determined

Table 2.3 Complete list of implementation-defined features of Standard C (*Continues*)

Integers

15. The representation and sets of values of the various types of integers.

Medium (in practice)	Static/Dynamic	Semi	Abuse detectable

16. The result of converting an integer to a shorter signed integer, or the result of converting an unsigned integer to a signed integer of equal length, if the value cannot be represented.

Severe	Static	Automatic	Avoid

17. The results of bitwise operations on signed integers.

Severe	Static	Automatic	Abuse detectable

18. The sign of the remainder on integer division.

Mild (in practice!)	?	?	Avoid

19. The result of a right shift of a negative-valued signed integral type.

Severe	Static	Automatic	Avoid

Floating-point

20. The representations and sets of values of the various types of floating-point numbers.

Medium (in practice)	Static/Dynamic	Semi	Much abuse detected

21. The direction of truncation when an integral number is converted to a floating-point number that cannot exactly represent the original value.

Probably mild	—	—	—

22. The direction of truncation or rounding when a floating-point number is converted to a narrower floating-point number.

Severe	Static	Automatic	Avoid

Arrays and pointers

23. The type of integer required to hold the maximum size of an array—that is, the type of the `sizeof` operator, `size_t`.

Probably mild	—	—	—

24. The result of casting a pointer to an integer or vice versa.

Potentially severe	Static	Automatic	Avoid

25. The type of integer required to hold the difference between two pointers to elements of the same array, `ptrdiff_t`.

Probably mild	—	—	—

Registers

26. The extent to which objects can actually be placed in registers by use of the `register` storage-class specifier.

Nil	—	—	Ban register

Structures, unions, enumerations and bit-fields

27. A member of a union object is accessed using a member of a different type.

Severe	Static/Dynamic	Semi/Automatic	Inspect all unions

Table 2.3 Complete list of implementation-defined features of Standard C (*Continues*)

28. The padding and alignment of members of structures. This should present no problem unless binary data written by one implementation are read by another.

Nil	—	—	—

29. Whether a 'plain' int bit-field is treated as a `signed int` bit-field or as an `unsigned int` bit-field.

Medium	Static	Automatic	Ban bit-fields

30. The order of allocation of bit-fields within a unit.

Mild	Static	Automatic	Ban bit-fields

31. Whether a bit-field can straddle a storage-unit boundary.

Mild	Static	Automatic	Ban bit-fields

32. The integer type chosen to represent the values of an enumeration type.

Mild	—	—	Could ban enum

Qualifiers
33. What constitutes an access to an object that has volatile-qualified type.

Medium	Static	Automatic	Inspect all volatile

Declarators
34. The maximum number of declarators that may modify an arithmetic, structure or union type.

Nil (in practice)	—	—	—

Statements
35. The maximum number of `case` values in a `switch` statement.

Nil (in practice)	—	—	—

Preprocessing directives
36. Whether the value of a single-character character constant in a constant expression that controls conditional inclusion matches the value of the same character constant in the execution character set. Whether such a character constant may have a negative value.

Nil	—	—	—

37. The method for locating includable source files.

Nil	—	—	—

38. The support of quoted names for includable source files.

Nil	—	—	—

39. The mapping of source file character sequences.

Nil	—	—	—

40. The behaviour on each recognized #pragma directive.

Severe	Static	Automatic	Ban #pragma

41. The definitions for _DATE_ and _TIME_ when, respectively, the date and time of translation are not available.

Nil	—	—	—

Table 2.3 Complete list of implementation-defined features of Standard C (*Continues*)

Library functions

42. The null pointer constant to which the macro NULL expands.

Nil	—	—	—

43. The diagnostic printed by and the termination behaviour of the assert function.

Nil	—	—	—

44. The sets of characters tested for by the isalnum, isalpha, iscntrl, islower, isprint and isupper functions.

Medium	Dynamic	Automatic	Wrap for consistency

45. The values returned by the mathematics functions on domain errors.

Severe	Dynamic	Automatic	Wrap for consistency

46. Whether the mathematics functions set the integer expression errno to the value of the macro ERANGE on underflow range errors.

Severe	Dynamic	Automatic	Underflow detectable

47. Whether a domain error occurs or zero is returned when the fmod function has a second argument of zero.

Severe	Dynamic	Automatic	Wrap for consistency

48. The set of signals to the signal function.

Severe	Static	Automatic	Ban signal

49. The semantics for each signal recognized by the signal function.

Severe	Static	Automatic	Ban signal

50. The default handling and the handling at program startup for each signal recognized by the signal function.

Severe	Static	Automatic	Ban signal

51. If the equivalent of signal(sig, SIG_DFL); is not executed prior to the call of a signal handler, the blocking of the signal that is performed.

Severe	Static	Automatic	Ban signal

52. Whether the default handling is reset if the SIGILL signal is received by a handler specified to the signal function.

Severe	Static	Automatic	Ban signal

53. Whether the last line of a text stream requires a terminating new-line character.

Nil (in practice)	—	—	—

54. Whether space characters that are written out to a text stream immediately before a new-line character appear when read in.

Nil (in practice)	—	—	—

55. The number of null characters that may be appended to data written to a binary stream.

Nil (in practice)	—	—	—

Table 2.3 Complete list of implementation-defined features of Standard C (*Continues*)

56. Whether the file position indicator of an append mode stream is initially positioned at the beginning or end of the file.

Severe	—	—	Wrap for consistency

57. Whether a write on a text stream causes the associated file to be truncated beyond that point.

Nil (in practice)	—	—	—

58. The characteristics of file buffering.

Mild (in practice)	—	—	—

59. Whether a zero-length file actually exists.

Nil (in practice)	—	—	Wrap for consistency

60. The rules for composing valid file names.

Medium	—	—	Portable file model

61. Whether the same file can be open multiple times.

Severe	?	?	Avoid

62. The effect of the `remove` function on an open file.

?	—	—	Wrap for consistency

63. The effect if a file with the new name exists prior to a call to the `rename` function.

?	—	—	Wrap for consistency

64. The output for %p conversion in the `fprintf` function.

Nil (in practice)	—	—	Could ban

65. The input for %p conversion in the `fscanf` function.

Severe	Static	Automatic	Ban it

66. The interpretation of a – character that is neither the first nor the last character in the scanlist for %[conversion in the `fscanf` function.

Severe	Static	Automatic	Ban it

67. The value to which the macro `errno` is set by the `fgetpos` or `ftell` functions on failure.

Medium	—	—	Wrap for consistency

68. The messages generated by the `perror` function.

Mild	—	—	Wrap for consistency

69. The behaviour of the `calloc`, `malloc` or `realloc` functions if the size requested is zero.

Severe	—	—	Wrap for consistency

70. The behaviour of the `abort` function with regard to open and temporary files.

Mild (in practice)	—	—	—

71. The status returned by the `exit` function if the value of the argument is other than zero, EXIT_SUCCESS or EXIT_FAILURE.

Mild	—	—	Wrap for consistency

Table 2.3 Complete list of implementation-defined features of Standard C (*Concluded*)

72. The set of environment names and the method for altering the environment list used by the `getenv` function.

Mild (in practice)	—	—	—

73. The contents and mode of execution of the string by the `system` function.

Severe	—	—	Ban it

74. The contents of the error message strings returned by the `strerror` function.

Nil	—	—	—

75. The local time zone and Daylight Saving Time.

Mild	—	—	Wrap for consistency

76. The era for the `clock` function.

Mild	—	—	Wrap for consistency

2.5 LOCALE-SPECIFIC BEHAVIOUR

This section refers directly to Appendix F.4 of the C Standard categorizing each feature appropriately (see Table 2.4), as was done for the unspecified, undefined and implementation-defined features tabulated above. This section is rather smaller than the others, containing only six items.

Table 2.4 Complete list of locale-specific items in Standard C

1. The content of the execution character set, in addition to the required members.

Nil (in practice)	—	—	—

2. The direction of printing.

Nil (in practice)	—	—	—

3. The decimal point character.

Nil (in practice)	—	—	Use ASCII

4. The implementation-defined aspects of character testing and case mapping functions.

Mild (in practice)	—	—	Use ASCII

5. The collation sequence of the execution character set.

Mild (in practice)	—	—	Use ASCII

6. The formats for time and date.

Mild	—	—	Wrap for consistency

2.6 ACCIDENTALLY UNDEFINED BEHAVIOUR

Although the C standard explicitly delineates those issues which it either declined to comment on, refused to define or left up to the implementor, practical use of language over a period of time continues to throw up strange behaviour from issues which the committee unintentionally missed out or defined incompletely. Language standards committees are kept together to deal with at least some of these issues, or *interpretations* as they are called. An interpretation is issued following a query from some user or set of users as to the exact meaning of some feature of the standard. Most such queries arise from compiler writers trying to write a compiler for the language. A good short article describing the process is Jones (1993a).

To illustrate some of the problems, examples of accidentally undefined or incompletely defined issues follow:

(a) The value of

```
sizeof(lvalue_designating_a_bit_field)
```

is explicitly undefined by the C standard, whereas the equivalent for an `rvalue`

```
sizeof(rvalue_designating_a_bit_field)
```

is not mentioned and must therefore be taken as accidentally undefined.

Note that in C an rvalue is a recipe for obtaining the value of some object expression (other than an 'array of'), whereas an `lvalue` is an expression denoting an object which can be used with the `&` address-of operator (there are some exceptions to this!). An `lvalue` may or may not be modifiable, but an rvalue cannot be modified. An example of an `lvalue` is a variable name.

Finally, note the relationship rvalue $\supset$ lvalue, i.e. every lvalue is an rvalue, but not the other way round.

(b) The following issue, raised by D. Jones, ANSI doc X3J11/90–056, can be construed in two different ways:

```
#define    f(a,b)     a+b
#if f(1,
          2)
#endif
```

Reading the relevant portions of the standard raises the question as to whether the `#if` directive ends at the new-line after `f(1`, or whether it is treated as white space, allowing the expression to be completed. The committee decided that the former was the case and the line-splice character '\' must be used if a `#if` directive spans more than one line.

(c) In the following, the first declaration U, is the type of a parameter to a function returning type T, but what about the second declaration?

```
int    x(T    (U));

int    y(T    (U (int a, char b)));
```

The standard states in Section 3.5.4.3 that 'in a parameter declaration, a single typedef name in parenthesis is taken to be an abstract declarator that specifies a function with a single parameter, not as redundant parentheses around a declarator'. According to this, there are two interpretations of U, but the committee decided on a general principle not enunciated in the standard: 'Whenever a typedef name could be taken as such in a declaration, it is so taken', so again the latter is chosen. *Note that a result of this is that the C language is defined by the standard* **plus** *the interpretations.*

(d) Another example of ambiguity in the preprocessor:

```
#define     f(a)    a*g
#define     g(a)    f(a)
main()
{
        int   j = f(2)(9);
}
```

This can be interpreted either as 2*f(9) or 2*9*g. The C committee has decided on more than one occasion not to condone this type of macro replacement and therefore *not to specify what happens in this case.* So either is OK as far as the standard is concerned.

Some of the examples given above and others besides are collected together in the article by Jones (1993a), to which the reader is referred for more details.

2.7 EMPIRICALLY DETERMINED MISBEHAVIOUR

In addition to the above, many features of a language are found to cause problems with use, even though their behaviour is well-defined or when abuse is not obvious. A vast body of experience has built up over the years for C, as well as certain practices which have proved fallible in all languages in which they are implemented. Such issues are the subject of the present section, which is split into certain classic types.

2.7.1 Errors of misplacement

An example of such a feature can be found unpleasantly frequently in C graphics code making use of graphical systems such as X11:

```
Widget       Thingy;
...
void Do_Something_Graphical( void )
{
        int   i    = AN_INT_CONST;
        int   pi   = &i;
        ...
        Thingy.int_point = pi;
        ...
}
```

Here, the pointer to the automatic i is stored in a structure with wider scope. If any attempt is made to use this after the function has been exited, very strange things can happen. A typical manifestation of this problem is when some functional component works on the first entry but fails, usually catastrophically, on the second and subsequent entries. On a compiler which is fairly sloppy and implements automatics statically, it may even work, until of course the code is moved to a more compliant compiler. It is, however, a difficult problem to find on any machine without specialized tools, even though it is detectable statically, and has caused much wasted time. Standard C itself explicitly states that pointers to automatics are meaningless when the automatic goes out of scope, however, abuse of this may be difficult to detect. The assignment of pi to the Thingy structure in the fragment above is entirely legal and well-defined; it is the use to which the Thingy structure is then put which can cause the problem. It is a humbling thought that this problem can take an experienced developer days to find, as the author has observed on more than one occasion.

2.7.2 Errors of omission and addition

Other examples of features likely to lead to problems but which are entirely legal and well-defined include the following classics known to most C programmers, but which still occur frequently in production code.

```
...
if ( a = b )
{
...
}
```

Here the compound statement {...} is executed only if $b \neq 0$. This occurs once every 3306 lines on average in commercial C code. Although occasionally meant, it is usually a case of the programmer typing = instead of ==.

```
a == b;
```

This is the opposite, whereby == was written instead of =. As a result the statement causes the compiler to evaluate the expression, return 1 or 0 dependent on whether it is true or not, and then discard the answer. In short, the statement does not do anything. This occurs about once every 12 325 lines in commercial C code.

```
...
if ( a == b );
{
    ...
}
```

This one always executes the compound statement {...} because of the trailing semi-colon after the predicate, which terminates the scope of the predicate. This can be awfully difficult to spot after a long day's code inspection. For example, in one package analysed, as reported later, this occurred about once in every 53 lines, breaking the local coding standards, which were only enforced manually.

Examples of all these and many more besides can be found in the wonderful book by Andrew Koenig (Koenig, 1988), but the author's point in quoting them here is that in spite of the reasonably widespread understanding of these little featurettes, *they still occur frequently in production C code*. The information is simply not being disseminated.

There is a further class of features which, although perfectly legal and perhaps sensible, are known to be related to unsafe behaviour. These might be termed errors of logical incompleteness. For example, consider the following fragment:

```
...
if ( a == b )
{
      ...
}
else if ( a == c )
{
      ...
}
...
```

This fragment is missing an else clause. Hence, if a is neither b nor c, the program will continue without executing either of the guarded compound statements. This may be what the programmer means, but the property of being neither b nor c covers an infinite set of possibilities and failure is frequently associated with the above when a program is changed during maintenance. This is allowed in many languages and forbidden by a tiny minority. This eventuality can be avoided by simply forcing the programmer to complete the clause by requiring that all block if statements shall have an else clause. In the above, this might appear as:

```
...
if ( a == b )
{
      ...
}
else if ( a == c )
{
}
else
{
      /*Why am I here ?*/
      assert( (a == b ) || (a == c ) );
      abort();
}
...
```

The use of the assert macro above will generally produce a standard message (the format is implementation-defined), locating the source of the assertion failure at the tiny expense of re-testing the predicates. A frequent use of this kind of construct might be in range checking inside a function to ensure that all input arguments lie within their defined ranges.

For precisely the same reason, programmers should be required to supply a default clause with all switch statements. Note, however, that the related issue of whether programmers should be allowed to let control fall through consecutive case labels by leaving out the terminating break statement which transfers control to the end of the switch is contentious. There are good reasons for using this construct occasionally, but equally truly, many spectacular program failures have resulted from a forgotten break statement. Perhaps the best solution in a safety-related environment is to flag all such fall-throughs automatically and force the programmer to sign off the occurrences and document the precise reason for fall-throughs. Alternatively, they could be forbidden and the programmer required to call the same function from within related case statements individually.

It is quite understandable if the C programmer thinks of the above as a definite overreaction to potential unreliability and that problems are unlikely. It should be enough therefore to state that an error resulting from the above was reported to the author at a software quality conference as being responsible for one of the largest telephone outages in history.

Note that the above two errors of logical incompleteness are not the sole preserve of C. In Ada, for example, an if .. elsif .. elsif .. end if statement is permitted without a mandatory else clause. The same is true in FORTRAN 77 and FORTRAN 90. In an effort to remove this kind of problem a small number of modern languages, for example, Occam, a parallel language favoured in certain kinds of control system, mandate the presence of complete logical structures for block if and switch type statements. In such languages it is *syntactically* illegal to omit the else or default clause. It is fair to record that programmers brought up with more traditional languages find such restrictions difficult to deal with at first.

2.7.3 Floating-point misbehaviour

Many C systems in the safety-related environment use floating-point arithmetic, in spite of the fact that such arithmetic is essentially indeterminate, and many famous problems have occurred in most languages because of it. For example, Keller (1993) reported that a round-off of a floating-point comparison propagated into a logical comparison of floating-point values led to a robot arm falling into the wrong quadrant ($360 - 0.000\,001$ degrees instead of $360 + 0.000\,001$ degrees) in the NASA space shuttle software. Another example, reported in Neumann (1993) caused a Patriot missile to miss a Scud missile in the Gulf War, with the loss of over 90 lives. Yet another example was reported by Hatton (1988), whereby a single comparison of floating-point numbers occurring occasionally within a 70 000 source line program caused a four significant figure drop in agreement of the same software package on two different platforms and took some three months to isolate.

It is very simple to formulate a methodology to handle such comparisons portably and deterministically. In essence, a number of the above problems boil down to C fragments of the following nature:

```
float a, b;
/*    Intermediate calculations on a, b    */
if ( a == b )
{
 ...
}
else
{
}
 ...
```

The problem is quite simply that the result of the comparison of a and b is not predictable in advance and may differ from machine to machine. To avoid the problem and render the comparison deterministic and portable, all that is necessary is to define a suite of floating-point comparison routines exemplified by the code fragment below:

```
#include "flcomp.h"
float a, b;
/*    Intermediate calculations on a, b    */
if ( flpcmp( a, "==", b ) )
{
 ...
}
else
{
}
 ...
```

where the header file flcomp.h contains function prototype declarations such as:

```
 ...
int    flpcmp( float a, char z[], float b );
 ...
```

and flpcmp is written to take account of the granularity of the floating-point arithmetic on a particular machine along the following lines:

```
#include "stdlib.h"
#define    YES  1
#define    NO   0

int    flpcmp( float a, char z[], float b )
{
       float       big;
       if (strcmp( z, "==" ) == 0 )
```

```
        {
                big = (fabsf(a) > fabsf(b)) ? a : b ;
                if ( abs( a-b ) <= (max(abs(a),abs(b))
                                        * FLT_EPSILON) )
                {
                        return( YES );
                }
                else
                {
                        return( NO );
                }
        }
        else if
        ...
}
```

FLT_EPSILON is the constant defined in Standard C to be the distance between 1 and the smallest float greater than 1, i.e. the granularity. The above is certainly not the most efficient way of implementing the concept, but the reader will get the idea and use of the routines can be mandated simply by forbidding programmers from explicitly comparing floating-point numbers, single or double precision, a statically enforceable and highly recommended issue. The same must be done for any for loops, as follows:

```
float a, b;
/*      Intermediate calculations on a, b  */
for( a=0.; a<b; a += 0.15 )
...
```

could be replaced by:

```
#include "flcomp.h"
float a, b;
/*      Intermediate calculations on a, b  */
for ( a=0.; flpcmp( a, "<", b ); a += 0.15 )
...
```

Alternatively, the use of non-integral loop variables could be simply banned. It may be useful to note for C readers that iteration loops defined using non-integral loop variables are candidates for eventual *removal* from the FORTRAN language.[10] The implications of the use of floating-point arithmetic in safety-related C are discussed further in Section 2.13.2.

This section concludes (Table 2.5) with a short list of items, including the above, empirically found to cause trouble in C programs, either directly or indirectly in the sense that they are frequently associated with unreliable practice. There are others, but most are statically detectable by the tools described in this book.

---

[10] Regrettably, one of the very few things that is. Take a feature out, add another 433....

Table 2.5 Example items in C likely to lead to problems in practice. A number of these items actually appear in Appendix E of the C Standard

1. Using relational or logical comparison operators in a `switch` expression is likely to lead to problematic behaviour.
2. Local declarations hiding more global declarations.
3. Floating-point comparisons for equality and also inequality and non-integral loop variables.
4. Wrapping round of unsigned arithmetic in constant expressions.
5. Implicit conversions to narrower types[11] or between signed and unsigned types.
6. Any use of precedence, given the 15 distinct levels in C.
7. Falling through cases within a `switch`.
8. Missing `default` in `switch` statements and `else` clause in `if... else if...` structures.
9. Assignment expression in control structures.
10. Jumping into a block containing initialization of an object with automatic storage.
11. A statement with no side-effects is encountered.
12. A function has `return` with and without expressions.
13. Testing for an unsigned value to be negative.
14. Non-matching `#if... #else... #elif... #endif` in same file.
15. Unreachable code.
16. Static function declaration with no definition.
17. `if` blocks without enclosing braces, especially nested ones.
18. Appearance of old-style assignment operator.

2.8 UNEXPECTED BEHAVIOUR

To the above categories can be added those features that are well-defined, portable but look exceedingly odd or are frequently misunderstood.

2.8.1 Multi-threaded behaviour

Although not part of Standard C, a Posix compliant function call which leads to very strange looking code to the formally minded is the `fork()` command:

```
if ( fork() )
{
      printf("True\n");
}
else
{
      printf("False\n");
}
```

The author came across this code fragment courtesy of Tim Hopkins, one of whose colleagues used it as a C test for prospective programmers at the University of Kent. In some sense, the question is a little unfair, as unless the programmer had

---

[11] A staggeringly expensive occurrence of this was reported as being responsible for the shuttle *Endeavour* failing to rendezvous with the Hughes/Intelsat 6/F3 spacecraft in 1992. The problem was traced to a loss of precision when a double-precision floating-point value was inadvertently stored in a single-precision variable. This is statically detectable and appears as a forbidden construct in several C standards that the author has seen.

heard of the fork call, they would never have dreamed of the true behaviour. Of course, the bizarre answer is that *both* branches of the predicate are executed, one by the parent and one by the child process which is spawned by the fork() call. This is one of many reasons why multi-threaded code can be so much more difficult to reason about and check than single-threaded code. Code fragments such as the above require a considerable depth of understanding, even though they can in theory be assessed formally. If the notions of setjmp, longjmp and signal handling are added to the above cocktail, however, all bets are off. Such features should either be banned from safety-related C or localized and formalized to such an extent that the developers had wished that they had been simply banned.

2.8.2 Evaluation order and precedence

Although hinted at earlier, the relationship between *order of evaluation* and *precedence* will be discussed in more detail here because the relationship is very frequently misunderstood in the programming standards that the author has reviewed.

It is painfully common to see these two concepts treated as essentially synonymous in misleading statements such as:

... use precedence to force the order of evaluation ...

Although related, the two are independent concepts and must be treated as such. From a Standard C viewpoint, the distinction is very clear. Precedence is clearly and consistently defined in terms of the order in which *operators* are applied, and order of evaluation, which relates to the order in which operands in expressions are evaluated, is deliberately undefined except at a few key points known as the *sequence points*. To illustrate the two concepts, consider the following expression, which should be familiar to all programmers:

```
a * b + c
```

Here the * multiplication operator has a higher precedence than the + addition operator, so that the compiler implicitly parenthesizes the expression as:

```
(a * b) + c
```

The programmer can change the operator application order by using parentheses explicitly, as:

```
a * (b + c)
```

However, evaluation order concerns the order in which items are evaluated within an expression (actually between sequence points). So in the example

```
a * (f() + g())
```

although the addition is done before the multiplication, *the order in which f() and g() are evaluated is undefined*. This can cause terrible problems in an expression in which there are side-effects, as for example in:

```
a = i + b[++i];
```

Since C does not define in which order the two operands of the + are evaluated, the ++i could be done before the addition with i on some machines and after on other machines *completely legally and therefore silently*. If i was equal to 2 before this statement then, the two entirely legal alternatives on different machines might be:

```
a = 2 + b[3];
```

or

```
a = 3 + b[3];
```

This represents a debugging nightmare, quite apart from making a mockery of any attempt at formal verification, because the fundamental law of commutativity of addition does not hold. The practice of relying on order of evaluation of operands in between sequence points must simply be outlawed for safety-related systems (and indeed any other sensible system). Unfortunately, as will be seen later, such reliance is quite common in C programs. At the time of writing, the author came across several occurrences of the following example of this in a major new financial system, one of whose design goals is portability:

```
for ( i = 0; i < 100; a[i++] = b[i] )
{
    . . .
}
```

For reference, the sequence points of C, that is those points at which all side-effects are guaranteed to have been completed are:

- && and || after the left-hand operand has been evaluated.
- ?: after the first operand has been evaluated.
- The "," operator after the first operand has been evaluated.
- The function call operator after all the arguments and the function designator have been evaluated but *before* control is actually passed to the called function.
- After every full expression. A full expression in C is an expression which is not itself part of another expression. In other words, it is either:
    —an initializer
    —the expression in an expression statement
    —the controlling expression of an if, while, do or switch statement
    —each of the three optional expressions of a for statement
    —the optional expression in a return statement

The 15 levels of operator precedence defined in C can be looked up in the excellent C reference (Jaeschke, 1991). The 22 levels of operator precedence (yes, 22) defined in the current draft of C++ can be looked up in Sexton (1993), a highly recommended text which will fit in a pocket, unlike some C++ books, which require a wheelbarrow.

The point of this discourse on this apparently arcane but lethal subject is that any dependence on implicit operator precedence or order of evaluation of operands should be absolutely forbidden in safety-related systems on the grounds that it is unlikely that many people will understand it properly and the penalties for getting it wrong are so high. That this is a reasonable thing to require is evidenced by the fact that such dependencies are statically detectable and there are tools available which can detect them. This is a classic example of something whose equivalent in another profession would lead to immediate ostracization by the engineers concerned, but which in software engineering encourages some programmers at least to write the most abominable expressions. Many C programming standards, while frequently making misleading statements about such abuse, do place some kind of constraints on it.

In defence of C, this particular problem is by no means the sole preserve of C. In fact the C standard is rather better than most in that the concept is defined sufficiently well as to render the problem statically detectable and therefore enforceably avoidable. Pascal, FORTRAN and Ada, as well as C++ of course, all share precisely the same problem. For example, in FORTRAN, a frequently encountered item in safe programming standards is the requirement that functions shall not set either arguments or global variables (COMMON block variables). In Ada, functions can only have IN arguments to circumvent this very problem. Unfortunately, in Ada, functions can set global variables, leaving the back door open. A good discussion of this pernicious problem can be found in Ghezzi and Jazayeri (1982). Surprisingly, many language books are rather light on this subject.

Even for the speed merchants, such side-effects are unpleasant, as they also inhibit the compilers ability to optimize by computing common sub-expressions only once, as the common sub-expressions may not be common, owing to side-effect pollution from other parts of the expression.

2.8.3 Arrays are not always synonymous with pointers

Asymmetries in a language are a considerable thorn in the side of safety-related software developers. Unfortunately, most languages are rife with them. A glance through the recently standardized FORTRAN 90 standard reveals many constructs with long lists of exceptions. One such example in C which has caused many problems is the relationship between arrays and pointers. The problem here is that the relationship between them changes across file boundaries. It is rather like travelling from the UK to the USA: the language remains the same, but the rules change.[12]

Within the same file, the C Standard guarantees that array subscripts are converted immediately to pointers. The array notation is merely a convenience. So for example, the two function prototype declarations

```
void func( char * a );
```

and

```
void func( char a[] );
```

are *exactly* equivalent. If the second form is used, the compiler converts it to the first.

Extending this, but still within the same file, declaring an array statically or dynamically via a pointer to which storage is attached using the standard C function

---

[12] Actually, this can occur in the UK alone within a distance of about 20 km.

`realloc()` allows the entity to be accessed either by array or pointer notation:

```
char      a[100];
...
a[3]    = ...
*(a+3)  = ...
```

and

```
char *      a;
...
a      = (char *) malloc( (unsigned int) 100);
...
a[3]        = ...
*(a+3)      = ...
```

However, if an entity is declared using array notation in one file and pointer notation in another file, chaos ensues. The two notations do not mean the same across file boundaries, as in:

```
file 1.c
char *      a;
...
a      = (char *) malloc( (unsigned int) 100);
...
a[3]        = ...
```

and

```
file 2.c
...
char              a[];
...
a[3]              = ...        /* CHAOS !!      */
```

Note that compilers make no comment about this practice, although a good static checking tool will correctly flag this as an incompatible type.

2.8.4 Obscure issues in the C standard

To the cocktail of difficult issues discussed in this chapter can be added features which, although well-defined in the standard, require considerable thought to work out what they actually mean. An example of this can be seen in the code fragment:

```
typedef    int    table[];

table      one = {1};
table      two = {1,2};
```

A request as to the meaning of this was raised by M.S. Ball, Doc X3J1190–044. The issue is whether the declaration of two is illegal. In fact, it is perfectly legal, and the types of the two objects one and two are completed even though the type table itself is never completed.[13]

Another example of this concerns scope and was raised by R. Peterson, in ANSI document X3J11/90–008. The issue is whether the following code fragment is conformant:

```
static      int    i;
main()
{
      extern      int    i;
      {
            extern      int    i; /* Scope ?    */
      }
}
```

The C standard (Section 3.1.2.2) states 'If the declaration of an identifier for an object or a function contains the storage class specifier extern, the identifier has the same linkage as any visible declaration of the identifier with file scope'. However, in this case, the second declaration of i hides the first, and so there is no visible declaration at file scope. The result is undefined behaviour, as Section 3.1.2.2 says later that 'If, within a translation unit, the same identifier appears with both internal and external linkage, the behaviour is undefined'.

From a safety-related viewpoint, the answer to both of these is that a precise parse of the program against the standard, such as is available in some of the tools discussed later, reveals the meaning.

2.9 PORTABILITY

Portability is a very wide subject and of increasing importance as the growth of open systems continues unabated. It is a very frequently misunderstood concept. In essence, a program is fully portable if it can be taken from one machine, compiled without change on another machine and run without any change in the output. Such a Utopia is rarely if ever achieved, for many reasons. The reason for its importance in safety-related systems is that a program can compile correctly but perform differently at run-time. If portability is a necessary feature of a safety-related system, such behaviour would be absolute anathema. There are many subtle reasons why such misbehaviour might occur, including the issues discussed under the heading of floating-point misbehaviour above. The implication for safety-related systems which must be portable is that there should be *no* dependence on implementation-defined or empirically determined non-portable features. Such a requirement is likely to lead to Draconian restrictions on the use of C. A reasonably satisfactory weakening of this requirement is discussed in Section 5.1.1.

Portability can be split into three types, intrinsic, conceptual and peripheral. This split is not standard nomenclature, although it is convenient and is discussed in considerably more detail by Hatton (1988). For an in-depth discussion of portability

---

[13] In practice, this is so badly supported that applying a typedef to an unsized array should be forbidden.

from many different viewpoints, the reader is recommended to consult Jaeschke (1988) for C in particular and Wallis (1982) for a more general account.

2.9.1 Intrinsic portability

Intrinsic portability is here taken to mean the portability of the language statements actually used. As has already been intimated in the discussion of implementation-defined features in C, a substantial chunk of the language can legally behave entirely differently on different architectures. Intrinsic portability is achieved by avoiding *all* such features. In C, these may be formally unspecified, undefined or implementation-defined behaviour.

Note that the above use of *architecture* can quite reasonably include the *same* machine with different releases of its C compiler. This fact is not generally appreciated, as portability is synonymous in many developer's minds with different hardware. The notion that implementation-defined features can change between compiler releases on the same hardware platform and can have just the same catastrophic effects on system behaviour is unpleasant but no less true. The author recently came across an example of this in a major commercial system, fortunately before the system failed as a consequence. The problem arose as a result of upgrading the compiler to the latest ANSI-compliant version. Note that this does not necessarily mean that the compiler was formally validated. It is simply market-speak for the fact that some attempt has been made to comply with some of the requirements of the ISO standard. The offending fragment appeared as:

```
#include <math.h>
...
r = (float) atof(string);
compute_values( r );
```

Here atof() is the standard C function for converting its single character argument to a floating-point number to be passed to the compute_values() function as its actual parameter. The problem arose when the code was recompiled with the new compiler. One particular feature of its ANSI compliance was that the declaration of atof() moved correctly from its pre-ANSI location of math.h to the location required by the ANSI standard, stdlib.h, which of course is not included by this particular fragment. As a result, the function atof() is no longer explicitly declared and defaults to type int completely silently, according to the default declaration rules (a particularly nasty loophole in C). What happens next can safely be left to the imagination, but it is sufficient to say that a perfectly normal int is generally an extremely bizarre float.

This problem can be avoided simply by requiring that implicit declarations are forbidden before compilation takes place. In contrast, finding such a problem at run-time can be particularly difficult.

2.9.2 Conceptual portability

Conceptual portability is rather more subtle. It is perfectly possible to do something in a language which, although the code is intrinsically portable, the action of the code is so closely linked to the underlying architecture, for example, that the resulting program would not run on any other architecture. An example frequently encountered is the act of referencing a file by explicitly giving its name, as follows:

```
#include "sys/special.h"
```

This statement is intrinsically portable, but would not work in general on those machines with a different file system model from UNIX, although MS-DOS and DEC VMS now translate this correctly.

Another classic source of conceptual non-portability involves almost any use of the standard UNIX call system('command') as the single argument to system is in the command-line format of the target machine.

A more exotic example might involve conversing with a mailbox system on a machine through system calls which, although the calls themselves are intrinsically portable, have no equivalent on another platform. This form of non-portability is extremely difficult to police, although restricting interfaces to those defined in Posix, for example, might be of significant help.

2.9.3 Peripheral portability

This category of portability simply refers to communication with external devices, for example, graphics devices, where such devices can be software or hardware. It is convenient to think of this problem as being largely solved since the advent of standard and *de facto* standards, but it remains an immense problem in the author's experience. A classic example of this can occur even with something so simple as communicating with an MIT X11 component. If the target computer happens to implement a different version of X11 than expected, many irritating problems can follow.

The author has been witness to major organizations considering portability as simply the problem of moving from one type of operating system architecture to another, for example, from Digital VMS to UNIX. The portability of the programs themselves was considered irrelevant, even though most of the work involved reduced to the solution of this problem, incorporating all three of the above types of portability.

2.10 C/C++ COMPATIBILITY

Many companies around the world are showing great interest in the language C++ (Stroustrup, 1991). It is directly derived from C, with the addition of Simula-like classes, and has arguably the fastest growing user base in the world with a reported doubling every 7 months currently. In some cases, users are 'graduating' from C and in others they are moving directly to C++ from some other language. The key attraction of C++ is that it is considered an *object-oriented language* and the programming community has decided that objects are now the way to go. It is far from clear that this is the case at this stage, owing to a breathtaking lack of evidence in its favour, but the potential user must accept at face value that this is the way the computer industry works. The author's view is that it will either happen or will be replaced by some other methodology, and as a former physical scientist, he is wildly unimpressed that such momentous decisions can be made on such little evidence. Meanwhile, around the world, programmers are being forced to write safety-critical systems in whatever the computer industry decides is the language of the moment, and currently without any protective international safety standards. This is not really good enough.

In the author's experience, C++ is very widely believed to be a superset of C, presumably because early C++ compilers first translated the C++ to C before conversion to object code via a C compiler. However, the two languages are clearly being developed by separate committees, but the simple marketing ploy of calling it C++ has reinforced this view. Unfortunately, C++ is categorically *not* a superset of C and contains numerous features which behave differently. This is emphasized by Bjarne Stroustrup, the originator of the C++ language, the ANSI C committee and the majority of the ANSI C++ committee according to Jones (1993b). In normal circumstances, this would have no particular impact on C users generally, as C is a standard defined language and C++ is an evolving language which is unlikely to be standardized before around 1997–1998. However, it is far from clear whether the two languages will remain distinct, and it seems quite possible that either C++ will replace C at some stage, or that, looking ahead 5–10 years, there will be two C-like languages available which are incompatible with one another. Either way, those users whose C code contains the very features that are currently defined differently in C++ will have a nasty surprise when their code is compiled with a C++ compiler instead of a C compiler.

As before, this has subtle implications for safety-related applications. The differences between C and C++ split neatly into those which would be detected and rejected by the compiler and those which would not, but which would lead to different run-time behaviour. If an issue is rejected by the C++ compiler, it is not dangerous in that it cannot creep into the final system, even though discovery at this late stage may be expensive to correct. However, those issues accepted by the compiler but which have different semantics in C and C++ are exceedingly dangerous, as it is more than likely that testing will not find them. The safety-related developer therefore has the following choices:

- Mark the product as being compilable only with a Standard C compiler.
- Mark the product as being compilable with either a Standard C or suitably assessed C++ compiler, but guarantee that the product contains no features of C which have a different definition in C++. Ironically, at the time of writing of this book, they are all statically detectable. It might be thought that a guarantee that only those features with different run-time behaviour be absent would be sufficient. However, it is always possible that the C++ compiler might miss something, as such compilers are unlikely to be formally validated for several years. In addition, the standard is of greater complexity (i.e. length) than that of C and is indeed of similar complexity to that of Ada, so an equally large number of interpretation requests is likely (~50 in C, ~2000 in Ada so far).[14]

---

[14] This topic is a recurring theme in this book: the complexity of a language is proportional to the thickness of its standards document. The most complex standards using this metric invite by far the most interpretation requests. Languages with large numbers of interpretation requests should be avoided if at all possible in safety-related developments.

In the spirit of the earlier section on statically-detectable, implementation-defined and undefined behaviour, those features currently defined differently in the two languages are listed below:

- The following are keywords in C++: asm, bool, catch, class, const_cast, delete, dynamic_cast, false, friend, inline, mutable, namespace, new, operator, overload,[15] private, protected, public, reinterpret_cast, static_cast, template, this, throw, true, try, typeid, using, virtual, wchar_t.
- The following reserved words are effectively keywords: and (&&), or (||), xor (^), bitand (&), bitor (|), compl (~), and_eq (&=), or_eq (|=), xor_eq (^=), not (!), not_eq (!=). The symbols in brackets show their equivalent.
- All functions must be declared before use in C++, removing the error-prone implicit declaration of type int in Standard C.
- Empty declarations in C++ mean that there are *no* arguments, not any number as in old-style function declarations in Standard C:

```
extern int f();    /* No arguments in C++ */
```

- Function prototype definitions are mandatory in C++. The old-style definitions with separate declarations for arguments is illegal.

```
void
function blobby(a,b)
int    a;
int    b;                /* Illegal in C++ */
{
    . . .
}
```

- The visibility of items declared as const is different in C and C++.

```
const int    i;    /* File visibility only in C++, but    */
                   /* external visibility in C.           */
```

All such global declarations should be qualified by extern or static in C to make the linkage explicit.
- In C++ it is illegal to use an empty return statement (i.e. return;) in functions returning types other than void. It is legal in C.

These are some of the better publicized ones. However, at a recent BSI C++ meeting, which the author attended, he was horrified to notice that in the current draft (January 1994) the wording is so incomprehensible that it is not even clear in which direction a floating type truncates when assigned to an integer type, especially negative ones. In Standard C, it is defined such that the fractional part is truncated

---

[15] Currently treated as a keyword by some implementations and best avoided in a C++-compatible C program.

(Section 3.2.1.3 of the standard).

```
int    i;
int    j;

float x = 1.3;
float y = -3.9;
...
i    = x;        /*   i = 1 in C and ? in C++    */
j    = y;        /*   j = -3 in C and ? in C++   */
```

It seems almost pointless to consider the esoteric issues of templates, overloading and memory models when something as basic as this is not addressed. The average user does not care which way it goes, so long as it is defined and therefore suitable for informal or formal reasoning.

2.11 EXTENSIONS

Safety-related C development should not contain extensions to the C standard. Although the standard itself contains a list of common extensions as Appendix F.5, their definition is not guaranteed and their portability poor. They are not necessary and there is simply no justification for their use whatsoever, particularly for a safety-related development. The most common classes of extension which the author has come across are:

- Those related to C++ features, such as the // form of comment. Although there is an obvious reason for such a feature, representing, as it does, evolution of a C compiler by its developers to encompass C++, such features must be avoided because their definition is not subject to careful scrutiny by a language standards body and there may even be unpleasant side-effects.
- Those related to the memory model of a PC or compatible which introduce extended keywords, near, huge and far.[16] In an age where it is quite common to find 16 Mbyte on a portable computer, with typical application sizes of 4 Mbyte, the days of the PC memory model, representing as it did times when memory was much more restricted, must be numbered. The idea that a techno-logical limitation lasting perhaps 10 years at most should affect the longevity of software of otherwise effectively unlimited lifetime is ridiculous. If the reader baulks at the notion of software of effectively unlimited lifetime, he or she should consider a library function, for example. Supposing such a library function were written in a standardized and safe way following the restrictions outlined in this book and accompanied by an expensive formal correctness proof. What possible justification could there be for throwing it away at *any* stage, provided it remained capable of use within a proposed application?

---

[16] To which can be added various others such as cdecl, pascal, fortran, fastcall, stdcall, interrupt, loadds, saveregs, import and export, all with various combinations of zero, one or two prefixing '_' characters. Others such as segment occur only with prefixing '_' characters.

- Those associated with the Digital C compiler on VMS, such as allowing the use of '$' as a legal identifier character. There are several significant extensions in this dialect, all of which have severe portability implications. The motives of any manufacturer including extensions such as this to a C compiler should be carefully questioned.

A classic example of the deleterious effects of language extension on the longevity of the resulting application software can be found in the various FORTRAN dialects common following publication of the FORTRAN 77 standard, X3.9–1978. Manufacturers were almost falling over themselves to extend the language. Some dialects were so far removed from the base language that it was almost impossible to recognize them as FORTRAN. This had many unfortunate effects, one of which was probably a strong contributor to the next version of the standard, FORTRAN 90, being years overdue. In addition, the author alone has come across an unhealthily large number of major software packages which have had to be thrown away because a recent need for open systems was completely inconsistent with the way the code had developed in the presence of uninhibited use of available language extensions by its developers. The price for years of 'freedom' is now being exacted with a vengeance. A frequently encountered reason for an organization moving to C from FORTRAN is portability. This is in spite of the fact that it is probably at least as easy to define a portable subset of FORTRAN as for C. What is missing, of course, is enforcement.

In the next chapter, the relationship of complexity to inherent safety and intellectual manageability will be explored and methods of measuring it defined.

2.12 LESSONS FROM DELIBERATE OBFUSCATION

For a number of years now there has been an annual Obfuscated C competition, the object of which was to write a truly awful C program in a number of categories. The nature of some of these can be gleaned from the following categories used in the 1988 contest (Libes, 1993):

- *Best of Show*
  This stunning program is guaranteed to cause irreversible brain damage to anything higher up the evolutionary ladder than a hamster. The judges noted that it involved such a warped use of the C preprocessor that the GNU C preprocessor took 45 seconds whilst the Amdahl C preprocessor took 75 minutes. Other preprocessors just fell over after running out of space—a truly cathartic preprocessing experience.
- *Best Abuse of System Calls*
- *Best Visuals*
- *Best Small Program*
- *Least Likely to Compile Successfully*
  This program, apart from being ghastly, had the unusual distinction that its compressed form was bigger than its uncompressed form.
- *Most Useful Obfuscation*
- *Best Abuse of C Constructs*
- *Best Abuse of the Rules*

This program consisted simply of

```
#include "/dev/tty"
```

- *Best Layout*

The hilarious nature of some of the entries has made it easy for critics of C to label the language (and frequently its users) as unsuitable for 'serious' development. The author takes completely the opposite view and considers it a very healthy sign that the language is explored in such depth. Indeed, the stated objectives of the contest have serious intent and are:

- To show the importance of programming style, in an ironic way.
- To *stress* C compilers by feeding them unusual code.
- To illustrate some of the subtleties of the C language.
- To provide a safe forum for poor C code.

Such introspection exists for no other language, and understanding the entries in this competition (which is no mean feat!), teaches the reader very important lessons about the weaknesses and strengths of the language. This competition alone may be a strong contributing factor to the fact that so few interpretations have been necessary for the C Standard in comparison with other languages. If exploring a particular semantic loophole in such an environment demonstrates its dangers to the programming community at large so that it will not be used inadvertently in a live system, this author, at least, is all for it.

In their own right, as can be seen from the above categories, these entries often function as formidable tests of the quality of a particular compiler in ways never even dreamed of by the authors of the various validation suites, which are discussed next. A compiler which can digest the standard validation suites (see below) as well as the above without getting computational ulcers would give great confidence in its implementation quality.

2.13 VALIDATING THE ENVIRONMENT

2.13.1 C validation suites

As has been seen in Chapter 1, one of the key requirements for use of a language in a safety-related environment is a national or international standard definition. Of course, the existence of such a standard is no guarantee that implementations actually conform to it. In order to provide this guarantee, validation suites are used to ensure that an implementation is indeed conformant. Such validation is not easy to achieve, and many implementations are economical with the truth and make claims such as 'ANSI-compliant' without any hard evidence that this is true. There are actually two commonly used validation suites, and the USA and Europe use different ones, of course. Such is the march of progress.

The National Institute of Science and Technology (NIST) (formerly known as the National Bureau of Standards) in the USA has selected the Perennial validation suite for procurement validation for US government agencies. In Europe, the British Standards Institute (BSI) and other standards bodies chose the Plum–Hall validation suite. The European choice was made first and the first formally validated compilers appeared there. The author is not aware of any compiler which has formally passed both validation suites. In any safety-related environment, it would considerably weaken a safety argument if an unvalidated compiler was used. Unfortunately, especially in cross-compiler environments, not many compilers have been thus validated at the time of writing.[17]

2.13.2 Floating-point validation

Although validation suites consist of many hundreds of different files of test source programs, they can't of course test everything. One area of particular interest is the treatment of floating-point arithmetic and the scientific functions in the run-time library. The C standard does not currently define floating-point manipulations precisely, although they are being considered by the Numerical Extensions Group, as already discussed earlier in this chapter. As noted in Section 2.2.4.2.2 of the Rationale in the ANSI version of Standard C, however, the C committee have made use of the floating-point expertise available in the FORTRAN community, which has been built up from extensive use of numerical computation over some 30 years. The need for validation suites there arose out of occurrences such as the following, communicated to the author by Dave Sayers of NAG some years ago:

- In a well-known mainframe, given $x = 6 \times 10^{-79}$, then $y = x * x$ returned 0.004 82.
- In a well-known supermini, dividing certain numbers in double-precision often led to 5 figure accuracy rather than the expected 15.
- In a well-known supercomputer, if $x = 0.0$ and $y = 1.0 - 1.0$, then the machine reported $x \leq y$, $x \geq y$ and $x \neq y$ simultaneously.
- In a well-known minicomputer, where the square of a number, $\mathrm{sqr}(x) \neq x * x$ for some values, including $x = 2.0$, which actually gave $\mathrm{sqr}(2) = 2$.

All were fixed of course, no doubt after a certain amount of panic among the scientific users of the machines.

For C, several exercisers are available to assess the quality of the support for floating-point computation on any particular compiler/machine combination. Probably the best known of these is paranoia. This was originally developed in Basic by W. M. Kahan of the University of California at Berkeley and has been translated into C by David Gay of AT&T Bell Laboratories and Thomas Sumner of the University of California at San Francisco from the Pascal version written by Brian Wichmann of the UK National Physical Laboratory. It is available as a C program by sending the message send paranoia.c from paranoia to the Internet address netlib@research.att.com. The resulting source file can be compiled for the local machine and run as appropriate. In essence, the following issues are examples of what is uncovered:

- Adequacy of guard digits for multiplication, division and subtraction
- Whether arithmetic is chopped, correctly rounded or something else for multiplication, division, subtraction, addition and square root.

---

[17] NIST supplies names of validated compilers in its 'Validated Products List'. The April 1993 edition, NIST IR5167, listed validated compilers on about a dozen machines. This list is updated regularly.

- Whether a sticky bit is used correctly for rounding.
- Whether underflow is abrupt, gradual or fuzzy.
- Whether infinity is represented.
- Whether comparisons are consistent with subtraction.

In addition, square root is tested for accuracy, although y^x, extra-precise sub-expressions and decimal to binary conversion are not yet in the author's version.

paranoia is run interactively and terminates with a statement as to the quality of the floating-point implementation on the machine in use. On the author's vintage 1993 Sparc Classic running OS 4.1.3 and a non-validated version of the C compiler, the terminating message was:

```
...
No failures, defects or flaws have been discovered.
Rounding appears to conform to the proposed IEEE standard P754.
The arithmetic diagnosed appears to be excellent!
END OF TEST
```

Well done, Sun! With the growth in availability of IEEE 754 floating-point standardized arithmetic, the situation is rather better than it used to be when machines would regularly fail this test for one reason or another. Nevertheless, if at all possible, paranoia should be run on any machine on which safety-related developments are intended to run, in addition to the recommended use of a validated compiler. Ideally, it should be run at regular intervals as a health check, to provide continuing reassurance. On some of the older technology supercomputers, such as the Cray-1, a similar floating-point health check ran in the background providing a continuous screening of the hardware. This process used a few per cent of the machine's available performance and it was common in the author's original company at least to switch it off for long periods to squeeze a little bit of extra performance from the then fabulously priced machine! The dubious rationale for this was that human observation of the results (which were largely graphical output of processed geophysical data) would detect floating-point failure sufficiently quickly. This of course would only be cost-effective provided the average job duration was no more than a few per cent of the mean time between failures, which was by and large the case, and the author was unaware of any problems resulting from this rather cavalier practice at the time. Meanwhile, 10 years later the ability of a geophysicist to detect problems graphically has been severely called into question by Hatton and Roberts (1992), who showed that there was a natural variation in these data in the first significant figure, i.e. some 10 000 times worse than was realized, due to errors in the software implementations, so the author hopes that this practice has now ceased!

Other floating-point validation suites are available in the comprehensive text by Plauger (1992), and, for the reader interested in more details, the same author reviews the work being done on floating point in the Numerical C Extensions Group in Plauger (1993). He finishes off with a favourite quotation from R. W. Hamming: 'Nobody should have to know that much about floating-point arithmetic; but I'm afraid sometimes you might'.

As a final note, the author in recent years has found C floating-point implementations at least as good as FORTRAN implementations and will add a favourite quote of his own made to him some years ago by the distinguished American geophysicist Jon F. Claerbout at Stanford: 'If you need double precision, you got the physics wrong'.

Given these caveats and suitable validation, the author now believes that C floating-point implementations are at least adequate and that most errors in the use of floating-point arithmetic arise through the programmer's inadequate understanding of the numerical properties of the algorithm, rather than deficiencies in the floating-point implementation itself. The following points give some support to this view:

- The rapidly growing number of implementations which use at least some of the IEEE 754 standard for floating-point arithmetic. This is usually supplied in the chip set and is language independent. Some chip sets, such as the INMOS T800 Transputer have a formally proven conformance to this standard.
- The results of Hatton and Roberts (1994) in a comparison of nine different FORTRAN packages totalling some 6 million lines of code, all implementing the same requirements and using the same input data, showed that natural variations in implementation of algorithms were some 10 000 times worse than the underlying variation in floating-point arithmetic implementation reported by Hatton (1988) when porting one of the packages between different platforms.
- Watt *et al.* (1987) note, when considering floating-point implementation in Ada, that, in practice, the major cause of inaccuracy in floating-point computation is not underflow (which does not raise an exception in Ada), but the cancellation of nearly equal values.[18] This is strictly in the preserve of numerical analysis and is a language-independent problem.

2.13.3 Other forms of validation

Other sources of material suitable for additional validation are available. As was referenced above, Plauger (1992) demonstrates an implementation of the Standard C library with a number of test harnesses to exercise such an implementation. The code for this is available and provides a useful extra source of validation material.

It is worthwhile noting that for safety-related software no amount of validation is too much, and the author believes that continuous self-checking, as described above, should be present in all safety-related systems.

---

[18] This can occur, for example, when a Hilbert matrix is inverted.

3

THE INFLUENCE OF COMPLEXITY ON SAFETY

Complexity is a fundamental property of computer programs. The central issues are how much of the complexity is justified by the underlying algorithm and how it is distributed. All too often the *natural* complexity of the algorithm is amplified by poor implementation to give a corresponding computer program of considerably greater *actual* complexity. Close attention to design can minimize the difference between the actual complexity of the computer program and the natural complexity of the algorithm, which of course, sets a lower bound on the actual complexity, and this indeed is one of the primary goals of design. This is of the greatest importance, as needless complexity is an old enemy of good engineering practice and it is the *actual* complexity which affects the maintenance costs of software throughout its life cycle.

This chapter is about complexity and its potential effects on safety. The effects are indirect but profound. The rationale for discussing this topic is that limiting the complexity of functional software components is believed to improve the reliability, and therefore safety, of a system. The measurement of complexity will be described, along with some well-known studies of complexity, which give strong hints as to how needless complexity can be avoided. Some measurements are highly language-specific, while others are much more generic in nature. Early experiences with object-oriented languages such as C++ suggest that there is a tendency to move complexity from control structures to data structures, and the study of complexity in such systems is still in its infancy. At the end of the chapter, a theoretical model will be presented to support the empirical results of complexity experiments. Chapter 4 then describes the results of extracting various complexity measurements among many other attributes from a large population of C and FORTRAN from many industries around the world. The FORTRAN results included there are essentially language non-specific, and so their discussion in a C context can be justified. The results presented there will be used to recommend complexity limits at the end of the book.

As the complexity of computer programs is a relatively new and inadequately understood area, it tends to generate rather more heat than light in discussions with practising programmers, in the author's experience. Resistance to the use of such concepts in software development frequently utilizes the misconception that programming is an art form as opposed to an engineering discipline, the implication being that art, and for that matter, architecture and music, are unbounded, allowing free rein to artistic aspirations. A secondary, and far more reasonable objection, is that not enough is known about it to provide guidelines to the practice of programming and this book is all about actual practice. Therefore this second objection will be addressed in detail later in this chapter. The first will be addressed now, whereby compelling evidence will be presented that art, architecture and music are far from unstructured, and indeed the detailed structure common to their practice would put many software developers to shame.

3.1 A DIGRESSION ON DISCIPLINE, FORM AND STRUCTURE

Complexity abounds in all systems. The standard solution in software engineering has been to meet complexity head-on by testing, rather like a gorilla greeting a competitor, while in every other engineering discipline the hard-earned answer is to avoid it. Confrontation is almost certainly one of the symptoms of an immature engineering discipline. As time goes by, no doubt software engineers will also learn how to avoid complexity wherever possible, but this is probably many years away, given the length of time it took to learn the lesson in more mature engineering disciplines. It is interesting to note that leading experts in software reliability are now suggesting that safety-critical systems may even have to avoid software in certain circumstances because of the currently insuperable problems of producing it to a guaranteed level of reliability (Littlewood and Strigini, 1992a).

Software engineers must relearn fallibility, because, as many software managers will know, strong emotional threads run through even the most orderly software development environments. Such emotion has always wreaked havoc in the attempts to introduce standardization. Even during the preparation for this book, the author has come across an environment where a senior development manager of a major company involved in the development of safety-related systems has said things like '*I* don't believe in standards'. The reader should note the emphasis on the word 'I'. Such people cost their organizations untold amounts of money and should be pensioned off as quickly as possible or convinced otherwise. Things are now maturing quickly, however, with most organizations beginning to suspect the benefits of an orderly and repeatable software engineering environment controlled by well thought out pragmatic standards. It is worthwhile digressing for a little while to investigate working solutions to the problems of complexity in other application areas, in the hope that they will shed light on a way forward for software engineering.

There is an immediate and strong analogue with spoken languages here. In spoken languages, redundancy of expression is deliberately sought to avoid repetition, while ambiguity is exploited frequently in jokes and by politicians. Such redundancy and ambiguity make some languages very difficult to learn, quite apart from the effects of dialects (akin to language extensions). As a child, the author spoke a dialect of English common to south-east Manchester, in the north of England. In that dialect, the word while means the same as the English until. There is a possibly apocryphal story of a man killed on a train crossing there because the warning said (in normal English), do not cross *while* the red lights are flashing. He duly waited until they did and then crossed.... In contrast, Esperanto, a deliberately entirely regular language intended to be of universal appeal, can be learnt remarkably quickly because it lacks redundancy and ambiguity, and as a consequence few people speak it. In comparison, English, which is fast becoming a standard language (certainly in technical circles), is full of redundancy and is remarkably readable even whnllthvwlsrmssng. Programming languages should be entirely regular like Esperanto and not arbitrarily irregular like English. Language committees please note.

Two example areas will be discussed in more detail now, both of which are generally considered to be artistic in essence and therefore frequently mistaken to be synonymous with a lack of design. The two areas are architecture and music, and nothing could be further from the truth. This may come as a surprise to programmers who believe that software design is an essentially artistic discipline necessarily devoid of standards and form.

3.1.1 Form and structure in architecture

In architecture, testing is absent as a quality assurance measure.[1] Buildings are no longer built first to see if they will fall down. The emphasis instead is on design and the utilization of principles of simplicity and good practice which have been learned the hard way over thousands of years by watching inadequate ones fall down and then finding out why at the inquest. Indeed, the three bywords of architecture are *firmness*, *construction* and *delight*. A wonderful example of these principles is the Pantheon in Rome, as shown in Fig. 3.1. The first reaction to this marvellous building is to wonder how the delicate tracery and intricate complexity of the exterior columns can possibly hold up the enormous dome. The simple answer is that they don't. Instead, a twenty-feet-thick concrete wall behind them has done the job most satisfactorily for the last 2000 years. Here intricacy adds delight but not structural strength. Even with an intricate building, as it is approached, it becomes apparent that the harmonious whole is by and large, the sum of a very few types of regular building element, for example, the bricks are regularly shaped and there are very few different sizes. This is simply the end-product of thousands of years of experience, which have shown that in order that the whole may be more easily visualized and realized, *the component parts must be simple*. After all, a flying buttress is no more than an architectural subroutine.

One of the few examples of architecture in which local complexity is mixed with global complexity is the dry-stone wall, which is quite simply a wall made without

---

[1] Actually, this isn't quite true. After the great storm of October 1987 in southern England, the structural integrity of some wind-damaged bridges was tested by presumably highly-paid volunteers driving trucks over them to see if the cracks grew!

Figure 3.1 The Pantheon in Rome. Here exterior beauty and complexity merely embellishes interior strength and simplicity.

concrete. Such walls are commonly found enclosing fields in Northern Europe, especially in Northern England. They exist because of an originally missing technology—concrete. As a result, irregularly shaped stones are used to construct the wall, locking it together to give it structural strength. If regularly shaped stones were used it would not last very long. Building such a wall requires great experience or it simply falls down. The problem is that the builder must keep the local and global perspectives in mind at the same time, and, as a result, there are many false starts, even among experienced builders. It is a real skill, the implication being that its construction requires a guru because of the necessary duality of perspective. Many false starts are made and many walls fall down. The analogy with software is plain to see.

3.1.2 Form and structure in music

The value of music as a medium relevant to this discussion is that unlike writing, where a misspelt word does not really detract from the quality of the text, a single 'misspelt' note can sometimes render an entire phrase excruciating. The magnificent naturalized American performer Victor Borge raised this to an art form. On other occasions, if the 'misspelt' note happens to be closely related to the harmony at that point, it will have a much lesser effect and may even enhance. Such errors occur frequently, for example, in the transcription of medieval lute and other music from its original tablature to standard musical notation. Often, the transcriber must make an intelligent guess.[2] Software textual errors are closely analogous. A single character mistake can have no effect whatsoever or, as in the case of the first US interplanetary spacecraft, *Mariner 1*, ultimately cause the vehicle to veer off course, necessitating the destruction of both spacecraft and rocket shortly after launch. This was truly a 'bum' note. Put into a more modern context, both music and software development are *chaotic*, since small changes to their state can lead to no effect at one end of the scale or to pathological change at the other. For a general discussion of this fascinating topic, see Gleick (1988) for a populist approach or Thom (1975) for a detailed original treatise.

At first hearing, what the reader might consider simply a nice tune frequently turns out to be a masterpiece of design and construction. This is a classic example of good intrinsic quality implying good external quality. Music takes many classical forms, such as the fugue, the raga, the symphony, the madrigal and opera. More modern aspects of music such as the compositions of John Cage and Karlheinz Stockhausen have experimented with a lack of structure as we know it, to the point that one of Stockhausen's compositions (a vocal work of 76 minutes duration based on the major ninth chord) moved Stravinsky to comment that it showed the need for the musical equivalent of a parking meter. However, it remains true that many pieces of music considered great by the majority abound with good structure. In music, the equivalent of a building falling down is that nobody listens to the music any more. The author would guess that Mozart's 41st Symphony gets listened to rather more often than Stockhausen's mighty ode to a parking meter.

Composers have always felt a need to impose order on their work. Stravinsky (1970) expressed this need vividly as:

> The creator's function is to sift the elements he receives from [his imagination], for human activity must impose limits upon itself. The more art is controlled, limited, worked over, the more it is free.

These are extraordinarily powerful and relevant words to the current state of software engineering. As an example of the truly awesome structure and design in otherwise 'nice tunes', consider the first movement of Beethoven's 5th Symphony in C minor. Few would disagree with the view that Beethoven was a towering genius. One of the many ways in which this genius manifested itself was in the ability to build beautiful musical structures. The 5th Symphony was a landmark in composition and is one of the most famous examples of a form known as the *sonata principle*. In its simplest terms, the point of the sonata principle is to set up a conflict in a piece of music between two keys, usually tonic and dominant, and then resolve it by merging the two keys into one, the tonic. The overall form consists of two pieces, the first of which is known as the *exposition* and the second of which is itself split into the *development* and the *recapitulation*.

---

[2] There is a marvellous example in Beethoven's Appassionata sonata. The pianist Vladimir Horowitz was convinced that one of the thousands of notes in this piece was wrong. He traced it back to Beethoven's original manuscript to discover that he was correct and it had been transcribed incorrectly in the many editions down the years.

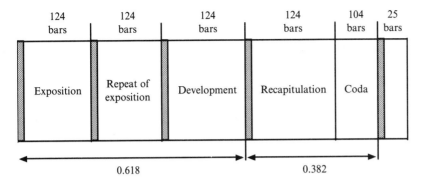

Figure 3.2 A schematic illustrating the amazing symmetry of the first movement of Beethoven's 5th Symphony. The golden section is the ratio 0.618:0.382. The five basic parts of this sonata form are shown with the motif (the 'da-da-da-daaa' bit) shown shaded. The piece is exactly in the golden ratio as shown if Beethoven had rounded it to 0.62 and if the 'extra' bar in the coda is discounted (a one-off error?!). In addition to the above, note that several of the main landmarks in this movement also occur at or near multiples of 62.

Listening to the 5th Symphony is a breathtaking experience. Studying it is even more breathtaking because of the almost supernatural underlying structure. In the late 18th and 19th centuries, it was quite common for composers to integrate ideas from mathematics, such as Fibonacci sequences and the golden ratio (approximately 1/0.618 or 0.618/0.382...) first discussed by Euclid and re-discovered by Fibonacci. The golden ratio plays an intimate part in the 5th Symphony as can be seen by studying Fig. 3.2, which shows its various sonata sections.

Just as in the architectural examples, the underlying building blocks, especially the harmony, are simple. Mozart's 40th Symphony is similarly constructed around the golden ratio, as is much of Bartok's music. Another important point to make is that even with underlying simplicity, composers (and especially Beethoven) may have rewritten their compositions many times before they were satisfied. Early versions of a number of Beethoven's pieces exist and give strong evidence of being written by a mere mortal; indeed, some are extraordinarily naïve. *Greatness emerged only after considerable refinement.* At the other extreme, the late, great and highly influential rock guitarist Jimi Hendrix, forever associated with blistering and seemingly impromptu stage performances, was known to be fastidious in his preparations, spending many hours making performance notes for himself and the other band members before an appearance. This leads to a powerful reminder for software developers not to be satisfied with something that only *seems* to work. An example of the benefits of this is provided by the UNIX filter `diff` (McIlroy and Hunt, 1976), where the developers were not satisfied, and as in Beethoven's work, real elegance and reliability emerged by successive refinement. As McIlroy is quoted in Kernighan and Pike (1984): 'I had tried at least three completely different algorithms before the final one. `diff` is a quintessential case of not settling for mere competency in a program, but revising it until it was right'. One of the triumphs of UNIX as an operating system is that such careful development can be easily utilized as a building block in more complex algorithms. The author long ago lost count of the number of times he has used `diff`, both directly and as part of a larger algorithm. He has never encountered a problem with it.

In case the reader thinks that only classical music is built around tight structure, a final example, that of the blues, might help. Although the blues is an archetypal area for improvisation, the improvisation is essentially based around a five-note scale known as the *minor pentatonic* scale plus a flattened fifth, with the usual panoply of decorations, such as note bending, slides and so on. So although it may be difficult to appreciate this, particularly when listening to a searing guitar solo by the likes of Stevie Ray Vaughan, Albert King, Buddy Guy, Eric Clapton or Gary Moore, it is nevertheless true, and is one of the earliest things a budding blues guitarist learns. Here again, beautiful, complex and highly emotional structures are built from extraordinarily simple components. For another recent similar diatribe to the above, see Mody (1992), who cites numerous additional supporting examples that music must be structured to be free. The same goes for computer science and computer scientists.[3]

So, it can be seen that two disciplines more popularly known for their artistic content are highly structured and carefully designed. There is indeed a lesson in this for all software engineers, for whom the opposite is all too frequently true. The structural integrity of a software system is often highly complex, rather than relying on the simple but powerful principles of simplicity and reuse. It is not as though simple and elegant solutions do not exist. For example, *Communicating Sequential Processes* (Hoare, 1985) offers such a paradigm for concurrent systems. It is more because the simple solutions are still considered to be inferior in some sense, a throw-back to when the mighty, proprietary and generally incomprehensible mainframe ruled the world with its acolytes and arcane practices. Fortunately their days now at last seem to be numbered, and the growth of open systems promises to bring some sunlight into a historically dark age. Occam's razor is the most powerful tool in the engineer's tool-chest.

To conclude this digression and return to the point, a profoundly important step in the maturity of a discipline is the enforcement of hard-learned previous experience and the recognition that complexity must be strictly controlled to that which is necessary and no more. In major systems, the architecture must be simple and there is no place for artistic licence because, to paraphrase Shostakovich, *software, like music, must be constrained to be free*. Only then is there a chance of producing something which works well and responds benignly to the ever-present requirements for change.

In the remainder of this chapter, the measurement of complexity and weakness in software systems will be addressed and put into a theoretical framework. In Chapter 4, some population complexity metric distributions from real systems will be presented, and in Chapter 5 the automatic limitation of complexity in practical software development will be enlarged upon. Metrics are frequently classified into structure metrics, linguistic metrics and hybrid metrics (Beizer, 1990). Linguistic metrics are taken to mean those which consider the program text to be a series of tokens, but which ignore the meaning and order of the tokens, such as in the Halstead metrics (Halstead, 1977). One of the main points of this book is to add a new category, deep-flow metrics, which are linguistically associated but are *entirely* based on the meaning and order of the language components.

---

[3] Especially those like the author, who sit on language standards committees.

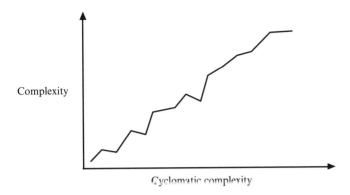

Figure 3.3 Although complexity increases with increasing cyclomatic complexity, it is probably not monotonic.

3.2 METRICS OF COMPLEXITY AND WEAKNESS

The search for valid software complexity measurements of good predictive power has continued unabated for a number of years, starting with the seminal work of McCabe (1976) and others. Unfortunately, not a lot of progress seems to have been made so far. Fenton (1991) gives an excellent summary of the current state of the art and a sound theoretical basis for such measurement, but in comparison with other measurement sciences, software measurement should be considered at best rudimentary as yet. The measurement of software properties is widely known as *software metrication*. There is no shortage of things to measure, but there is a dire shortage of case histories which provide useful correlations. What is reasonably well established, however, is that there is no single metric which is continuously and monotonically related to various useful measures of software quality, such as maintenance cost, reliability or malleability in all spheres of application. It is quite likely that there isn't even a monotonic measure of any kind. The popular measure of graph complexity known as cyclomatic complexity (McCabe, 1976), exhibits this property. For example, there is no case whatsoever for arguing that a program with a cyclomatic complexity of 2 (i.e. one decision in a *proper* program) is simpler than one with a cyclomatic complexity of 3 (two decisions). There is, however, a very reasonable case for arguing that one with a cyclomatic complexity of 2 is simpler than one with a cyclomatic complexity of 100. In other words, complexity is not strictly monotonic with cyclomatic complexity, but is generally monotonic, as illustrated in Fig. 3.3.

As a result, statements concerning the raw values of such metrics are of little value owing to the inadequately understood relationship between the many metrics extant and software maintenance properties in general, and there is therefore a need for sensible comparative measures to make some progress. Demographic or population analysis concerns the extraction of metrics of proven significance in some context from large populations of code. The advantage of this is that it can give such comparative measurements of quality, which, although somewhat coarse, are far more compelling. Provided that the metrics used have good predictive quality, a statement to the effect that a functional component is in the worst 10 per cent of all code measured in a particular population is far more relevant than informing a programmer that the component has a cyclomatic complexity value of 43!

The author first used such a technique in 1989 in a form known as Demographic Quality Analysis, using metrics which had proven significant in a prior analysis of the NAG library, described shortly. Put to use on many packages, the following properties became obvious:

- Functional components lying in the bottom 20 per cent using a combined metric were frequently observed to consume the lion's share of the maintenance resources and were responsible for most of the errors.
- Different populations of code differed markedly in their overall distribution. This led directly to the notion that it is very important to measure a package against something relevant. For example, graphics code generally consists of large numbers of small components, whereas scientific code does not. There are also linguistic differences, with FORTRAN components containing around four times as many executable lines on average as C components (Hatton, 1994a). The notion of using different population sectors for appropriate measurements may seem obvious in light of the vast amount of attention this gets in advertising initiatives, where 'targeting' to a particular demographic sector is crucial to success, but it is nonetheless worth repeating. Measuring the quality of a FORTRAN scientific package against a C graphics demographic is as irrelevant as targeting a skateboard campaign at the over-100s.

The technique should not be taken as strictly quantitative and has been used as an experimental technique so far, albeit heavily, in qualitative terms only. In essence, the values of several key metrics are measured in large populations of software. The metrics are monotonic in the sense that higher values are associated with poorer software. For each metric, the population distributions are split up into percentile node-points as follows:

$[a_0, a_1]$ contains the worst 10 per cent of all values.

$[a_0, a_2]$ contains the worst 20 per cent of all values.

$\vdots$

$[a_0, a_{10}]$ contains the worst 100 per cent of all values, i.e. all of them.

where a_i is the appropriate value of the metric.

An example of demographic quality analysis for one particular metric in a package is shown in Fig. 3.4. In this figure, the distributions of five metrics are shown for a medium-sized package. The histogram indicates the number of functions (top three metrics) and files (bottom two metrics) which fell into each bin—the more displaced to the left, the lower the quality.

In general, the metric values are not distributed uniformly with percentile, but they appear to have considerable predictive potential, as evidenced by the following example, one of many similar which the author has conducted. (Examples of distributions of various well-known complexity metrics taken from population measurements on both C and FORTRAN are shown in Section 4.2.)

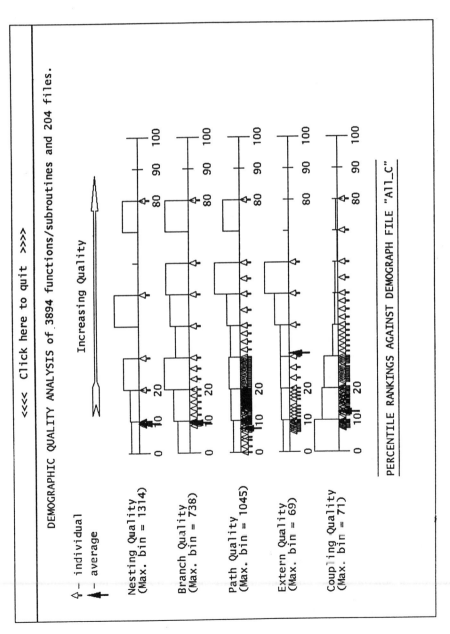

Figure 3.4. Demographic analysis of a large C system comprising some 200 000 lines. The metrics, from top to bottom, are maximum depth of nesting, decision count, static path count, number of variables of external linkage and a data-flow metric.

Table 3.1 Comparison of the number of bugs reported with ranking of corresponding components in a database product

Worst four modules	Average percentile ranking by DQA	Ranking by client in number of bugs reported
Module A	6.40	12
Module F	6.48	15
Module S	6.52	10
Module Z	6.59	8

Table 3.1 shows the distribution of reported errors in a widely used database product as supplied by the user, compared with the ranking of the corresponding components by population analysis. In this case, the package concerned was subjected to Demographic Quality Analysis and the worst few functions, as judged by a combination of decision count, maximum depth of nesting and static path count, were ordered in increasing average percentile ranking, i.e. worst first. Simultaneously and independently, the authors of the package compiled a list of the worst few functions in terms of maintenance cost and errors so far discovered. As can be seen, although the order is slightly different, the worst four in terms of cumulative error rate coincide with the worst four as judged by population comparison using the statically-computed metrics.

The results reported here seem on the face of it to support the notion of modularization, practised in the computing industry for many years. Modularization, or step-wise decomposition, of systems involves breaking them down into simpler components, which is then thought to lead to a more reliable system. This of course, could only be true *if the resulting interfaces are self-consistent.* Many languages, although mandating that interfaces must be consistent, provide no mechanism for enforcing this. C is an example of such a language with two distinct ways of defining interfaces. One of them involves the notion of *function prototypes* and is enforced, but the other, which is only included for backwards compatibility, is not. As will be seen shortly, interface faults arising as a result of using this second mechanism rather than the first are rife in C programs generally. Languages such as C++ and Ada mandate interface consistency. Other more subtle implications of the above results and their relevance to the practice of modularization will be analysed in more detail in Section 3.3.

3.2.1 Control and structural complexity

Probably the first studies of the actual complexity of software concerned decision structure and control. A widely known paper by McCabe (1976) described the measurement of one particular metric, *cyclomatic complexity*, along with case histories of its use. The argument was presented in the paper that functional components with more than 10 decisions were strongly associated with unreliable behaviour. This particular metric has had a profound effect on the development of metrication in software, and unfortunately engendered the belief in some quarters that one metric is enough to determine whether a functional component is good or bad. It is widely believed today, however, that no one metric exists or is likely to exist with these universally beneficial properties. Rather, combinations of metrics will be required as is noted by Beizer (1990), for example. A method of doing this is described in Chapter 4, and some fruitful combinations described.

There are many popular metrics in use today for measuring structural complexity. Some of the few which have proved of repeatable value in the author's experience are:

- *Cyclomatic complexity*, as described above. The simplest way of calculating this in general is that it is the number of decisions plus one, providing all parts of the program are reachable. Following the work of McCabe (1976), a suggested maximum is 10 in very tightly controlled environments, with perhaps a slackening to 20 with sign-off.

- *Static path count*. This is a measure of the testability of a program and simply counts all the paths through a program, assuming that all predicates are independent. In essence, parallel flows add and serial flows multiply. This was used by Hatton and Hopkins (1989) to measure properties of the NAG scientific subroutine library, described shortly.

  A similar metric was analysed by Nejmeh (1988) who reported that a value in excess of around 200 was observed to be highly correlated with problematic modules. This is strikingly similar to the values of around 1000 reported by Hatton and Hopkins (1989) given that the range of values they studied ran up to 500 000 000. A suggested maximum would be somewhere in the range 200–1000 according to the above studies.

- *Fan-in/fan-out*. In essence, this is the number of times a function is referenced (fan-in) and the number of functions it in turn references (fan-out). This is exemplified by Ince *et al.* (1993) as providing a means of measuring whether there is a missing level of design, as is likely to be the case if the fan-in/fan-out was unusually large. This is frequently calculated as:

$$\text{fan-in} \times \text{fan-out}$$

which unfortunately gives zero if either is zero, whatever value the other has. The author prefers to use:

$$\text{fan-in} + \text{fan-out} + (\text{fan-in} \times \text{fan-out})$$

which avoids this behaviour. The author uses a high fan-in/fan-out value to indicate components which are structurally tightly coupled to the design. In other words, changes which would affect components with high fan-in/fan-out can be expected to be traumatic. Furthermore, any component which had such a fan-in/fan-out *and* exhibited symptoms of poor quality via other measurements can be expected to cause severe problems and requires early corrective action. There do not appear to be any recommended limits for this in independent studies but the author notes that anything much above 30–40 represents a 'busy' component.

Metrics such as those described above are intimately associated with measuring the testability of components, and can be used to guide the design of test suites. They all share the same fascinating property that they are statically measurable and can therefore detect testing black spots long before unit testing is even entered.

Given the difficulties and inadequacies of much testing, such use alone more than justifies their mandatory use in a safety-related environment. To make one last point on the use of metrics, a picture is always worth a thousand words (or numbers in this case). The author knows of one company which practises a very effective complexity-limiting scheme by simply pinning the control graphs of functions on the door of the author responsible and shaming them into writing simpler code. To see how effective this can be, Figs 3.5 and 3.6 show the control graphs of various functions from the widely-used GNU `diff` package. Figure 3.5 has a rather complex component in the centre, which will exceed the metric limits recommended above. In the same package, the same component appears in the top left-hand corner of Fig. 3.6. By comparison, the component below it completely dwarfs it, continuing at this scale for several metres in both directions.[4]

Before the next section, it is probably worth mentioning that one C construct poses special problems with programming staff when attempting to enforce the kind of complexity limits in safety-related development recommended at the end of this book. That construct is the `switch` statement. This statement very rapidly builds up both the cyclomatic complexity and the static path count and yet its homogeneous nature strongly suggests that complexity does not build up linearly. Certainly two functions with the same large static path count, but one of which contains mostly `switch` statements, do not appear to the experienced programmer as equally complex. The best course of action seems to be to treat its complexity less than linearly, and perhaps logarithmically, since a 20 branch `switch` statement is not in practice twice as complex as a 10 branch `switch`.

3.2.2 Data and object complexity

One of the biggest criticisms of the structural complexity metrics is that they do not contain information on data structures. The definition of metrics for data structures such as occur frequently in object-orientated systems such as the C++ class system is in its infancy. Given that this book concerns only C, little more will be said on this, and the reader is advised to watch the literature. The author will merely note that object-orientated systems appear to transfer system complexity from structure to data, and he has seen a number of C++ systems with ridiculously simple functional components and a labyrinthine class system which caused the mind to boggle. When plotting the class hierarchy of such a system recently from a major communications package, the lines joining the various classes were in such abundance that all the white pixels between the boxes representing the class names disappeared after about twenty minutes plotting on a blisteringly fast work-station, prompting the package's designers to burst out laughing, and confirming their view that things had got a little out of hand! The system did not even use multiple inheritance, one of the most effective ways in C++ of obfuscating data structure and the object of much unflattering attention in most C++ programming standards.

---

[4] Such components might goad a hard-pressed safety-related software manager into leaving a gun and a single bullet on the desk of the programmer responsible to avoid having to fit a larger door.

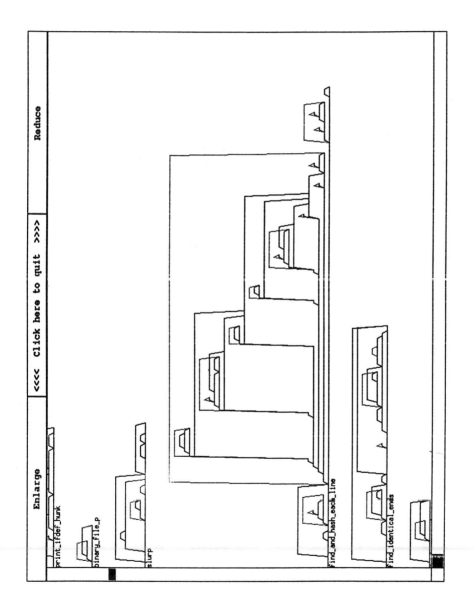

Figure 3.5 Control graphs of functional components of the GNU diff package.

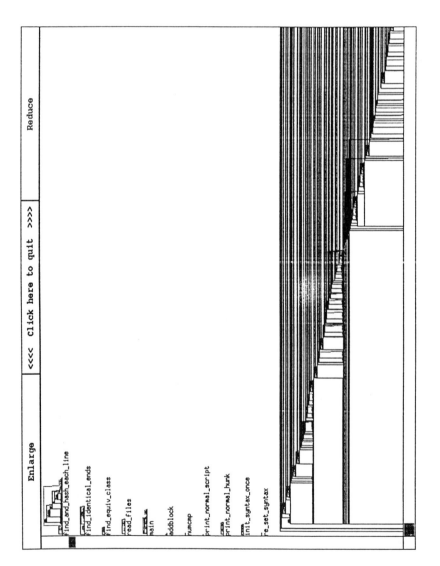

Figure 3.6 More control graphs from the GNU diff package. The complex component in the middle of Fig. 3.5 now appears as the tiny hieroglyphic in the top left corner, if the reader is holding this book in a shop, the one at the bottom would go out of the door. (This leads directly to the important new complexity metric that if you could paper the side of a house with the control graph, it's probably too complex.)

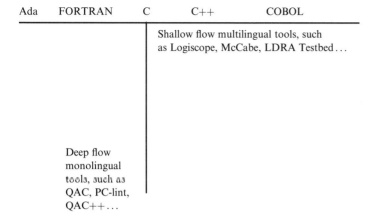

Ada	FORTRAN	C	C++	COBOL

Shallow flow multilingual tools, such as Logiscope, McCabe, LDRA Testbed...

Deep flow monolingual tools, such as QAC, PC-lint, QAC++...

Figure 3.7 Diagram illustrating the difference between shallow flow and deep flow tools.

There are a number of basic data metrics which are candidates for use in screening problematic components in C. These include the widely-studied Halstead metrics (Halstead, 1977), which consider the program text, operands and operators as a stream of tokens. Beizer (1990) reports that these metrics have a good history of prediction, but the many studies are not in a form allowing direct recommendations to be given for safety-related development. Of all the other possibilities, perhaps the one with most intuitive appeal, at least for C, is a count of the number of variables having external scope. Over-scoping variables is a common problem in C as it works in direct opposition to the notions of data-hiding. C programmers frequently overscope such variables by failing to use the `static` keyword for variables with file scope, increasing the probability of a clash between two items of the same name and also increasing the scope for inadvertent modification. There is some evidence that systems with unusually large numbers of variables with external scope are more resistant to easy change. However, the evidence is by no means strong, and so no direct recommendations will be made at this stage.

3.2.3 Shallow vs. deep analysis

It is worthwhile discussing practical metrics extraction briefly. In terms of language parsing, software quality measurements generally fall into two distinct classes, the relationship between which appears as Fig. 3.7.

- *Shallow flow metrics*. Although important, such metrics by definition make few demands on the language parser. Examples include both the conventionally defined metric types of *structural* metrics, such as cyclomatic complexity, and *linguistic* metrics, such as the Halstead metrics. Such metrics are common in multi-lingual measurement tools as a direct consequence of the fact that their extraction requires only a shallow look at the language.
- *Deep flow metrics*. In contrast, the deep flow metrics, such as statically-detectable fault rate, described by this book can only be extracted by a very detailed look at

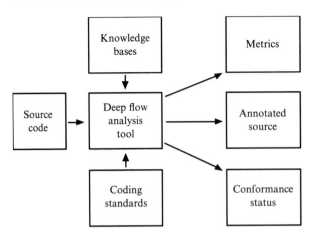

Figure 3.8 The structure of a deep flow static analysis tool.

the language syntax and semantics. Such measurements place enormous demands on the language parser and as such are produced only by tools specializing in one language. Such tools are themselves quite large and are typically of the order of 50 000–100 000 lines of C. The architecture of such tools is shown in Fig. 3.8. Such a tool must be able to parse the appropriate language at least as thoroughly as a compiler *as a starting point*. The depth of this parsing means that shallow flow metrics can simultaneously be extracted with little additional effort. The drawback when multilingual systems are in use, of course, is that each language requires its own tool.

Notice that the output of deep flow static analysis consists of annotated source for the programmer to study as well as metrics information and conformance status, i.e. whether or not the component analysed conforms with the standards supplied to the analysis tool, for use in an automated change and configuration control system. In contrast, deep flow dynamic analysis involves a deep parsing of either the source language directly or its object code equivalent, but the output in this case is typically a highly edited form of the original, which tracks dynamic conformance issues as described in detail in Section 5.3.

Note that shallow flow tools tend to be aimed at test planning and coverage rather than intrinsic reliability and consistency.

3.2.4 The calibrated package

After reading the above, the reader could be forgiven for wondering just how much has been achieved in software measurement. There is no question that progress has been made, and certain metrics exhibit essentially repeatable and largely monotonic relationships with various software maintenance attributes. However, the biggest single problem facing software measurement scientists is the lack of calibrated packages. In this context, a *calibrated package* is a software package which contains a comprehensive and accurate history of change, preferably in machine extractable form. Such history should contain a complete record of all error occurrence, including the error type, as well as where and how it happened. Only then can sensible correlations be made between the maintenance history and intrinsic complexity properties of the software, such as its decision count. Without such correlations, only bland, non-specific and generally unconvincing statements can be made. In several years of study, the author has come across very few such calibrated packages.

One particularly good package to study was reported by Hatton and Hopkins (1989). This involved the internationally known NAG FORTRAN scientific subroutine library, totalling around a quarter of a million executable lines. This particular package is around twenty years old and has been under continuous development since its early days. Its huge advantage in measurement terms is that there is a complete machine extractable bug and maintenance history built into the comment header for each component. Using this history Hatton and Hopkins were able to demonstrate that the static path count defined earlier in this chapter was very highly correlated with the number of bugs detected so far in the life-cycle of each component. Studies are continuing with this package to compare evolution of error distributions with differing release, as the releases of the product are broken up into a series of *Marks*.

3.3 COMPLEXITY, MAINTENANCE AND RELIABILITY

So far, the tenor of this chapter has been that complexity measurement is an important part of the software process, that some obvious measures exist and, finally, some studies support their use in software development. Furthermore, some form of complexity limiting forms a part of all of the safety-related standards initiatives described in Chapter 1. However, the author would like to point out a fundamental inconsistency between the long-held notion that modularization is 'a good thing' in large systems design, and the results of some recent case histories. Until this inconsistency can be resolved by public debate, the author will continue to recommend that complexity limiting takes place in line with state-of-the-art thinking as described in Section 7.3.

The inconsistency involves the following strands:

(a) The seminal work of Miller (1957) shows that humans can cope with around 7 ± 2 pieces of information at a time through the mechanism of the short-term memory. Note that this appears to be independent of the information content of the pieces. For example, a binary sequence contains inherently less information than a sequence of denary numbers but the length of the sequence that can be absorbed and manipulated is around the same. Miller also described the notion of *chunking*, by which a problem is systematically broken down into chunks which fit into short-term memory during the understanding process.

This a strong argument for using highly expressive compact languages, provided the nomenclature is familiar. Miller's work can relate to the depth of the dependency tree associated with a statement or small group of statements in a programming language. If the depth is very small, for example as in functional languages, reasoning should be easier than if each statement or group of statements requires understanding of many other statements or side-effects to understand it. There is a good analogy here with spectral analysis and resolution, (Kanasewich, 1981): in order to see something clearly, the effects of its surroundings must first be removed.

(b) Shneiderman (1980), in a detailed analysis, argues that chunking is how programmers understand programs.

(c) Hilgard *et al.* (1971) argue that the short-term memory requires a *rehearsal buffer* which continuously refreshes its contents. These authors also describe the standard memory model, whereby a long-term memory backs up the short-term memory but acts in a fundamentally different way, in that its contents are in a coded form and to all intents and purposes are never lost, even though the recovery codes may get scrambled in various conditions. There is very considerable psychological and physiological evidence to support this model.

(d) Sommerville (1984) referencing the work of Greeno (1972) and Shneiderman (1980) endorses the chunking model and argues, amongst other things, that the presence of the goto construct inhibits such chunking, explaining its appalling reputation for obscuring code. He also goes on to describe a further working memory in the brain which backs up the short-term memory during program understanding, although there appears to be no psychological evidence for such a model.

(e) Compiler optimization experiences suggest close analogies with chunking and complexity. For example, Bornat (1974) makes the following observations: 'Much of the demand for code optimization is caused by the widespread use of inappropriate programming languages', p. 174; and 'Structured program design teaches us (amongst other things) that gotos are Harmful to the Brain. Experience in language implementation shows they are Hard to Implement and Not Particularly Efficient Either'.

(f) In practice, as is discussed in a case history cited in Section 5.1.1, the only statement which appeared to conflict with simple complexity measures was the switch statement, whose complexity appears empirically to be a logarithmic rather than a linear function of its decision count. Hence, even though a switch statement can have arbitrarily many cases (in theory), its homogeneity appears to render it a simple chunk.

(g) Analogous complexity measures arise in speech processing (Pylyshyn *et al.*, 1983). Two speech complexity measures of particular relevance to programming language complexity are:

1. The number of possible sentences of L words that can be constructed from a vocabulary of size N words. If words can arrive in unrestricted order, this gives N^L sentences.

2. The branching factor, which is the average number of words that can follow each of the words in a sentence.

Higher values of these two measures lead to rapid degeneration in the accuracy of automatic speech perception. It is entirely reasonable to expect the same from program texts.

Now, any model of complexity must distinguish between c_n, the *natural complexity* inherent in a problem, and the potentially greater complexity used to implement its solution. This latter will be termed c_a, the *actual complexity*, to distinguish it here. Whatever measurement framework eventually emerges, the following inequality should hold:

$$c_a \geq c_n$$

It appears to be exceedingly difficult to measure the difference between natural and *actual* complexity, as is evidenced by the time it takes human programmers to understand some programs, and also by the dramatic differences in productivity which have been measured in different individuals. It is beyond the scope of this book to investigate this subject, but suffice it to say that it is believed that 'good' design' by definition, minimizes the difference.

For the purposes of the following analysis, it will be assumed that the design is sufficiently well thought out that c_a and c_n are the same and only the implementation is at issue. Given this, points (a)–(g) all tend to support the view that 'simplest is best', which is consistent with conventional engineering doctrine. However, there is now recent, considerable evidence that *proportionately more errors are committed in small software components than large ones*. For example, the measurements of Hatton and Hopkins (1989), described earlier, suggested that the following relationship for components with larger static path counts held in their studies of the NAG library:

$$n_b = c \log_{10}(n_p)$$

where c is a constant close to 1, n_b is the number of bugs and n_p is the number of static paths. In other words, the more paths, the more bugs occurred during the life-cycle, but *logarithmically*. Herein lies the contradiction, for this observation leads directly to the conclusion that if a problem has a natural complexity of 100, it is better to have it as a single module of 100 than say, 10 modules of 10, because

$$\log_{10}(100)(= 2) < 10 \log_{10}(10)(= 10)$$

This then contradicts the fundamental assumption that modularization is an essential component of cost reduction in maintenance. Moreover, further recent evidence corroborates these measurements (Davey *et al.*, 1993), who found their results counter-intuitive also. Although this experiment referred to errors detected during internal testing of a newly developed package, as opposed to the NAG study, which included all errors reported in twenty years of use, analysis of these authors' data strongly supports the kind of logarithmic relationship reported by Hatton and Hopkins (1989). To illustrate this, Fig. 3.9 plots actual bug counts reported in a large C development by Davey *et al.* (1993) alongside a prediction of those bugs, assuming the same kind of logarithmic relationship for statement counts as is quoted above for static path count. In this case, the prediction was obtained by taking the basic relationship

$$n_b = c \log_{10}(n_s)$$

The right-hand side expression is plotted using the value of 1.6 for c just to normalize. The similarity is remarkable even though a different complexity metric, i.e. statement count, is used instead of static path count.

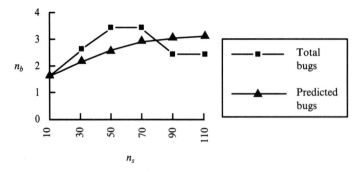

Figure 3.9 Total bugs versus logarithmically predicted bugs. The distribution of errors reported by Davey *et al.* (1993) plotted against a prediction using the logarithmic relationship reported by Hatton and Hopkins (1989).

Building on the above, Moller (1993) found precisely the same behaviour in a study of three versions of a large operating system. In addition, he found the following:

- Modified code had four to eight times more faults than new code.
- There were more faults in data flow (e.g. direction of variables) than in control flow.
- Interfaces were more fault-prone than internal complexity.
- 10 per cent of all faults were initialization errors.
- Complex logical decisions, i.e. those involving combinations of && and ||, were very prone to fault.

Given that these three important empirical studies all found the same counter-intuitive behaviour, it is worthwhile to explore this property a little further. It can immediately be seen that this holds for any functional behaviour of n_b which is less than a linear function of n_p, for this would require:

$$n_b(ij) < i \times n_b(j)$$

where i and j are integers. So if

$$n_b(j) = j^p$$

for some power p, then the inequality reads

$$i^p \times j^p < i \times j^p$$

and so

$$i^p < i$$

which implies

$$p < 1$$

The above leads to the inescapable conclusion based on the results of recent case histories that modularization does not improve reliability in terms of errors found. In fact, the opposite appears to be true. The reader may well ask if this contradiction can be resolved. There are at least three mitigating factors.

1. Maintenance is made up of three components, corrective, adaptive and perfective, which roughly correspond to mistakes; things which should have been done differently; and things that were forgotten. Lientz and Swanson (1980) found that these were in the ratio $17:18:65$. In other words, only 17 per cent of all maintenance was corrective. This suggests that although reliability might get worse with increasing modularization, other aspects of maintenance, such as the costs of enhancement, might drop sufficiently that the overall cost of maintenance goes down. However, in a safety-related development, where reliability is crucial, this may not be considered appropriate.

2. Increasing the number of modules and therefore interfaces for a given functionality without the use of tools to ensure the consistency of those interfaces leads to an increased static fault rate. This is discussed in detail in the next chapter. This may explain the tendency for small modules to contain proportionately more errors, *but only if there are an increased number of function references.* The author is unaware of any measurements which would throw light on this.

3. One of the central points of modularization is *to reduce the overall line count* by reusing common functionality. It is possible that if the count is reduced enough, the overall predicted bug rate would actually drop. This can be investigated by considering the following simple model.

   Suppose a package of L lines is implemented as a number, C, of components. It will be assumed without stretching the analysis too far, that these are of equal size: (L/C) lines.

   This, using the logarithmic model discussed above, with a normalizing constant of 1, suggests that the total number of errors, E, is given by

$$E = C \log_{10}\left(\frac{L}{C}\right)$$

Since it is the behaviour of E under change which is of interest, taking the two partial derivatives of this function yields

$$\frac{\partial E}{\partial C} = \log_{10}\left(\frac{L}{C}\right) - 1$$

and

$$\frac{\partial E}{\partial L} = \frac{C}{L}$$

Now ideally, in changing a system or even designing a new system, the idea is to reduce E. The independent variables are L and C, so that the number of errors can be influenced in this simple model either by changing the number of components or the number of lines. A reduction in E is achieved in the following circumstances:

(a) C is constant, L is *decreased* and $\partial E/\partial L > 0$. This corresponds to the obvious case that the overall number of lines is decreased for the same number of components, as would occur in software re-use.

(b) L is constant, C is *decreased* and $\partial E/\partial C > 0$. This corresponds to the less obvious and rather disturbing conclusion that the number of errors also decreases as the number of components is reduced for the same number of lines, i.e. fewer components containing more lines.

Interestingly, there is a third case whereby the number of errors reduces as follows:

(c) L is constant, C is *in*creased and $\partial E/\partial C < 0$. This corresponds to the case when the overall number of components is *increased* for the same number of lines. This would correspond to arbitrary breaking up of components without any attempt to reuse. This only leads to a reduction in errors if the partial derivative is negative, which gives the condition: $L/C < 10$.

In other words, it is possible to reduce the number of errors by increasing the number of components for the same total lines provided the components are sufficiently small in the first place. As such, this is a rather unlikely case, but if the error relationship was proportional to the log to base 20 or even 50 (a rather slower growth than implied by log to base 10), a realistic situation could arise. Object-orientated systems also tend to have small components.

Finally, it is interesting to note the relative sizes of the two derivatives. This might help to indicate which design strategy would be of most value: aim to reduce the number of components without affecting the total line count too much (fewer but bigger modules) or vice versa, (re-use). This corresponds to the ratio:

$$\left| \frac{(\partial E/\partial C)}{(\partial E/\partial L)} \right| = \left| \frac{L}{C} \left[\log_{10}\left(\frac{L}{C}\right) - 1 \right] \right|$$

When this ratio is large, monolithic design is favoured for reduction in errors, whereas when it is small, reuse is favoured. As can be seen, when the ratio $L/C \gg 1$, i.e. components are already quite large, then continuing the trend appears to be the best strategy, whereas when components are very small, reuse is the most advantageous.

Summing up the complete argument, an analysis of the recent results reported by Hatton and Hopkins (1989), Davey *et al.* (1993) and Moller (1993) gives strong indications that the long-held view that modularization is always beneficial, is an over-simplification. In most circumstances, for example, when modularization does not reduce the size of the system by very much, the overall reliability could be expected to *decrease*. One further issue in favour of modularization in safety-related systems, however, is that smaller components are simpler to reason about. This is of course only true if the components are not tightly coupled to their environment. Be that as it may, the situation is not clear, and until the above arguments are developed further by public debate, this book will continue to recommend that individual functional complexity is limited using the metrics described. This leads to a form of measurement rather like human medical health screening for such things as cholesterol levels, blood pressure and so on. The presence of such factors as a high cholesterol level do not guarantee that the possessor is going to suffer from heart disease; in fact some people seem naturally to have high levels with no adverse effects. However, the evidence is presented in such a way that *a high level should be avoided wherever possible in the certain knowledge that statistically, the chances of heart disease will be reduced*, although it is still somewhat controversial by how much. A rather more well understood statistic is the relationship between smoking and lung cancer, among other things. The relationship is unquestionable and yet smokers still live long lives sometimes, although they will probably spend a higher percentage of it with some form of ill health. Unfortunately, *most* smokers will die younger than non-smokers.

So, when a software component is found to have high complexity using multiple metrics which have proved to be strongly correlated with high maintenance and/or unreliability on calibrated packages, the author would argue that their use is relevant and closely analogous to the above. In a large system, for example, complexity screening will find those modules likely to be most problematic with considerable accuracy. However, how they should then be treated is not yet resolved. Given that the above metrics can all be measured statically, i.e. before the code is compiled, their use in safety-related development should be considered a fundamental part in *anticipating* problems and therefore in building a simpler and safer system. Ince (1991) also supports the view that enough is understood about some of the metrics described above to apply them routinely. However, detection is one thing and treatment another.

An example of complexity screening and its overall effects on complexity metric distributions will be given in the next chapter.

4

POPULATION STUDIES OF C PROGRAMS

In the last few years, the author has been involved with two large-scale measurement initiatives. The relationship between these is indicated in Fig. 4.1. The object of the cross-bar part of the 'T' was to make *static* measurements of unsafe items, such as those described in Chapters 2 and 3, to find their distribution across both C and FORTRAN code from many different industries around the world. Two separate languages were chosen to estimate the degree of linguistic dependence of items in the study and to allow for comparison between those items which were essentially language-independent.

In contrast, the vertical bar of the 'T' concerned a very large N-version programming experiment in one of these industries—seismic data processing—to assess run-time consistency of identical algorithms with identical parameters and identical data programmed independently in the same programming language. The results of this latter experiment, which covered only FORTRAN, are described in Hatton and Roberts (1994)[1] and will not be discussed further here.

This chapter concerns the cross-bar of the 'T', for which the author has carried out static measurements on large amounts of commercial C software from the following application areas:

- Graphics
- CAD/CAM
- Language parsing

---

[1] For the reader impatient to know the answer, the agreement between nine packages, each exercising some 150 000 source lines, all ostensibly implementing the same algorithms, degraded at the staggering rate of approximately 1 per cent per 1000 lines of implemented code.

Static consistency analysis of many different disciplines

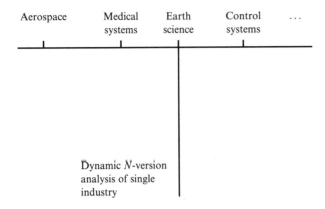

Figure 4.1 A schematic of the relationship between the two large-scale measurement initiatives described in this chapter.

- Games
- Communications*
- Database
- Electrical engineering
- Geographic information systems
- Medical systems*
- Systems analysis
- Financial systems
- Control systems
- Network management
- Aerospace*
- Insurance
- Image processing
- Public utilities*

The application areas marked with an asterisk included safety-critical code, and the population as a whole included companies with and without ISO 9001 status. The statistics of the population analysed during 1993, the last complete year before this book was written, are shown in Table 4.1.

It is interesting to note that the average C function is typically four times smaller than the average FORTRAN function (Hatton, 1994a, b), in spite of the fact that C

Table 4.1 Statistics for the whole population studied in this chapter

Number of packages analysed	54
Total number of application areas	17
Total number of preprocessed lines	1 583 104
Total number of executable lines	1 133 869
Total number of function references	244 918
Total number of functions analysed	29 723
Average function size in number of preprocessed lines	53
Average function size in executable lines	38

has invaded application areas traditionally employing FORTRAN in the last few years. Most of the code in the above study is less than three years old, but all of it is in commercial use. No beta or earlier code was analysed.

4.1 STATIC NON-CONFORMANCE RATES IN REAL SYSTEMS

This section is rather dense and full of statistics. The author's only defence is that he knows of no other source of such information and the results are very illuminating and particularly relevant to the implementor of a safety-related system. The notion of non-conformance is used in the above title to cover all those features that are likely to lead to problems of one kind or another, and they are split here into a number of categories.

As will become apparent to the reader, the probability of a fault leading to a failure can vary from the extremely unlikely to the inevitable. However, a fault can only become a failure if it is executed, so even a fault which would lead inevitably to a failure may never occur as the code in which it lurks is rarely if ever illuminated. The following discussion will attempt rather loosely to attach a probability of failure, *given that the code is executed*. The issue of whether the code is ever executed is a matter for testing stratagems, and will be discussed in more detail later.

4.1.1 Inline faults

An inline fault is defined here as a fault which is not associated with an interface. Historically, languages have developed in such a way that statically-detectable faults in interfaces have been much more common, owing to the availability of independent compilation without any requirement for interface checking. For example, in FORTRAN 77, statically-detectable inline fault rates are less than statically-detectable interface faults by a factor of 10 or so (Hatton, 1994b). C is, however, an unusual language in this regard, as the category of inline faults is regrettably very wide. Nevertheless, interface faults are still frequently encountered, even though Standard C incorporates a way of guaranteeing their consistency via the medium of the function prototype. Regrettably this is optional to maintain compatibility with the old-style declarations and definitions.

Table 4.2 contains a list of typical inline faults and their occurrence rate in the population described at the beginning of this section. Note that not all detectable inline faults are shown, only some of the more serious ones. A mixture of well-defined but abused features is included along with some symptomatic of clutter, such as variables unused within scope. The severity column is subjectively split up as S(evere), M(edium) and L(ow). It would be reasonable to require that none of these should appear in a safety-related application, given that they are both statically detectable and symptoms of disorder.

Note that items 6, 8, 9 and 10, as marked with an asterisk, indicate particular faults which could be due either to the differing promotion rules between K&R and Standard C or through different implementations of plain char (whether it is signed or unsigned is implementation-defined).

Table 4.2 Inline static inconsistency items and their occurrence rates

Ref.	Inline fault and standard reference if relevant	Severity	Transgression rate in executable lines
1	Casting a pointer to a narrower integral type; 3.3.4	S	1 : 16 923
2	Modified more than once between sequence points—dependence on evaluation order; 2.1.2.3	S	1 : 41 995
3	Modified and accessed between sequence points—dependence on evaluation order; 2.1.2.3	S	1 : 113 387
4	Operand of sizeof has side-effects which will not take place; 3.3.3.4	S	Never recorded
5	Jump avoiding local initialization; 3.1.2.4	S	Never recorded
6*	Test for unsigned value < 0;	S	1 : 94 489
7	Non-matching #if ... #else ... #elif ... #endif in same file	S	Never recorded
8*	Test for unsigned char < general negative constant	S	1 : 1 133 869
9*	Test for unsigned value < general negative constant	S	1 : 26 369
10*	Unary—on an unsigned expression gives an unsigned result which can never be negative; 3.3.3	M	1 : 103 079
11	Control expression is an assignment	M	1 : 3306
12	Variable may be unset at this point	M	1 : 846
13	Statement has no side-effects, it can be removed	M	1 : 12 325
14	Cast between pointer and int type; 3.3.4	L	1 : 149
15	Text after preprocessor directive; 3.8	L	1 : 26 369
16	Switch without default clause	L	1 : 1597
17	Fall-through from one case to next	L	1 : 6709
18	No else in if—else if block	L	1 : 888
19	Nested comments; 3.1.9	L	1 : 984
20	Left-hand operand of ',' does nothing	L	1 : 113 387
21	Unreachable statement	L	1 : 1236
22	Variable unused in scope	L	1 : 491
23	Static function declaration but no definition	L	1 : 16 923
24	No definition given for structure tag	L	1 : 125 985
25	Declaration hides a more global declaration	L	1 : 1153
26	Nested if blocks with no braces	L	1 : 12 740
27	Presence of horrors such as i+++j	L	1 : 7411
28	Appears like old-style assignment operator	L	1 : 12 325

4.1.2 Interface faults

As was mentioned above, the optional nature of the function prototype has led to a significantly higher average interface inconsistency rate than would otherwise have been the case. This is such that any safety-related application *must* mandate the use of function prototypes. If the compiler does not support these (and some surprisingly still do not), then the use of a tool that can check the consistency of old-style interfaces must be mandated. The need for this is emphasized by the statistics below.

In the population under study here, the distribution of old-style definitions and implicit declarations (i.e. no declaration in scope), was as shown in Table 4.3. From these figures, a *function prototype efficiency ratio* can be defined as

$$100\left(1 - \frac{D_{\text{old}}}{D_{\text{total}}}\right)$$

Table 4.3 The distribution of old-style declarations and definitions

Item	Total number	Occurrence rate in executable lines
Old-style definitions (i.e. with separate parameter declarations)	12 670	1 : 76
Functions referenced without an explicit declaration in scope and therefore defaulting to type int	23 660	1 : 41

where D_{old} is the number of old-style definitions encountered and D_{total} is the total number of definitions encountered. The higher this number the better.

Similarly, an *implicit declaration risk ratio* can also be defined as

$$100 \left(\frac{R_{imp}}{R_{total}} \right)$$

where R_{imp} is the number of implicit declarations encountered and R_{total} is the total number of function references encountered. The lower this number the better.

Using the above figures, Table 4.4 shows these two ratios for the population analysed here.

Table 4.4 Function prototype use and implicit declaration occurrence percentages

Item	Ratio (%)
Function prototype efficiency for whole population	57.4
Implicit declaration risk ratio	9.7

The function prototype efficiency ratio of 57.4 per cent is particularly disappointing considering that all of the packages analysed have been developed since function prototypes appeared in the C language. The implication is that approximately half of all interfaces encountered in this population leave themselves effectively unprotected. In fact, only 6 of the 54 packages achieved 100 per cent use of function prototypes. Some were dismal. The risk of default int declaration, the correct response of a compliant compiler to the complete absence of any declaration, is also high at 9.7 per cent. In order to see the scale of interface inconsistency, Table 4.5 analyses serious fault rates in interfaces for this C population. Of all the statically-detectable faults discovered in this population, 25.8 per cent are in the interfaces. The more that function prototypes are used, the lower this gets. Given the average function prototype efficiency ratio of around 57 per cent, this suggests that in the absence of function prototypes, roughly half of all statically-detectable faults would lie in the interfaces, emphasizing the importance of the function prototype efficiency ratio as a measure of C consistency.

It should be noted that even those packages that used function prototypes 100 per cent, exhibited the occasional interface inconsistency because the prototypes were not visible at both the definition and the call. This occurs whenever the declaration and function call are in one file and an (inconsistent) function definition in another. For example, functions called with too few arguments appeared in one, while one example of a declaration and definition returning a different integral type occurred in another. There remain intrinsic loopholes in interfaces of course, even when the

Table 4.5 Interface static inconsistency items and their occurrence rates

Ref.	Interface fault if relevant	Severity	Transgression rate in executable lines
1	Definition returns int but declaration returns something else probably due to a missing type specifier in the definition	S	Never recorded
2	Function unintentionally called with too few arguments	S	1 : 3489
3	Declared function is also defined as an external variable name	S	1 : 1 133 869
4	Declared variable is also defined as a function	S	Never recorded
5	Integral type is passed to a floating type	S	1 : 39 947
6	Integral type is passed to a struct type	S	Never recorded
7	Integral type is passed to a union type	S	Never recorded
8	Pointer is passed to a floating type	S	Never recorded
9	Pointer is passed to a struct type	S	1 : 1 133 869
10	Pointer is passed to a union type	S	1 : 8125^2
11	Floating type is passed to an integral type	S	1 : 566 935
12	Floating type is passed to a pointer type	S	Never recorded
13	Floating type is passed to a struct type	S	Never recorded
14	Floating type is passed to a union type	S	Never recorded
15	Struct type is passed to an integral type	S	Never recorded
16	Struct type is passed to a pointer	S	1 : 226 774
17	Struct type is passed to a floating type	S	Never recorded
18	Struct type is passed to a union type	S	Never recorded
19	Union type is passed to an integral type	S	Never recorded
20	Union type is passed to a pointer	S	1 : 283 467
21	Union type is passed to a floating type	S	Never recorded
22	Union type is passed to a struct type	S	Never recorded
23	Static function call with different number of arguments to definition	S	1 : 36 576
24	Argument has different type to definition of function	S	1 : 766
25	Argument has different type to previous calls	S	Never recorded
26	Function called with variable number of arguments	S	1 : 1454
27	Function does not return value but calls to it check the result	S	1 : 113 387
28	Incompatible argument	M	Never recorded
29	Non-zero constant is passed to a pointer	M	1 : 16 675
30	Literal will be truncated	M	1 : 17 444
31	Function returns a value which is sometimes ignored	M	1 : 2613
32	Function returns different integral type in definition and declaration probably due to implicit declaration.	L	1 : 812
33	Function returns pointer but declaration assumes int	L	1 : 5323
34	Function defined to return int but declared to return other	L	1 : 283 467
35	Function has different return type at point of call	L	1 : 87 221
36	Function called with unintentionally too many arguments	L	1 : 1364
37	Argument is struct or union but definition is variadic	L	1 : 49 299
38	Pointer to function has different return type to definition	L	1 : 6872
39	Declared function is also defined as a macro	L	Never recorded
40	Macro is also defined as a function	L	1 : 2662
41	Macro is also defined as a variable	L	1 : 125 985
42	Declared variable is also defined as a macro	L	Never recorded
43	Integral is passed to pointer type	L	1 : 10 499
44	Integral type is passed to a narrower type	L	1 : 866
45	Pointer is passed to an integral type	L	1 : 1366
46	Integral type is passed to a wider type	L	1 : 1003

^{2} All occurrences of this fault appeared in the same safety-related package!

Table 4.6 The distribution of some incompatible items between C and C++

C/C++ incompatibility	Severity	Transgression rate in executable lines
Use of C++ keyword	S	1 : 22 263
Function not declared before use	S	1 : 29
Empty parameter list declared for 1 or more arguments	S	1 : 51
Old-style definition	S	1 : 2729
return; in a function not returning void	S	1 : 2920
Presence of __STDC__	S	1 : 4567

function prototype has apparently secured everything, as for example, if a macro is also defined as a function, which occurred in one of the packages 100 per cent protected by function prototypes.

4.1.3 C/C++ incompatibility rates

Although there is a widespread belief that C++ is a superset of C, this is not the case as was discussed in more detail in Section 2.10. Of the known incompatibilities, some should be detected by a C++ compiler, but others will not, leading to unexpected run-time behaviour. Given that C++ may well replace C at some stage, the presence of such features, particularly those likely to lead to differing run-time behaviour, should be considered problematic to say the least. While C++ is still evolving and many parts are still undefined, the presence of any known incompatibility should be considered severe. It is prudent in general software engineering to avoid these. In a safety-related application this has no unpleasant implications provided it is stated clearly that the code is not to be compiled with a C++ compiler under any circumstances. If this should ever be the case, the code must be developed avoiding all such features.

Section 2.10 gave some advice on dealing with this, and Table 4.6 shows typical occurrence rates of some features in a subset of the above population totalling about a fifth of the code.

4.1.4 Use of extensions

The use of extensions in C has already been covered in Section 2.11. In the population analysed, extensions occurred whenever the compiler allowed it. Their transgression rates have not been tabulated as they are a specific problem rather than a general problem, and should simply be banned.

4.1.5 Programming standard violations

For a number of the software systems analysed as part of these large population studies, written programming standards were available. This provided the opportunity to measure the degree to which the standards were enforced in the code. As is discussed later, the degree of enforceability of standards varies dramatically, with anywhere between 20 per cent and 100 per cent being automatically enforceable. Hence in the studies here, the number of categories which were monitored is recorded

Table 4.7 The distribution of C programming standard transgressions in a package developed by an ISO 9001 certified company

Standard item (6 out of 30 categories)	No. of transgressions	Line rate
All macro bodies must be parenthesized	360	1 : 500
No gotos must be present	8	1 : 22 513
No implied declarations	6086	1 : 30
One statement per line	135	1 : 1337
No hidden null statements	3382	1 : 53
Consistent indentation must be used	10	1 : 18 010
Totals	9981	1 : 18

but the degree of enforceability of the standard is not precisely defined, so the transgression rates reported should be considered as a *lower* bound.

Table 4.7 shows the transgression rates in a major piece of C development totalling some 200 000 lines developed by a company validated to ISO 9001.

Table 4.8 shows the transgression rates in one component of a major safety-related package totalling some 16 000 lines. Note that inspections in this case were done for all code and had been effective in enforcing some parts of the standard, but not others.

A third case history is shown in Table 4.9 in a somewhat different format. Here, the standard was split into rules and guidelines. Rules were mandated and guidelines were recommended. In addition, the developer agreed to a supplementary set of rules and guidelines against which the source code, totalling some 9000 lines, was also audited. Again, transgression rates are very high.

To put the above case histories into context, programming standard transgressions are not the sole preserve of C developers. Table 4.10 illustrates transgression rates measured by the author when auditing a very large FORTRAN 77 package consisting of 344,777 executable lines. In this case, the standard was well written, considerably detailed, the result of a considerable effort and, like its C stablemates

Table 4.8 The distribution of C programming standard transgressions in one component of a safety-related package

Standard item (13 out of >100 categories)	No. of transgressions	Line rate
#include syntax must be conformant	246	1 : 65
Function prototype definitions only	83	1 : 191
No implied declarations	351	1 : 45
Indentation must be consistent within file	357	1 : 44
Declarations must be consistently indented	23	1 : 690
Variables if set must be reused	4	1 : 3969
Variables must be used in scope	9	1 : 1764
Return value of function must be checked	69	1 : 230
Variables must be initialized before use	5	1 : 3175
Declarations must not hide more global ones	5	1 : 3175
Expressions must not rely on precedence rules	5	1 : 3175
Functions must be less than 120 lines	7	1 : 2268
No implementation-defined pointer casts	1	1 : 15 900
Totals	1165	1 : 14

Table 4.9 Table of transgression rates of rules and guidelines in a case history totalling some 9000 lines. The first two rows suggest that rules are adhered to some 3–4 times better than guidelines

	Total number of items	Number of items tracked in audit	% of standard	Transgression rate in lines
Base rules	28	10	36	1:12
Base guidelines	18	8	46	1:3
Sub-total	46	18	39	1:2
Supplementary rules	14	1	7	1:420
Supplementary guidelines	22	7	32	1:78
Sub-total	36	8	22	1:64
Interface rules	67	4	6	1:91

above, hopelessly maintained. The standard was transgressed at the rate of once every 66 lines, even though only 6 out of 40 categories in the standard were being monitored.

The overall average transgression rate reported across a wide variety of both C and FORTRAN code is 1 transgression every 71 lines, with C being generally less well-adhered to than FORTRAN (Hatton, 1994b), although this is probably due to the fact that C standards are typically wildly over-ambitious and voluminous compared with their FORTRAN counterparts.

The author has frequently noted the phenomenon seen in the above case histories whereby one or two items are responsible for massive numbers of transgressions. In general, it is easier to accept a large number of transgressions being missed when they are made up of a small number of transgressions of a large number of rules. It is much less easy, however, to accept the phenomenon above, where it could reasonably be expected that the standard would be easier to enforce. This is, however, in agreement with the author's general observation that in many companies no real effort is currently made to enforce programming standards, and such effort as there is, tends to focus on stylistic issues such as indentation standards rather than reliability issues. This is rather like surveying a house before purchase to see if it is the right colour rather than if it has any structural weaknesses. It is a symptom of inappropriate engineering priorities.

Table 4.10 The distribution of FORTRAN programming standard transgressions in a typical company

Standard item (6 out of 40 categories)	No. of transgressions	Line rate
All variables must be declared	1088	1:317
No ANSI transgressions	1484	1:232
No floating-point comparisons	2546	1:135
No named COMMON blocks	58	1:5944
No R/L interface type mismatches	48	1:7183
No char/non-char type mismatches	35	1:9851
Totals	5259	1:66

Table 4.11 The distribution of depth of nesting for the whole population in percentiles

Percentile value	Maximum depth of nesting
0	121
10	4
20	3
30	2
40	2
50	1
60	1
70	1
80	0
90	0
100	0

4.2 COMPLEXITY METRIC DISTRIBUTIONS

Of the many complexity metric distributions extracted from the population analysis discussed in this chapter, it would be inappropriate to the main aim of this book to cite them all. Instead, only the metrics which have been discussed in Section 3.2 as being most relevant to complexity limiting are shown here.

Table 4.11 shows the whole population distribution of the maximum depth of nesting in percentiles. The highest depth of nesting achieved in this population was a staggering 121! Quite apart from the fact that Standard C requires no more than 15 for a conforming implementation, it is interesting to speculate what was going through the programmer's mind in the design process (an illegal substance perhaps). Apart from the extreme nature of the bottom 10 per cent of the population, the overall distribution is reasonably consistent with code for which it is feasible to design test suites.

Table 4.12 shows the equivalent distribution for cyclomatic complexity, as discussed in detail in Section 3.2.1. Again the bottom 10 per cent is extreme. In this case, the worst function managed to contain 2224 independent decisions. Such a

Table 4.12 The distribution of cyclomatic complexity for the whole population in percentiles

Percentile value	Cyclomatic complexity
0	2224
10	13
20	8
30	5
40	4
50	3
60	2
70	2
80	1
90	1
100	1

Table 4.13 The distribution of static path count for the whole population in percentiles

Percentile value	Static path count
0	500 000 000
10	200
20	30
30	10
40	6
50	4
60	2
70	2
80	1
90	1
100	1

function represents a formidable Achilles' heel in any system. It is complex beyond any reasonable hope.

Table 4.13 shows the whole population distribution of static path count. As discussed in Section 3.2.1, this is a good metric of testability. Values much greater than about 200 lead to problematic functional components. As can be seen, again the bottom 10 per cent contains the functions giving most concern.

It is useful to compare the worst 10 per cent of the population distribution of externally visible variables (i.e. variables declared with extern scope) as shown in Table 4.14.

The distribution of external variables is a file-based metric in C (unlike the first three, which are function-based metrics), as extern refers to visibility across file boundaries. Although excessive use of extern scope is frowned upon in C as it works against information hiding and simple interface design, there is far less quantitative evidence of this representing a problematic practice than of the three function-based metrics above, but if the 10 percentile limits naturally emerging from these are used, *any files with more than 15 external variables should be treated with suspicion*. This would be a good starting point to assess the predictive capabilities of population analysis given a suitable calibration package. This technique

Table 4.14 The distribution of external variable count for the whole population in percentiles

Percentile value	Number of external variables per file
0	134
10	15
20	6
30	3
40	2
50	1
60	0
70	0
80	0
90	0
100	0

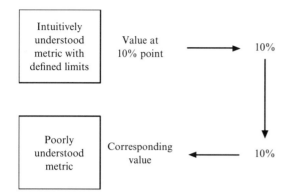

Figure 4.2 A way of predicting trigger points for metrics that are less well understood intuitively using population-derived of better understood metrics.

could be used with any metric which intuitively increases as quality decreases, and is shown schematically in Fig. 4.2.

Two other comparisons are of interest (see Tables 4.15 and 4.16). First, it is interesting to compare the cyclomatic complexity and static path count distributions

Table 4.15 Comparison of cyclomatic complexity distribution for package developed using complexity limiting against population as a whole

Percentile value	Cyclomatic complexity (package with complexity limiting in operation)	Cyclomatic complexity (whole population)
0	307	2224
10	8	13
20	4	8
30	2	5
40	2	4
50	2	3
60	1	2
70	1	2
80	1	1
90	1	1
100	1	1

Table 4.16 Comparison of static path count distribution for package developed using complexity limiting against population as a whole

Percentile value	Static path count (package with complexity limiting in operation)	Static path count (whole population)
0	500 000 000	500 000 000
10	24	200
20	6	30
30	2	10
40	2	6
50	2	4
60	1	2
70	1	2
80	1	1
90	1	1
100	1	1

Table 4.17 Comparison of cyclomatic complexity distribution for C and comparable FORTRAN populations

Percentile value	Cyclomatic complexity (FORTRAN population)	Cyclomatic complexity (C population)
0	642	2224
10	33	13
20	19	8
30	12	5
40	9	4
50	6	3
60	4	2
70	3	2
80	2	1
90	1	1
100	1	1

Table 4.18 Comparison of static path count distribution for C and comparable FORTRAN populations

Percentile value	Static path count (FORTRAN population)	Static path count (C population)
0	500 000 000	500 000 000
10	2 707 584	200
20	2 048	30
30	108	10
40	18	6
50	8	4
60	4	2
70	3	2
80	2	1
90	1	1
100	1	1

from the whole population above with the equivalent extracted for a single high-quality package where complexity limiting has been in operation. This is shown in Tables 4.15 and 4.16.

Examination of these tables shows that complexity limiting is proving effective in reducing the distribution of component complexity considerably in this case. Experience suggests that this will be beneficial over the lifetime of this package, although no empirical results were to hand at the time of writing.

The second illuminating comparison is to compare values of the same metric with populations written in different languages. This is shown next for the whole C population described above against a comparable FORTRAN population also measured by the author (Hatton, 1994a). Table 4.17 shows the distributions for cyclomatic complexity and Table 4.18 shows the same comparison for static path count.

These last two tables show a strong tendency for C programmers to write more testable functions than FORTRAN programmers, apart from a small percentage of massively complex functions in terms of decision counts.

STRATEGIES AND SOLUTIONS FOR SAFETY-RELATED DEVELOPMENT

5.1 DEFINING ENFORCEABLE STANDARDS

5.1.1 Programming standards and style guides

An overview

As was stated in Chapter 1, there is a strong initiative in the direction of product standardization and certification. This has grown naturally from process certification and the need for measurable aspects of product quality which can be fed back into the improvement of the process itself. One of the important instruments of product quality is the programming standard, and it seems most likely that, in the not too distant future, companies will have to define programming standards which their products must adhere to, and non-compliance will presumably lead to failure.

Programming standards have been around for many years. Unfortunately, it is the author's experience that they are usually 'shelf-ware' and have frequently been the focus of acrimonious dispute among the contributors. The following pattern seems to have been repeated in many companies:

1. Various interested parties meet with the good intention of producing a programming standard to standardize code production and improve implementation consistency, readability and therefore maintainability.
2. Many meetings follow of which the major part is devoted to stylistic issues such as identifier and component naming conventions and indentation standards.
3. Frequently bitter discussion follows about the many differences of opinion which occur on matters of style. The real function of a programming standard is forgotten and a voluminous document slowly evolves.
4. The voluminous document is released and ignored.

It is reasonable to ask why the above pattern is repeated so often. The common denominator quite simply is style. Style has a place, but is not the most important function of a programming standard, although it is of course the most subjective aspect. It is rather like failing to build a reasonable house because nobody can agree on the colour of the wallpaper.

There is a simple solution. *No programming standard should ever contain stylistic information.* Such information should be relegated to a *Style guide.* This view is endorsed for example by the draft safety standard IEC SC65A which specifically refers to these two items as separate documents.

What then is the function of a programming standard? Quite simply, it is to promote those aspects of the code which relate to reliability and simplicity. It must take account of state-of-the-art development experience in the corresponding language, but most of all it must be as *enforceable* as possible. Programming standards which cannot be enforced are not well adhered to, as was seen in the previous chapter, where even taking account of the fact that not all categories for potential non-conformance were checked, programming standards were found to be broken at least once every 71 lines on average. The property of enforceability is of universal benefit. For the software engineers, it means that the careful work of defining professional best practice is not wasted and can eliminate a particularly nasty class of fault. For the auditor, it gives a ready and unequivocal means of certifying an important aspect of product quality, and for the user it provides a reassurance that a certain level of quality has been met. The best standard in the world is of no use to anybody if there is no guarantee that its provisions have been carried out. On the other hand, if a standard can be guaranteed to have been 100 per cent enforced, a glance at the quality and completeness of the programming standard alone can give valuable information as to the intrinsic quality of the resulting products. This is closely analogous to the confidence which is inspired by a hammer manufactured to explicit quality requirements such as the 'kite-mark' of the British Standards Institute. The user can be reasonably confident that the head is not going to fly off. The author can remember in childhood days that this occurred unpleasantly often to his father, who is a carpenter, but not so in recent times as considerable progress has been made. The time has now come for software also.

To summarize the above, the following list illustrates the properties that a good programming standard must have:

1. It must contain features which specifically relate only to the reliability, portability or complexity of the software.
2. It must be automatically enforceable, and ideally its mandatory components should be 100 per cent enforceable. This will be explored in more detail below.
3. It should be evolutionary. A static programming standard will not take advantage of feedback either internally or externally. Eventually, it will be ignored by the programming staff who will quite reasonably argue that it is out of date. As a general rule, a programming standard should be assessed for effectiveness and updated as necessary every six months.
4. It should differentiate between *Standards*, which must be applied, and *Guidelines*, which are recommended behaviour, and provide *Justifications* for both. In the author's experience, justifications, preferably with examples, are important to

encourage the programmer not to be resistant. No programmer will resist a standard which prevents them wasting their time producing an inferior product. If the standard items are 100 per cent automatically enforced, the justifications can be lengthy, so that even if the programmer does not read all of them, they are available for reference and there is always the security that *nothing* will be missed. This is exactly akin to a good legal contract—it is rarely if ever needed, except perhaps for reference.

It is worth developing this last point a little, taking into account automatic enforceability. When creating a programming standard some if not all of the following features must be addressed:

- Items which must be enforced and are *automatically* enforceable.

   In C, an example of this would be that no dependence on expression order of evaluation was allowed (a potentially very nasty feature of C). These can be detected (or avoided) by a number of tools, and provided the software process guarantees that all items in the program library are subject to checking by such a tool and that no such occurrences are found, the item is enforceable. All that is required is to ensure that the process provides for the enforcement. Appropriate tools are available.

   From a safety point of view, the absence of the feature can and indeed must be *guaranteed.*

- Items which must be enforced and are *not automatically* enforceable.

   In C, an example frequently found in programming standards is the highly desirable requirement to check all returned file pointers for legal file operations, handling illegality in a standard way. Although in theory it is possible to design tools to check this, in practice it is very difficult, and a manual inspection is almost certainly required to ensure that it has been done. But it has already been seen that the best manual inspections will still make mistakes.

   From a safety point of view then, no guarantee can (or should) be made. The fallibility of human inspections must be recognized explicitly.

- Items which are desirable, i.e. recommended as a guideline, and are automatically enforceable.

   In C, an example of this would be that all declared local variables shall be used, thereby avoiding clutter. An option to detect these exists in a number of compilers.

   From a safety point of view, although the absence of the feature can be *guaranteed,* the item may still be present because it is covered only by a recommendation rather than a requirement. The author would question the point of having something only as a recommendation which was capable of automatic enforcement. After all, if a programming standard is seeking to standardize, it should do precisely that and not try to be nice about it. There is nothing nice about software failure, especially in a safety-related system. Perhaps the only argument in favour of the automatically enforceable guideline is the intention that, one day in the future, an escalation policy will lead to it becoming a standard, but to do so immediately might overload an existing culture unused to enforceable standardization.

- Items which are desirable and are not automatically enforceable.

   In C, many *stylistic* issues tend to fall into this category.

- Items which inform.

Many programming standards that the author has seen contain far too many irrelevant informative statements in the mistaken assumption that these are standard-inducing. This may seem odd, but there is little point for example, in defining the base document governing a programming standard as being the Standard C document and then including sentences within the standard which simply reiterate some feature of Standard C. This simply makes the standard bigger and therefore more intimidating. Such items are simply pointless baggage.

Absolute and relative standards

Once a standard has been developed, a policy of application needs to be set in place. One of the most frequently cited reasons to the author for not using a standard was the pre-existence of some vast body of non-conformant code which the development staff did not know how to treat. All too often, this overwhelms the will of the developers to do anything at all. It would be unreasonable for product certification initiatives to fail a company's efforts to improve its code by a systematic documented procedure largely because so much non-compliant code is already in existence. Although this is not guaranteed, certification, like the law, revolves around what is *reasonable*. It is entirely reasonable to recognize therefore that existing code has to be treated differently from new code, and this provides a solution to the problem. The required improvement can be achieved by the mechanism of *absolute* and *relative* standards.

By definition, an *absolute standard* makes specific non-comparative statements about the quality of the code. For example, for C, an absolute standard might be that there shall be *no* transgressions of the C standard, or (rather less emphatic in view of some of the more irritating requirements) fewer than x transgressions per 1000 lines.

In contrast, a *relative standard* might state that a new version of a program component shall contain *fewer* transgressions than its predecessor. This is a reasonable policy, is enforceable and will incrementally improve the quality of the code over some period. The rate of improvement depends on the required relative quality difference and the resources available to do the job.

Taken together, absolute standards for new code and relative standards for existing code cap the problem of non-compliance and systematically reduce it. This is entirely within the spirit of improvement and introduces the notion of *incremental improvement* into the development process. Of course, organizations will differ about what constitutes relative improvement, but to a certain extent this is irrelevant.

Introducing a programming standard

The author's experience of introducing policies of incremental improvement into companies suggests that the following phased strategy works well.

1. Convene a meeting of parties interested in defining programming standards.
2. Work through the problem areas of C as discussed in Chapter 2, highlighting the most relevant ones for the company's needs. For example, nobody would want to use features leading to undefined behaviour (although many inadvertently do);

however, an organization to whom platform independence was not important might reasonably ignore at least some of the implementation-defined features, given that these must be semantically well-defined and are therefore amenable to formal argument.

3. Pick out the top ten or so worst features which everybody agrees are fundamentally problematic and unwelcome in any developments by the company.
4. These will form the first release of the programming standard.
5. Agree an escalation policy whereby the 'screws can be turned' every six months or so. The ideal body for this would be the Software Engineering Process Group concept of the Carnegie-Mellon CMM (cf. Chapter 1).

The author has found that, provided the start is slow enough, culture shock is avoided and programming staff quickly become enthusiastic as the immediate benefit is obvious. Agreed unpleasant features are being recognized and avoided. The pace of improvement can always be quickened later. If all else fails, the simplest C programming standard the author has so far implemented is the following one-liner:

Thou shalt use function prototypes exclusively.[1]

As was seen in Chapter 4, if enforced, this reduces the number of statically-detectable faults on average by around 26 per cent, a dramatic improvement in intrinsic quality, and yet on average companies only achieve a little over 50 per cent utilization of this highly desirable feature. The use of function prototypes is also a significant step forward in the software design process and is considered an important feature in modern languages generally because of the explicit definition of component interfaces. For example, C++ mandates function prototypes and the C standard itself actually borrowed the concept from C++. In C++, however, the old-style definitions and declarations are simply forbidden. Some form of this concept is present in Ada, Modula-2/3 and FORTRAN 90, as well as other languages.

An example of incremental improvement

As an example of programming standards enforcement and the benefits to be gained, Hatton (1993a) describes a case history which encompasses all of the above and adds other features, such as the explicit treatment of reusable components in an automated standards enforcement environment. This particular case history took place over a two-and-a-half year period, during which time the standards were tightened four times and simultaneously broadened to take account of the accumulated experience. The claimed benefits were very impressive and it is worth describing in more detail because the degree of automation used would be necessary in a safety-related environment, where the absence of certain features must be guaranteed.

Programming Research Ltd (PR:QA) is a relatively small organization which develops product quality measurement tools for C, C++ and FORTRAN (QAC and QAC Dynamic,[2] QAC++ and QA FORTRAN) and a process manager (QA Manager) which automates significant parts of levels 2 and 3 of the Carnegie-Mellon CMM. These products are used at many sites around the world in numerous

---

[1] And thou shalt make sure that they are in scope by forbidding implicit declarations.
[2] This product was restricted to internal use only.

industries including both safety-related and non safety-related ones. There are many external users and effective process control was considered critical.

In January 1991, PR:QA had implemented an internal process automated by QA Manager whose goal was to guarantee compliance with key parts of the CMM and to form a basis for ongoing metrics extraction. Other goals included a systematic improvement policy for existing software (written in either C or C++), a rigidly defined although then unambitious programming standard for new code, and a mechanism to encourage reuse.

In essence, the process manager used the product measurement tools to determine whether software components complied with the current standards. If not, the component was unequivocally rejected. As the process manager was responsible for change and configuration control, the result was that if components made it onto the libraries, they were guaranteed 'clean'. The architecture is essentially as depicted in Figs. 5.2 and 5.3 (see Section 5.2). The various phases of improvement are described below.

Phase 1: July 1991–September 1991 The first stage undertaken was to define a *relative* programming standard for *existing* code and an *absolute* programming standard for *new* code, along with a mechanism for systematically evolving these standards (the Software Engineering Process Group (SEPG), a CMM concept), i.e. turning the screws periodically. The importance of this has been discussed already.

To define the forbidden constructs, a number were selected and split up into different levels: internal standards transgressions (level 4), complexity warnings (level 7), standard violations (level 8) and Standard C constraint violations (level 9). The C measurement tool QAC was configured to detect just those. The constraint violation category might be surprising, but some so-called ANSI compilers were found to allow even some constraint violations in C. The standards for new and existing code were defined as follows:

- *New code*

$$(l_4 + l_7 + l_8) \times 50 \leq L \qquad \text{AND}$$

$$l_9 = 0$$

where L is the number of executable lines and l_i is the number of occurrences of items at level i. In essence, this means no more than one item of any configured level per 50 executable lines and no constraint violations.
- *Existing code*

$$(l_4 + l_7 + l_8) \text{ must decrease} \qquad \text{AND}$$

$$l_4 \leq l'_4; \ l_7 \leq l'_7; \ l_8 \leq l'_8 \qquad \text{AND}$$

$$l_9 = 0$$

where l'_i corresponds to the previous release and l_i to the current release. Hence no level may increase and the total number of violations must decrease. Again, no constraint violations are allowed.

The process manager was then configured to run the measurement tool with these measurement criteria and reject any non-conformant components.

Phase 2: October 1991–December 1992   The first phase of the improvement program was relatively unambitious in order to facilitate cultural acceptance, although the automatic enforcement was perceived as a welcome but frequently unpleasant experience. The principle enemy of many attempts at standards maintenance is over-ambition, which normally results in complete rather than partial failure. When things are *guaranteed* to be found, the presence of too many non-conformances quickly causes confrontation. This is exacerbated in safety-related environments, where it can be argued that as much as possible should be included in the beginning because of the larger consequences of failure making it difficult to find the correct initial balance. In the case study, the second phase was considerably more ambitious than the first because cultural acceptance had been achieved and significant progress made. The company's SEPG then mandated the following.

More items were added at the previously enforced levels of internal standards transgressions, including indentation and other stylistic warnings (level 4), complexity warnings (level 7), standard violations (level 8) and constraint violations (level 9), and two new levels were added: unsafe features (level 3) and obsolescent and upwards compatibility features (level 5). This latter category included items which had a different meaning in different dialects both of C and C++. The effect of adding items is most felt on new code. Existing code is not so affected as it must simply be *better* than the previous version when *both are measured for the same items*. A final turn of the screw required the average occurrence rate on new code to be halved. The standards for new and existing code were then enforced as follows:

- *New code*

$$(l_3 + l_4 + l_5 + l_7 + l_8) \times 100 \leq L \qquad \text{AND}$$

$$l_9 = 0$$

In essence, this means no more than one item of any configured level per 100 executable lines can occur and there could be no constraint violations.

- *Existing code*

$$(l_3 + l_4 + l_5 + l_7 + l_8) \text{ must decrease} \qquad \text{AND}$$

$$l_3 \leq l'_3; \; l_4 \leq l'_4; \; l_5 \leq l'_5; \; l_7 \leq l'_7; \; l_8 \leq l'_8 \qquad \text{AND}$$

$$l_9 = 0$$

Again, no level may increase and the total number of violations must decrease. No constraint violations are allowed.

Again, the above required a simple change to the shell scripts driven by the process manager.

Phase 3: January 1993–September 1993   Yet more items were added at the previously enforced levels. In addition, a number of individual items from level 3 had emerged from analysis of many failures in C programs as simply too dangerous to allow at all. These became known as 'killer items'. These have already been discussed earlier in this book and no safety-related program should contain any occurrences of them.

It was also recognized during this period that the policy of increasing reuse would place much greater demands on the reliability of the reusable components, owing to their greater visibility. There is little point in reusing sub-standard components. The author has read many articles promoting the wondrousness of reuse without ever seeing the importance of high-quality reusable components mentioned. That such reuse does not naturally lead to more reliable systems is demonstrated in Canning (1993), for example. These issues are at the heart of good engineering. In the case study, a separate *absolute* standard twice as difficult as that for normal new code was therefore mandated for nominated reusable components (of which the process manager is aware). In addition, it was further required that incremental improvement was not good enough, so that all reusable code, new or old, must satisfy the absolute standard.

The standards were therefore enforced as follows:

- *Reusable code, new or existing*

$$(l_3 + l_4 + l_5 + l_7 + l_8) \times 200 \leq L \qquad \text{AND}$$
$$l_9 = 0 \qquad \text{AND}$$
No killer items

In essence, this means no more than one item of any level per 200 executable lines can occur and no constraint violations or killer items.

- *Non-reusable new code*

$$(l_3 + l_4 + l_5 + l_7 + l_8) \times 100 \leq L \qquad \text{AND}$$
$$l_9 = 0 \qquad \text{AND}$$
No killer items

In essence, this means no more than one item of any level per 100 executable lines can occur and no constraint violations or killer items.

- *Non-reusable existing code*

$$(l_3 + l_4 + l_5 + l_7 + l_8) \text{ must decrease} \qquad \text{AND}$$
$$l_3 \leq l'_3;\ l_4 \leq l'_4;\ l_5 \leq l'_5;\ l_7 \leq l'_7;\ l_8 \leq l'_8 \qquad \text{AND}$$
$$l_9 = 0 \qquad \text{AND}$$
No killer items

Again, no level may increase and the total number of violations must decrease. No constraint violations or killer items are allowed.

Again a simple change to the shell scripts driven by the process manager was all that was required. At this stage, after three phases of incremental improvement, these shell scripts totalled several hundred lines of UNIX Bourne shell-compatible commands. Since the C quality measurement tool was around the same speed as the compiler, the implied lag in returning a source code component successfully to the process manager was between 2 and 3 times the compilation time, this worst case arising for a return of a modified component, necessitating a quality *comparison*.

As a final point, it should be stated that no fewer than four separate quality tests, including the above code checking, were then in place. These comprised simple textual checks such as detecting the absence of valid program headers and copyright notices. The power of a modern workstation is such that very comprehensive checks could be carried out at this stage without impacting the development process.

October 1993–present   For this phase, *run-time failure rates* detected by a recently introduced dynamic reliability harness were being introduced into the quality improvement plan and measured during the now mandatory regression tests (enforced by the process manager). Such failures include the usual issues of illegally dereferenced pointers, array bound violations, use of uninitialized storage, arithmetic errors and so on. The standard was intended to be zero dynamic failures during the regression suites. Anything less would be inadequate.

Results   The following results were reported. First of all, dramatic reductions in the numbers of warnings, and especially the statically-detectable fault rate, were recorded in the various packages under the control of the process manager (which comprised some 250 000 lines of C and C++). This comes as no surprise, and although this is bound to have an effect on their reliability, this reliability could not easily be quantified for a number of reasons.

Second, and perhaps the most impressive statistic quoted, was an 80 per cent drop in support calls, leaving an overhead of only 30 per product per year, totalling 75 hours for all products, or around 2 per cent of total software overhead. While improving intrinsic quality was not the only contributing factor, it was certainly one of them. Perhaps more tangibly associated is the fact that the average porting time for *all* products fell to only three to six hours in total, depending on the machine speed, reducing effectively to compile, link and regression suite time, or around one hour per product. The reason for this is that features having debatable portability were ruthlessly and automatically purged during the period of the case history. In comparison, the average porting time for products of a similar size was reported in Unigram (1992) as being 42 hours, or 9 programmer days, on a sample of 71 sites. The author has heard of far longer times than this.

Third, it was frequently observed that enhancements that caused the number of complexity warnings to *increase* (necessitating action) forced the programmer to do something which normally is difficult to achieve: to inspect familiar code with the same critical eye as a third party. The reason for this is that unlike, say, a locally deprecated syntactic issue, complexity warnings arise on *structural* issues, necessitating a more global inspection. This was reported as being without exception beneficial, with many occurrences of the 'What on earth was I doing it that way for in the first place?' syndrome once the familiarity barrier was breached. This led to substantial reductions in complexity of previously over-complex components. *The programmer could not simply ignore it, as the process manager would not accept it unless the problem was resolved.* This is particularly difficult to achieve in manual environments, and was a noteworthy if initially unexpected step. The noted software process expert Watts S. Humphrey also singled this aspect out in Humphrey (1993).

Finally, a less obvious but highly desirable benefit was a dramatic increase in the average programmer's fluency with C and, in particular, knowledge of its strengths and weaknesses, as non-conformant code was efficiently but ruthlessly rejected.

Table 5.1 Reuse of code

Product	Reusable lines	Total lines	Reuse ratio %
QAC	40 900	82 300	50
QA FORTRAN	34 000	73 000	47
QA Manager (X)	18 300	50 100	37
QA Manager (Motif)	18 300	52 700	35
QA C++	40 900	82 900	49
QA C Dynamic	11 500	30 400	38

A number of other benefits were reported to have accrued from the automated process control and process and product metrication. First and foremost the average effective reuse ratio of 10 per cent soared to around 40 per cent, in the sense that for every 60 lines of a new product which had to be written, 100 lines were delivered. Even very different products, such as the process manager itself and the product measurement tools had reuse ratios of 35 per cent. The last reported reuse figures (as of 6 May 1994) are given in Table 5.1. One likely cause for this very high and increasing reuse ratio (quite apart from the written policy), was that recreating the wheel was often more difficult than using an existing solution because the absolute coding standard was so high! In other words, if the programmer needed to recreate the wheel, it had to be a very good wheel. This fact, coupled with the requirement that all code was maintained by the process manager (QA Manager), giving easy browsing access to all components, appeared to be compelling reasons for *not* recreating the wheel. Furthermore, the higher quality requirements for reusable components appeared to avoid the problems of reusing poor items, ameliorating the problems intimated by Canning (1993).

The eventual goal of this continuing study is to converge to the following theoretically achievable goals:

- Zero detectable static faults.
- Systematic and progressive documented re-engineering of existing over-complex code and control of complexity in new code.
- Verifiable adherence to a set of well-defined standards known to improve product reliability, portability and maintainability.

Safety-related C standards

At this point, it is reasonable to ask what should be in a safety-related C programming standard. This is a difficult question, as even safety-related software has commercially oriented pressures, such as product delivery and budget. However, the arguments considered in this book so far and the case history above suggest that the following should be achieved as a very *minimum*:

- There should be no statically-detectable reliance on undefined features.
- There should be no statically-detectable transgressions to the programming standard which covered the development. Why otherwise would a programming standard be present? Its *raison d'être* is to protect the developer from problem areas of the language while encouraging easy maintenance.

- There should be no statically-detectable reliance on implementation-defined features whose behaviour is different on that class of machines on which a portable program is intended to execute. Alternatively, the program should be implemented and tested in full on each relevant platform. It should be remembered that implementation-defined features are *well-defined* from the programmer's viewpoint and therefore could be amenable to a formal argument of correctness. However, their definition may differ from machine to machine, necessitating a rework of the formal argument as well as different coding from machine to machine. If the same functionality could be implemented portably, which is nearly, if not always, the case, it would be foolhardy not to do so.

As was discussed at length earlier, the reason why the above features are restricted to *statically-detectable* items only is that this is the only class of items whose absence could be *guaranteed* by appropriate tool support. Items that are dynamically detectable only cannot be guaranteed to be absent, owing to the limitations of testing, which will be discussed next.

The sections in a safety-related C programming standard might reasonably be organized as follows:

- A justification for the use of C, with associated literature.
  Given that the language has known problems which affect reliability, it is strongly recommended that this be admitted by the standard and a justification for use of the language be given. This justification would include reasons as to why C was being considered as the implementation language and what steps were being taken to constrain the developers to avoid ambiguity
- The scope of the standard should be described in the sense of defining which development was covered by the standard. In addition, the base standard, for example, the Standard C document, should be defined, along with an intended escalation policy for regular review and, if necessary, tightening of the standard.
- The nomenclature of the standard should be defined, particularly with regard to which items are mandatory and automatically enforceable, which items are mandatory but manually enforceable, and which are simply unenforceable recommendations.
- The items covered by the standard should be covered in some reasonable order, perhaps, for example, that of the C standard itself. If possible, these should be defined such that all mandatory requirements are automatically enforceable.
- Test coverage strategy and dynamic reliability failure rates should be set. For example, the standard might require 100 per cent statement coverage and that there should be no illegally dereferenced pointers during the execution of some defined regression suite.
- Complexity limits should be set for functional components. As was seen in Chapter 4, there is more than enough empirical evidence now to suggest that such limits beneficially affect both maintenance cost and reliability.

Finally, the standard must bear evidence of version numbering, revision history and QA functions, such as multiple sign-off, to make it both authoritative and unequivocal. Such a standard will go a long way towards convincing an external auditor that due care and professional attention has been paid, quite apart from the direct benefits to the development itself. The author's experience suggests that, so far, few standards approach the above model.

5.1.2 Dynamic testing standards

Testing is a very big subject in software development and many books have been written on the subject, following the pioneering book by Myers (1979). The discussion here will be limited to those issues of particular relevance to safety-related systems.

Test coverage

A great deal of work has been done on the subject of test coverage and there are various forms in regular use. A range of strategies, in increasing order of achievability is defined by Bache and Mullerburg based on work by themselves, Prather and McCabe, and is quoted by Fenton (1991) as follows:

(i) *All paths testing*. This requires each path to be tested at least once. In the case of loops, this includes each iteration and for infinite loops is of course unattainable.

(ii) *Visit-each-loop paths testing*. This exercises a subset of all paths taking flow past the loops and at least one iteration of each loop.

(iii) *Simple path testing*. This is defined by Prather and requires execution of each path which does not contain the same edge more than once.

(iv) *Structured testing*. This strategy is defined by McCabe and requires execution of a linearly independent set of paths.

(v) *Branch testing*. This requires that each edge in the flowgraph be visited at least once.

(vi) *Statement testing*. This requires that each node in the flowgraph be visited at least once.

Fenton (1991) goes on to quote Hennel, who has shown that even for the most modest category of *statement testing,* the percentage of statements covered as a function of all possible statements frequently does not exceed 40 per cent in industrial systems. The author emphatically believes that for safety-related systems a *statement coverage* of less than 100 per cent is unthinkable, with the exception only of those statements which conventionally appear in proofs by assertion and assert that in essence, execution of that statement cannot happen without a gross failure in correctness of the program. An example would be

```
#define      IMPOSSIBLE_STATE(x)  \
fprintf(stderr,x),fprintf(stderr," Line %d",_LINE_),abort()
...
if ( ... )
{
      ...
}
else if ( ... )
```

```
{
        . . .
}
else
{
        IMPOSSIBLE_STATE("Correct program cannot be here ...\n");
}
```

In this case, the statements guarded by the else clause would be excluded from the 100 per cent statement coverage requirement, as to execute them requires the kind of program failure which must be avoided. The abort statement and use of the _LINE_ concept of Standard C simply causes the program to stop with an indication of where the assertion failed. The macro makes it clearly visible to the maintenance programmer. Such correctness-supporting enhancements to the C language are discussed in more detail in Section 5.4.5.

Programmers are generally not well informed about test coverage procedures and very few companies in the author's experience perform them systematically. It is, however, an explicit requirement of many quality initiatives, such as the Carnegie-Mellon CMM (Section 1.2.1.2), as well as safety initiatives such as IEC SC 65A (Section 1.3.1) and Def Stan 00–55 (Section 1.3.2), and so it should be! There are numerous tools on the market that can provide this capability including such things as tcov, which is a standard feature on Sun workstations and gct, a GNU utility. These are discussed further in Section 5.3.5.

The author agrees with Fenton again in that high targets for the more demanding targets, such as 80 per cent branch testing coverage, should be defined and met. In fact, Def Stan 00–55 defines the following requirements for test coverage:

- All statements.
- All branches for both true and false as well as all branches of a case statement including the default branch.
- All loops for zero, one and many iterations with regard to initialization and typical running and termination conditions, whatever 'many' means.

Such targets are, however, not without their cost, and achieving them can take a great deal of effort. The author has personal experience of a nuclear engineering site in the UK which took 18 months to achieve 100 per cent path coverage of 3 per cent of their code. Note also the $15 million spent in Canada on proving 1200 lines of code correct, again in the nuclear industry as noted in Section 1.2.1. The problem of course with these massive investments is that the requirements must be *fixed* before the testing starts.

Testing types

The draft safety standards also refer directly to the types of testing which must take place, as shown in Table 1.7. These cover the traditional types, such as boundary values, singularities, special values, range checks and so on. The reader should consult Myers (1979) or Beizer (1990) for more details. Such tests have a background in human fallibility stretching into the distant past, far before software intruded into the world.[3] Good testing requires careful planning and should be built into development so that the test plan evolves with the code. The best codes are *designed* to be testable just like the best engineering structures.

To summarize, testing unfortunately never naturally terminates, and perhaps the best that can be achieved is to set a budget for testing using the best available tools for the design of test strategies to achieve the most comprehensive coverage and test planning possible within that budget. It is certainly true that no safety-related system can reasonably set a target of perfection given the current state of know-ledge, although there are some very ambitious projects, such as the A320 airbus fly-by-wire systems which set a Mean Time Between Failures target of no more than once every 10^9 hours! Unfortunately, conventional testing procedures, whereby fault rates are monitored continually and used to predict final system reliability using *reliability growth models*, can give us no confidence that such ambitious targets have been met, limiting predictability to around one failure in around every 10^5 hours (Littlewood and Strigini, 1992a).

5.2 INTEGRATING SOFTWARE PRODUCT QUALITY INTO PROCESS CONTROL

It is comforting that so many of the classic problems associated with C development can be avoided. The problem in a safety-related environment is how can it be absolutely guaranteed that they have indeed been avoided. This section will discuss the software process in more detail, following on from the introductory discussion in Chapter 1, and, in particular, how the process needs to be modified to guarantee that the software product is free from the many potential defects described in this book.

As any would-be maintainer of a large software package will agree, the first observation that can be made is that software is not really soft at all if preservation or enhancement of the original functionality is required. Old, large packages can be very hard indeed in the sense that they are highly resistant to premeditated change. It is reasonable to ask if this is the case at all points in the life-cycle, however. The answer is, of course, no. *Observation of many developers suggests that software is soft until the code is compiled.* Given that the only software 'tool' available to most developers today is the compiler, the inevitable result of compilation is that the programmer enters 'testing'. It is as if a mental watershed is passed at the successful compilation stage, such that afterwards the programmer is unwilling to change things for any other reason than issues arising directly from the testing process itself.

Put another way, all the intrinsic quality that is likely to be built into a code component must be built in before compilation, while the software is still soft. So if statically-detectable faults are to be eliminated, programming standards enforced and component complexity limited as described in previous chapters, these must be done **before**

---

[3] The author was reminded of this recently when reading a book on the Salerno landings in Italy in September 1944. The German High Command had anticipated and planned for a surrender by Italy both *before* and *after* the landings took place. Unfortunately, the surrender occurred *during* the landings, throwing the German High Command into considerable initial disarray.

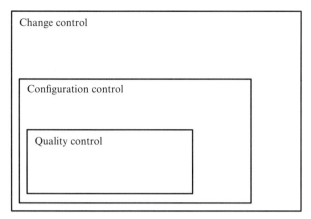

Figure 5.1 Schematic showing the relationship between change, configuration, and quality control in the software process.

compilation. After compilation, the software becomes brittle and the costs of building in intrinsic quality together with programmer resistance, rise considerably.

Software process control can be viewed like the layers of an onion as shown in Fig. 5.1, and consists of at least change, configuration and quality control, of which the most obvious process attribute to the software engineer is change. In the next sections, process control will be described in more detail and an architecture described within which guaranteed enforcement of the concepts outlined in this book can be achieved.

5.2.1 Change control

Change control is the most visible part of the software process and encompasses the entire spectrum of items making up a product, from designs through to the system documentation. In Section 6.1.3.2 of ISO 9000–3, change control is required for all software items under configuration management. In addition, the following appears:

- Before a change is made official, its validity should be confirmed and the effects on other items should be identified and thoroughly examined.
- Methods to notify the changes to those concerned and to show the traceability between changes and modified parts of software items should be provided.

In essence, this latter states that there shall be no change without requirement.

A Request for Change (CR from now on in this book) will typically go through numerous states during its lifetime. There is unfortunately no standard nomenclature for the state names, but those shown in Fig. 5.2 are typical. The IEEE Software Engineering Standards provide more background (IEEE, 1989), and Whitgift (1991) is also recommended.

To give the reader some idea of what is involved, the above states will be described now.

- *Proposal* Any request for change will arrive as a proposal. In this form, it will be logged into the quality system for future treatment.

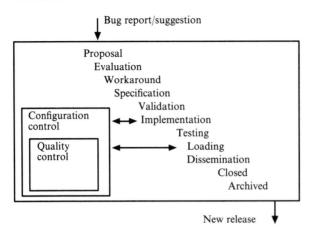

Figure 5.2 An example of the states a request for change to a software system can pass through.

- *Evaluation*   The proposal is evaluated for technical feasibility. A reported bug might be confirmed or an enhancement checked for suitability. Alternatively, a spurious report might be rejected.
- *Workaround*   In the case of a bug, a way of avoiding it might be found, or for an enhancement, some half-way house might be sought.
- *Specification*   At this stage, a systems analyst will design the nature of the change to the software items under configuration management, determining which are the affected components, the estimated time of change and, in a safety-related environment, any risks associated with the change.
- *Validation*   Here the specifications for software change are checked against the requirement. This would typically be done by an independent party.
- *Implementation*   Only at this stage can components associated with the product actually be changed. This might encompass documentation changes or changes to code components. The affected code components are borrowed for change. In most environments, these are reserved for change solely associated with this requirement. In less strict environments, they would not be so reserved and *parallel development* might take place with all the associated problems of merging independent and perhaps unrelated development strands later.
  On return, conformance analysis would be done to guarantee that items which successfully reach the libraries for testing *are already conformant*. Only in this way can the safety-related development manager *guarantee* that conformance testing has been done. Non-conforming items would be rejected before even entering testing. Note that even conformant items will not go to production libraries at this stage. They will go to the test libraries first.
- *Testing*   Here the changes would be tested independently to see if they satisfy the requirement. In addition, regression suites and any other test suites registered with the software items under configuration control would be run. Finally, integration testing would be performed.
- *Loading*   On completion of a successful testing phase, the software is loaded to the production libraries. A good automated system would require that updated test suites and documentation, if relevant, be loaded concurrently with the

software items. Conformance analysis might be repeated here in order to contribute to incremental improvement statistics.

- *Dissemination* In the dissemination phase, the originator of the CR would be informed that the request had been successfully implemented.
- *Closed* The CR is formally closed, i.e. completed.
- *Archived* The CR might be archived at a major system release milestone so that an automatic record of every contributing CR and all software items affected could be distributed with the product.

5.2.2 Configuration control

Configuration control is about the management of different versions of components such that any version can be extracted on demand, for example by supplying a date and time. Although the interface is rather primitive, the UNIX utilities sccs and the GNU utility rcs provide excellent basic features. Build control of a complete system is catered for by the UNIX utility make, for example. Note that there is nothing lightweight about these two tools, as with some modification they are used to maintain such formidable systems as the UNIX system itself, as well as the MIT graphics system X11.

Among other things, ISO 9000–3 has the following to say about configuration control:

The configuration management system should
a) uniquely identify the official versions of each software item;
b) identify the versions of each software item which together constitute a specific version of a complete product;
c) identify the build status of software products in development or delivered and installed;
d) control simultaneous updating of a given software item by more than one programmer;
e) provide coordination for updating of multiple products in one or more locations as required;
f) identify and track each change request from suggestion through release.

Although sccs and make provide the kind of basic facilities necessary to comply with this list, some considerable infrastructure is necessary around them to implement them satisfactorily. It is surprising how many companies, safety-related or otherwise, do not have this basic capability. The author believes that a deficiency here overrides virtually all other considerations in the software implementation cycle, as the fundamental principle of accountability is breached uncontrollably otherwise. There seems little point in doing software quality assurance when the deliverables are uncertain!

As a final note, the author would have preferred the word 'forbid' to replace the word 'control' in item d.

5.2.3 Quality control

It is impossible to guarantee that intrinsic quality checks have been carried out unless they are built into a defined and automated process such that all code is automatically subjected to such checks before it is released to formal program libraries. Figure 5.3 shows the life-cycle of source code components and the point at which intrinsic quality control checks must be applied to be effective. This is certainly sufficient to

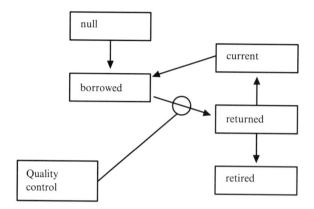

Figure 5.3 The life-cycle of a software item and the place of quality control.

guarantee that such checks have been carried out, but it is not the most cost effective place to discover that a component is non-compliant. Instead, it must be supplemented by an environment which allows the intrinsic quality checks to be run by the individual programmers before compilation.[4]

5.3 AUTOMATION AND TOOLS

Automation and tools go hand in hand. Once a manual process is defined, it can immediately be scrutinized for potential automation. As has been seen, if certain key intrinsic product quality measures are not made automatically, then human fallibility will guarantee certain faults appearing at some non-zero rate. For example, it was shown in an earlier chapter that programming standards, when manually enforced, are transgressed at the rate of once every 71 lines, with a much worse rate implied for C. Clearly automation is highly desirable. However, early automation, in the sense of attempting to automate a process that is not yet well defined, can be a serious mistake, Humphrey (1990). One symptom of this is the *tools vs. toys* or *shelf-ware* syndrome.

5.3.1 *Tools vs. toys* and shelf-ware

The shelf-ware syndrome is recognized by all software tool vendors. Beizer (1990) notes sadly that, even in enlightened companies, tool usage was very low, and typically less than five per cent. He ascribes this to poor training programs. This is only partly true. In the author's experience, a large chunk of blame is due to the software vendors and the way tools are sold on features rather than benefit, and this in itself is a symptom of the Western world's poor understanding of what really constitutes quality, as preached by Deming and others. In essence, the tool

---

[4] As a guideline, programmers in the author's company use a static analysis tool to enforce intrinsic quality every six minutes on average, although some 80 per cent of those invocations are done automatically by the process control system to carry out various tasks, including automatic verification of code compliance prior to loading to libraries.

vendor, working to slogans, exhortations, targets and numerical quotas (cf. Deming's 14-point plan in Section 1.2.1), sells a software tool to a customer, who uses it for a little while and then puts it on the shelf, where it languishes from then on. The tool satisfied no real need; it was merely a toy. In the long term, this benefits neither vendor nor customer, for the vendor will sell no more and the customer gains no benefit. Indeed, the customer may go on to develop an aversion to tools because of one bad experience. The author has even come across companies who categorize such disparate processes as dynamic testing and configuration management as the same in the sense of buying a tool for one *or* the other, a choice not unlike choosing between a dishwasher and a pair of skis. The continual hype of the software industry is largely responsible for this, as it replaces methodologies at regular intervals, thus confusing the customer to the extent that the great majority of them use only a compiler, reflecting a 1960s level of technology. The shelf-ware syndrome is singular if not unique to the software world.

In contrast, in longer established engineering disciplines, tools are expected to become long-term aids to solve a particular problem, because the particular problem is a side-effect of a stable well-defined process. The author's father is a carpenter and uses many tools. Some of these tools have been used so often, for example wooden handled saws, that they have assumed the same shape as the hand which grips them. Some of them are only used occasionally for special purposes. None are shelf-ware. The carpenter's processes are well-defined and automation has gradually come to play a large part, although by no means the whole and nor is it ever likely to.

The above is strongly relevant to the would-be developer of safety-related software in any language, especially C, which has an unusually wide range of supporting tools available. As has been seen in Chapter 4, without automation many faults occur which could have been prevented by available tools. It is in the best interests of everybody if safety-related software development environments:

(a) Have a sufficiently well defined process so that automation opportunities can be identified. ISO 9001 certification *and* level 2 and perhaps even level 3 of the Carnegie-Mellon CMM is probably a necessary condition for this.

(b) Make use of tools strategically, i.e. long-term, within their process. Methodologies should not be scrapped at regular intervals, otherwise the process will tend to resemble the fashion industry rather than an engineering industry. The author fully recognizes that new methodologies appear and will be of value, but only if they include previous good practice as a subset. For example, the existence and use of a CASE design tool should not mean that there is an excuse for releasing C code in the 1990s with statically-detectable interface faults, and yet every ninth interface, on average, contains such a fault, as was seen in Chapter 4.

5.3.2 The automation of code inspections

Code inspections have proven to be a very valuable but under-utilized tool (Bush, 1990; Humphrey, 1990). Probably the main reason for this under-utilization is their labour-intensiveness. During a code inspection, the inspector would typically be looking for the following:

- Transgressions of the house style.
- Transgressions of the internal programming standard.
- Dangerous use of the language.
- Non-portable use of the language if the application was intended to be portable.
- Highly complex components.
- Errors of the mind. In other words, things which, although self-consistent, are simply wrong.

The net result of this is that it is difficult to inspect more than around 200 lines per day thoroughly, although many organizations allow much higher rates than this, sometimes more than 1000 lines per day. At these speeds, inspections miss many things and are of cursory value only. This is a classic case where automation has a significant beneficial impact because *all of the items in the above list apart from the last are automatically enforceable*. In other words, if the human inspector is preceded by automated inspections using appropriate tools, such as are described in this book, human inspections can focus on the one area which is non-automatable and at which the human mind excels—irrational departures from the required functionality. This dramatically improves the efficiency of the inspection process as well as rendering it far more interesting.

5.3.3 Static vs. dynamic testing

At this point, it is perhaps worth drawing the reader's attention to a frequently misunderstood issue. Static and dynamic testing are often presented in an either/or light. They are, however, categorically *not* competitors. Part of the reason for confusion is the historical dependence on dynamic debugging as a technique for improving the reliability of a software application. The program is simply run and the programmer observes what happens, correcting it on the fly. This growth in the dependence on dynamic testing is somewhat unusual among engineering disciplines, in which static testing has a long and distinguished history. For example, in the rail industries it has long been the practice for an engineer to walk by the side of a stationary locomotive or passenger unit tapping its wheels with a hammer. This is extremely effective at detecting a wide variety of cracks which occur, and a skilled 'wheel-tapper' could not only detect such a crack but also detect its severity and even its position. Of course, some cracks only open up when the unit is in motion, requiring an expensive dynamic test rig to detect. Hence in railway engineering, static testing precedes the considerably more expensive and less effective dynamic testing, but both are necessary. A similar thing occurs in air transport, where skilled mechanics inspect airframes for cracks while the aircraft is stationary. Not carrying out such regular checks would be deemed unconscionable.

A result of the unbalanced emphasis on dynamic testing in software development is that, even today, many organizations do no static testing, in spite of the two enormous advantages that it enjoys:

- Static testing naturally terminates. For all but the most trivial of programs, dynamic testing only terminates when the budget (or the programmers) run out.

- It has been reported to be dramatically more cost effective than dynamic testing in eliminating program error. For example, Grady and Caswell (1987) report it as being some five times more effective, although Hetzel (1993), at least, is unclear as to exactly what this means.

Just as in railway or aircraft engineering, there will always be software issues that can only be detected dynamically, such as the general case of illegally dereferencing pointers. Again, the simple conclusion is that both static *and* dynamic testing play a fundamental role in improving the reliability of a program and neither should be missed out.

In the remainder of this chapter, a number of well-established static and dynamic tools, embodying much of the advice and techniques described in this book, will be described. Although the tools inevitably overlap in some places, the overall tool set described works together in harmony to ensure a sufficiently tightly controlled environment for safety-related development as to be comparable with that for any other language in regular use in the safety-related area. The reader should not be lured into thinking that one day there will be just one tool that does everything. Every other engineering discipline provides abundant evidence to the contrary!

5.3.4 Static analysis tools for C

There are several natural ways of ordering such tools. The author's immediate inclination was simply to list the tools and extol the features at length. However, on reflection, this mirrored the feature-rich, solution-poor environment in which most software tools are presented ('buy one of these, it must do something useful...'), and this book in general, and this chapter in particular, is supposed to be about solutions. It seemed more natural therefore to reorder things according to categories of problem-solving. As a result, some tools appear in more than one section.

Fault detection

It frequently comes as a surprise to developers coming new to C that static fault detection is not apparently part of the compiler environment. This is partly due to the fact that Standard C itself may allow constructs of a surprisingly dubious nature, as was seen in Chapter 2, and also because it is not traditionally the role of a compiler to provide such facilities. Compilers are usually designed around the notions of performance, both in the speed of the compiler itself and also in the efficiency of the generated code. This situation is not restricted to C, of course, as most FORTRAN users will confirm, but is perhaps more apparent than with some other languages. In spite of this, some compilers do provide a reasonable level of static checking, for example, the GNU compiler gcc from the Free Software Foundation. This particular compiler, using its -Wall (i.e. all warnings) option, provides such things as additional argument checking on the use of well-known functions such as printf and scanf, both sources of frequent problems.

Static fault detection is of course crucial to the developers of safety-related software in that any fault will mature into an error in the appropriate circumstances. This may not be for many hundreds of execution years, but if the fault is statically detectable, there is no excuse for it being in safety-critical code and the developers would be found wanting. If the static fault checking provided by the compiler is insufficient, which is almost certain to be the case for safety-related development given current compiler technology, there are a number of other widely available tools which can provide varying degrees of such checking. Perhaps the best known example of such a tool is `lint`, which is distributed as part of the UNIX system. `lint` is a classic example of a potentially very useful tool whose usefulness is somewhat limited by the obscurity of its user interface and frequency of spurious warnings. This is such that books, for example Darwin (1990), have been written solely to guide the user in how to understand its output, which is characterized by large numbers of frequently obscure messages and also some false negative and positive reports. In the author's experience, however, it still detects a wide class of commonly occurring faults in C code, and, given its widespread availability, its use or an equivalent package should be absolutely mandated for any C development, let alone safety-related development, with appropriate sign-off for any spurious messages. There is simply no excuse for not using it in a UNIX environment. The author can recall literally hundreds of occasions in his own early development experience where, in the absence of the more advanced tools discussed next, `lint` detected a legitimate problem while the compiler remained disturbingly mute.

`lint` can be used both for inline analysis of a single file, as in:

```
% lint file.c
```

or for multi-file analysis, as in:

```
% lint *.c
```

in which case it checks dummy and actual arguments in interfaces for consistency. Unfortunately, many versions do not yet support key standard features such as function prototypes, so in order to make full use of such tools, it is necessary to write interfaces in such a way as to be compatible with both old and new style function declarations and definitions, as is shown below:

```
#ifdef   USE_PROTOS
#define      NEW_DEF(type,parameter)              type parameter
#define      OLD_DEF(type,parameter)
#define      DECL_PROTO(arglist)                  arglist
#define      NO_ARGS                              void
#else
#define      NEW_DEF(type,parameter)              parameter
#define      OLD_DEF(type,parameter)              type parameter;
#define      DECL_PROTO(arglist)                  ()
#define      NO_ARGS
#endif

#define      IN
#define      OUT
#define      INOUT
   ...
```

```
/*      Example function prototype declaration with data flow   */
ray_trace_status *
inv_normal_ray DECL_PROTO( (
        IN      ut_triplet *        ut_col,
        IN      int                 n_segments,
        OUT     md_triplet *        md_col,
        OUT     xz_coords *         xz_norm_inc,
        IN      int                 max_segments
        ) );

/*      Example function prototype definition with data flow   */
ray_trace_status *
inv_normal_ray(
        NEW_DEF(    IN      ut_triplet *,       ut_col),
        NEW_DEF(    IN      int,                n_segments),
        NEW_DEF(    OUT     md_triplet *,       md_col),
        NEW_DEF(    OUT     xz_coords *,        xz_norm_inc),
        NEW_DEF(    IN      int,                max_segments)
)
        OLD_DEF(    IN      ut_triplet *,       ut_col)
        OLD_DEF(    IN      int,                n_segments)
        OLD_DEF(    OUT     md_triplet *,       md_col)
        OLD_DEF(    OUT     xz_coords *,        xz_norm_inc)
        OLD_DEF(    IN      int,                max_segments)
{
. . .
}
```

If the compiler flag USE_PROTOS is used the new-style declarations and definitions are visible, and if absent, the old-style equivalents are used.

At least two commercial tools are available whose use greatly exceeds the functionality provided by lint, but which are used in a similar way, albeit with vastly improved user interfaces. In the PC world particularly, PC-lint is a well known product (Stiles, 1992), although it is also available in other environments. Although still a command-line interface rather like a compiler, PC-lint has considerably better control of its input parameters as well as its output messages, and has the following features which are of particular relevance to the safety-related developer:

- It detects some 400 issues compared with the 100 or so in the 'standard' version of lint, many of which find immediate use.
- It features optional strong typing even when defined types differ but resolve to the same type, as for example in the code fragment:

```
typedef     int     Boole;
Boole               LesPaul;
int                 LeoFender;
. . .
LeoFender   = LesPaul;
```

PC-lint will, under option, flag the last statement as a type mismatch even though the underlying C type, int, is the same. Such extensions as this are very laudable and greatly improve the security of C code. Parenthetically, such 'strong' type mismatches are very common in X11 applications.

- To the author's knowledge, it is currently alone among static analysis tools in detecting unused header files. These are embarrassingly common in C systems (due of course to the absence of suitable tools!), and such clutter unquestionably degrades the comprehensibility to an extent, prejudicing both reliability and therefore safety.

- It can be used on big systems via the production of intermediate files to facilitate incremental static checking. The importance of this concept was underlined recently to the author by the experiences of a company which markets both FORTRAN mathematical libraries and software tools. Unfortunately, the libraries were too big to permit comfortable analysis by their own software tools. When the libraries were analysed by a tool capable of handling large systems, a considerable number of faults were detected. If the libraries had been smaller, all of these faults would have been detected by the company's own tools. No tool should ever have internal limits as to the size of application which can be analysed.

- Its output is configurable, avoiding the all too common situation whereby a programmer is so overwhelmed by messages about his or her code that they throw their arms up in despair and switch everything off.

Although not strictly a lint-like tool, QA C is based on the same validated parser as the Model C Implementation of Knowledge Software Ltd, and contains a number of lint-like checks alongside its central function of a C quality measurement tool. Of particular relevance to the safety-related developer is the fact that it detects the majority of the statically-detectable unspecified, intentionally or unintentionally undefined, and implementation-defined features cited in Appendix F of the C Standard, quite apart from a number of other problematic features. QA C has correspondingly far more messages than even PC-lint, but many of these relate to its optional formidably strict policing of the C standard. Perhaps the best description of the type of checks QA C performs is afforded by the fact that it was used to produce all of the C fault-rate and complexity statistics reported in this book. In addition, it contains many visualization facilities through its X-based interface. It contains no hard limits and is suitable for systems of any size.

It is certainly fair to say that any piece of C which survives both PC-lint and QA C is free of most if not all the known statically-detectable faults and both should be in systematic use in safety-related environments. Together, they arguably constitute the most powerful static checking capability of any language. Both products run at compiler speeds, removing the possibility of lame excuses for not using them based on slowness of execution. In addition, both are very highly configurable, removing the other frequently occurring lame excuse that there are 'too many' messages.

Programming standards maintenance

Given the importance placed on programming standards by all the major draft safety standards (cf. Chapter 1), their enforcement is of particular importance in safety-related development as a verifiable statement of good practice.

As is discussed elsewhere in this chapter, it is most important that standards be automatically enforceable to add weight to any warranties as to the absence of certain unpleasant practices. In essence, automatic standards enforcement involves carefully matching what can be enforced, what should be enforced and the degree to which an organization is capable of accepting enforcement, all of which are equally important. The enforcement then involves configuring a suitable tool and finally defining its position in the software process to guarantee that it is indeed being applied. The key requirement for the tool is therefore configurability, given that the tool can detect the requisite items.

Both PC-lint and QA C are capable of configurability at the individual message level and PC-lint goes even beyond this, allowing context-sensitive suppression of certain kinds of message, for example if they are associated with a certain identifier. This is a definite advantage in terms of ease of use and frequently requested by programmers, although any such mechanism is a serious disadvantage in a safety-related environment, as each such use represents a potential Trojan Horse with respect to reliability in that inadvertently leaving one in would disable any later automatic checking, negating any warranties about the guaranteed absence of certain features. One other noteworthy feature of QA C is its ability to enforce multiple standards simultaneously, a situation common in companies with both safety-related and non safety-related development.

Other tools with similar configurability exist, although generally without such comprehensive coverage of known problems, which a programming standard should seek to disallow for safety work.

ISO standards compliance

Arguably one of the strictest Standard C compliance checking tools in the world is the British Standards Institute Model C implementation produced by Knowledge Software Ltd. This implementation not only performs a detailed static check of C code for compliance but implements many run-time checks also in its role as a C compiler. QA C enjoys the same level of static checking by virtue of sharing its parser, but as a pure static analyser replaces the run-time checks with a wide knowledge base of complexity and empirical problems reported in C. It perhaps should be mentioned, finally, that Standard C conformance is extremely onerous in some ways and full compliance will inevitably lead to some unpleasant trade-offs against program clarity and reliability. For example, Standard C requires that identifiers with external linkage have no more than six significant characters, a consequence of the fact that there are still some antediluvian linkers around, so the rest of the world must pay the price.

Metrication and complexity limiting

The need for a mechanism for limiting individual component and system complexity has been discussed at length in Chapter 3. It was also stated there that individual metric measurements are of little use and that combinations of metrics and some way of comparing their values against each other or against other populations is vital. There are a large number of tools on the market which satisfy such requirements, as complexity metrics can usually be extracted by shallow flow analysis,

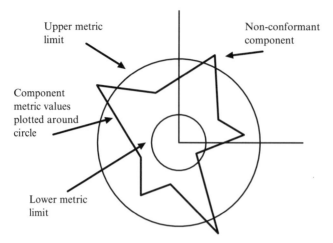

Upper metric limit

Non-conformant component

Component metric values plotted around circle

Lower metric limit

Figure 5.4 Schematic of a Kiviat diagram.

placing few demands on the language parser. Examples of tools include both shallow flow tools such as the McCabe toolset and Verilog's Logiscope, as well as deep flow tools such as QA C.

The method whereby individual modules are compared against each other or against populations varies from the Kiviat diagrams, favoured by Logiscope among others, to the graphical demographic analysis methods pioneered by QA C and discussed in detail in Chapter 3. There is a fundamental difference in these two diagrammatic forms, however. With Kiviat diagrams, low and high absolute metric boundaries are set as inner and outer radii of concentric circles and the individual values of each component analysed are plotted, each component corresponding to a unique angle. An example is shown as Fig. 5.4.

Demographic analysis, by contrast, does not display absolute metric values. Instead, it displays percentile values compared with a specific population. Population distributions are constructed by analysing large amounts of code from a specific application area and the metric values corresponding to the best 10 per cent, 20 per cent and so on are extracted. The process was described in detail in Section 4.1. Demographic analysis thus makes statements to the effect that a particular component lies in the nth percentile range compared with a given population, implying that it is at least as good as n per cent of that population. This method of display has the advantage of placing all metrics on the same linear scale, even though their underlying behaviour may be non-linear. For example, the range of cyclomatic complexity could be expected to vary between 0 and perhaps 1000 for a typical population, whereas that for maximum depth of nesting might vary between 0 and 50 for the same population.

5.3.5 Dynamic analysis tools for C

In the case of dynamic analysis tools, it is rather more revealing to categorize them as to *how they actually work* as this is closely related to what it is possible to achieve. In essence, they come in a number of different forms, as, for example, is discussed by Hunt (1993). They are discussed below.

Enhanced `malloc` functions

As the C programmer will be aware, `malloc/free` (and `calloc`) are the standard way in C of managing dynamic objects using the heap. This is such a prevalent part of programming in C that standard versions of `malloc` are highly optimized, which means that if anything goes wrong (as is frequently the case), little or no information other than a classic core dump is available. At the expense of a modest loss of efficiency, versions of `malloc` are available which provide significant information to assist where and what has gone wrong. These include the use of bounds markers for heap blocks which can be checked when memory is acquired using `malloc` and marking memory which has been released using `free` with some distinctive pattern. Such checks are of particular relevance in the development of graphical user interfaces, where such problems are exceedingly common. The value of such enhanced capabilities is that inconsistent use of the standard `malloc` usually manifests itself some time later in an entirely different location leading to awful debugging problems. All the developer has to do to make use of them is to link in the enhanced version of `malloc` instead of the system-supplied version. Enhanced versions essentially track such things as:

- Memory leakage through failure to release dynamic memory. The problem here is that nothing untoward happens until there is none left. The author has actually come across an example of this being a problem in a safety-related environment whereby the graphical user interface to a control system grew sufficiently during the operator's session that it aborted before the session was complete. The developer's immediate patch was to make sufficient swap space available that this did not occur during a session. The machine was simply rebooted each evening to reset everything. Plugging such memory leaks is a common and massively unpopular occupation among graphical user interface developers due to its extreme intractability.
- Freeing non-allocated memory. This is simply a dreadful error and generally leads to a quick and merciless end.

Given the seriousness of these kinds of problem, their absence should be guaranteed by tool support. A recommended strategy for this will be given later, but a typical example of a `malloc` debugging package is `dbmalloc`, which is widely available from many `ftp` archive sites, such as the University of Kent at Canterbury, UK.

Interpretive systems

Such systems *interpret* the C code checking various run-time attributes, such as array bound violations, line by line. Although they can be thorough, such systems are frequently very slow, as interpreting code can be 1–2 orders of magnitude slower than the compiled version. As such, their use on a large system can be very frustrating. The author once took two days using such a system to find a bug in a Motif graphical user interface. As this particular bug had defeated all other approaches, this was progress of a sort, although about as interesting as watching water freeze.

The excessive run-time is at least partially compensated by the higher degree of inter-action available and the insight provided by viewing the running program. Probably the most widely used example of such a system is Centerline (Kaufer *et al.* 1988).

Another notable and far more thorough example is OSPC (Open Systems Port-ability Checker), which is a sister product of the validated Model C implementation of Knowledge Software Ltd, which is probably the most comprehensive product of its kind, sharing its front end parsing with QA C. OSPC arguably has the most detailed run-time pointer tracking capability of any product in the world, while being very tight on Standard C conformance. It gives a remarkably sophisticated check of run-time conformance, including the library, for a performance penalty of only some 30–40 times slower than normal compiled code and is able to check most of the run-time detectable undefined issues discussed in Section 2.3.

Object code monitoring systems

Such systems work with the *object* code directly and this is at the same time both a great strength and a great weakness. The strength derives from the fact that:

- Multi-language systems can be handled much more easily, for example, C and C++.
- The fault occurrence rate of third party systems can be monitored even when the source is not available, which is of particular interest in a safety-related environ-ment, where dependence on such systems is common and actively encouraged in draft safety standards because of the general robustness of widely used libraries.
- It is easy to use.

The weaknesses derive from the fact that:

- Working with object code is conceptually non-portable; therefore such tools have limited platform availability.
- Numerous faults can no longer be detected after the source is discarded, for example, certain classes of array bound violation.

However, in spite of such weaknesses, the classes of fault which can be found by these techniques include:

- Most array bound violations unless they are well beyond the defined bounds of the array.
- Reading or writing to memory freed by `free`.
- Freeing the same piece of memory more than once.
- Reading and using uninitialized memory, although this may only be for local memory.

By far the best known tool using such technology is Purify (Hunt, 1993). The run-time overhead of using this product is said to be less than a factor of three, which is very impressive, allowing production versions of software to be released complete with a dynamic reliability harness built in. Care must be taken however to capture the output warnings in some sensible manner. The author's experience with certain windowing systems is that they can emit many such warnings *per second* while running! Given the expected increase in use of third party libraries, dynamic memory, client–server and network applications, the use of such tools is likely to increase considerably.

Source modification techniques

A source modification system works by placing assertions into a copy of the source code directly before it is compiled. In this it attempts to gain the best of both worlds in that although there is a compile overhead, the run-time overhead is about the same as object code monitoring systems, i.e. less than a factor of three, while at the same time, because it is working with source code, it can in principle detect nearly all possible transgressions, including the following:

- Detection of memory leaks.
- Array bound violation of strings and global, stack and parameter arrays.
- Illegally dereferencing pointers.
- Using most classes of uninitialized memory.
- Function call argument checking, including variadic functions and functions referenced by pointer.
- Run-time library argument checking.
- Arithmetic error detection, including over- and underflows.
- Incorrectly mixing pointers to data and pointers to functions.
- Dangling FILE pointer references.
- Bad arguments and pointer errors with stdio functions.

This is of course ideal if the source code is available. An example of such a tool is QA C Dynamic, which is built around the parsing technology originally produced in the product Safe C (Feuer, 1985). It should be noted that source or object code modification is not always suitable, as for example when timing is an issue.

To give the user some idea of how such a tool is used, the example below shows a typical session. The tool itself is invoked exactly like the compiler and any errors detected at run-time are automatically tagged with the line number so that the accompanying file viewer can stitch them together. This example illustrates detection of a number of different array bound violations:

```
% qa 1.c
% a.out
% qac2 1.c
output ...

char s[]="012"; /* four-element array */

main()
{
        int a[3];        /* three-element array */

        a[0];
        a[-1];   /* negative index out of bounds */
1.c(11) ++ WARNING ++: <=7=(1502) Pointer/Index out of range
         ptr=0xf7fffb60, range=(0xf7fffb64,0xf7fffb70) [12]
```

```
      s[3];    /* index of the null character */
      s[4];    /* beyond the end of the string */
1.c(13) ++ WARNING ++: <=7=(1502) Pointer/Index out of range
        ptr=0xe5b4, range=(0xe5b0,0xe5b4) [4]


      f(a);
}

f(b) /* when f is called with a, b has length 3 */
int b[];
{
      b[3];    /* 3 is beyond the end of b */
1.c(21) ++ WARNING ++: <=7=(1502) Pointer/Index out of range
        ptr=0xf7fffb70, range=(0xf7fffb64,0xf7fffb70) [12]
}
```

The next example illustrates detection of arithmetic overflow through addition:

```
main()
{
    short s = 32000;    /* short assumed to be 16 bits wide  */
    long l = s;
    unsigned u = s;

    printf("s=%-12dl=%-12ldu=%-12u\n", s, l, u);

    printf("s=%-12dl=%-12ldu=%-12u\n",
      s += 1000,l += 1000,u += 1000);
          /* signed short overflows */
18.c(12) ++ WARNING ++: <=3=(1532) Arithmetic overflow

    printf("s=%-12dl=%-12ldu=%-12u\n",
      s += 32000, l += 32000, u +=32000);

    printf("s=%-12dl=%-12ldu=%-12u\n",
      s += 1000, l += 1000, u += 1000);
                              /* unsigned never overflows */
}
```

Finally, the last example illustrates detection of various abuses of the run-time library, in this case relating to I/O:

```
#include <stdio.h>

main()
{
    FILE *fp;
    char buf[BUFSIZ];
```

```
      fp = fopen("16.c", "read");
16.c(10) ++ WARNING ++: <=4=(1526) Argument value out of range
         parameter 2 in call of fopen


      fp = fopen("16.c", "r");
      fseek(fp, 0L, 0);
      fseek(fp, -1L, 0); /* can't go neg from start of file */
16.c(13) ++ WARNING ++: <=4=(1526) Argument value out of range
         parameter 2 in call of fseek
16.c(13) ++ WARNING ++: <=4=(1538) Invalid argument
         in call of fseek, errno=22


      rewind(fp);
      fread(buf, sizeof(buf[0]), BUFSIZ, fp);
      fread(buf, sizeof(buf[0]), BUFSIZ+1, fp);
                                    /* reading 1 too many/
16.c(17) ++ WARNING ++: <=7=(1502) Pointer/Index out of range
         index=1024, limit=1023, for fread arg 1


      putc("A", stderr); /* arg 1 should be an int/
16.c(19) ++ WARNING ++: <=4=(1523) Bad argument to library
function
         parameter 1 in call of putc
         got char * expected int
}
```

Compiler options

Most compilers contain no such options for run-time checking. An honourable exception is the SCC/386 C compiler, which is a product of Salford Software Ltd and is a full compiler for the DOS world which in its CHECK mode inserts checks into the code to screen for the following (Jones, 1993b):

- A reference through a NULL pointer.
- A reference through an uninitialized pointer.
- A reference that does not point to a data object whose address has been taken in the program.
- A reference to an automatic object that has ceased to exist.
- A reference to an allocated object that has since been deleted.
- A reference that would alter a program constant.
- An attempt to treat a pointer to a function as a pointer to data, or vice versa.

The above checks slow down the code by a factor of 10 or so, which is rather more than similar products described above. It is, however, comforting to see C compiler writers putting in run-time checks which were once common in FORTRAN compilers but which were taken out gradually to satisfy users' urge for performance at any cost, including system failure. *It is a sobering thought for the speed merchants that today's workstation can execute C with every check known to computer scientists enabled faster than workstations of perhaps two years ago could run optimized code. Surely this is a more legitimate use of increasing performance!*[5]

Before leaving this section, it should be pointed out that dynamic analysis tools for C frequently find use in other languages. This is because of the wide use of C as an intermediate language in other language environments, for example in early FORTRAN 90 and C++ environments. This will of course present problems if there is no exploitable relationship between the source language and the generated C. However, the author has had personal experience with FORTRAN whereby use of the superb Bell Labs product f2c (Feldman *et al.* 1990) to convert FORTRAN to C followed up by the use of QA C Dynamic (discussed above) on the generated C leads directly to a dynamic analysis capability for FORTRAN because f2c preserves the relationship between the line numbers, allowing run-time detected errors to be related to the FORTRAN source lines at which they occurred. As was seen above, another example of this is provided by Purify, which works for both C *and* C++.

Dynamic test coverage

All of the tools discussed so far are concerned with finding static or dynamic inconsistencies in the language. However, given the rightful importance of test coverage in modern safety initiatives, as stated in Section 5.1.2, the subject is worthy of more discussion. There are many tools on the market, but their use is regrettably not widespread. However, the concepts involved in determining test coverage are very simple. What is less simple is determining what to do when the coverage is not high enough.

The very minimum level of coverage which should be guaranteed with a safety related system is 100 per cent statement coverage, with the exception of 'impossible' statements, such as are described in Section 5.1.2. An excellent example of a test coverage tool which can enable this to be achieved, tcov, is included with Sun workstations, so there is no excuse whatsoever for Sun users not to use it. The author has relied exclusively on this along with some shell formatting tools to process its output for some time on both small and large systems, and for the basic requirement of enabling 100 per cent statement coverage to be achieved it does an admirable job. The following shell script will give the reader an idea of how simple it is to integrate the use of tcov into a development environment:

```
#!/bin/sh
# Set the -a flag on the compiler to generate coverage data.
#
make "CDEBUG=-a" test_normal
#
# Run the program and build coverage.
```

---

[5] It is a non-trivial problem to decide whether to leave run-time assertion checks switched on in production code. The practice of removing them prompted C. A. R. Hoare to say that it was like using a lifebelt in practice but removing it for the real thing. However, in time-critical software, the presence of such assertions will grossly distort the time relationships. The author personally believes that for fly-by-wire systems assertions of illegal states should be left in, and any occurrences of such states should be registered in the plane's flight recorder.

```
#
test_normal < test_data1 > /dev/null
#
# Build coverage database using tcov.
#
tcov *.c
for file in *tcov
do
        base=`$file .tcov`
        echo "File .. $base.c"
        echo " Statement coverage"
        cat $file | tail -6
        echo " Unexecuted statements"
        cat $file | grep "#####"
done
```

A typical output of this would be as follows:

```
File .. fwd_normal_ray.c
  Statement coverage
      58 Basic blocks in this file
      47 Basic blocks executed
   81.03 Percent of the file executed

     306 Total basic block executions
    5.28 Average executions per basic block
 Unexecuted statements
##### -> IMPOSSIBLE_STATE("Illegal value found\n");
##### -> IMPOSSIBLE_STATE("Illegal value found\n");
##### -> IMPOSSIBLE_STATE("Illegal value found\n");
##### -> IMPOSSIBLE_STATE("Illegal value found\n");
##### -> IMPOSSIBLE_STATE("Illegal value found\n");
##### -> IMPOSSIBLE_STATE("Illegal value found\n");
##### -> IMPOSSIBLE_STATE("Illegal value found\n");
##### -> IMPOSSIBLE_STATE("Illegal value found\n");
##### -> IMPOSSIBLE_STATE("Illegal value found\n");
##### -> layers_to_print = trace_status->segment;
##### -> layers_to_print = trace_status->segment;
```

On studying the output above, it is immediately obvious that the last two statements were not illuminated by the test suite and further analysis of the predicates guarding them will be necessary to generate the appropriate test data. Such analysis teaches the author of the program a great deal about the nature of the implemented algorithm.

Another example of a freely available tool of wider availability is gct, from the Free Software Foundation (the GNU distribution). There are many commercially available tools which together provide considerable functionality, including the McCabe toolset, Logiscope and LDRA Testbed.

5.4 SUPPORT FOR FORMALISM

No book on safety-related systems would be complete without comment on formal methods. Unfortunately, as with any other activity in computing, the introduction of a 'new' technology such as formalism invites a competition among the various interested parties to establish a dominant strain, often for largely commercial reasons. Having seen the damage wrought on programming language standardization by pure commercial interest, this author has no vested interest in formal methods and does not care which one is used provided *appropriate* use is made of one to the limits of the development budget. As with all other things, there are caveats, however. The first thing to note is that there is nothing magical about formal methods. Using one does not guarantee success. Nothing guarantees success. A formal method is simply a method which is formally supported and therefore amenable to critique and measurement against some requirement. If the requirement is incomplete with respect to the system (external incompleteness), or if the formal argument is incomplete with respect to the requirement (internal incompleteness), there will of course be problems. The reader is also reminded of the incident described in an earlier section, whereby introduction of a formal methodology, SSADM, into an organization with an inefficient process was deemed to have actually degraded the situation rather than improved it.

Other disturbing evidence as to the efficacy of formal methods is cited by Hetzel (1993) in analysing the claims by advocates of formal methods that the application of formal methods (in this case Z) to the well-known IBM CICS system had resulted in a 50 per cent drop in failure rate for the release. He notes that the claims had originally been analysed by Norman Fenton, who with a number of others felt that the reason the CICS system had improved was simply because a number of troublesome modules had been recognized and redesigned, and not because a formal method had been used. The author would strongly subscribe to this view having had similar experiences in the past grappling with a million lines of FORTRAN (Hatton, 1988).

All of the safety standards, draft or interim, discussed in Chapter 1, require some kind of formal support for reasoning in the programming language, although they do not specify any particular one. For example, IEC 65A requires that the language or a suitable subset be completely and unambiguously defined (Clause 11.2.14) and also recommends various formal and semi-formal methods, especially at the higher levels of safety implication (Clause 9 and Table D8).

In comparison, Def Stan 00–55 states:

> The Safety-Critical System shall be programmed in a language, or a predefined subset of a language, which shall have the following characteristics:
>
> a) A formally-defined syntax
> b) A means of enforcing the use of any subset employed
> c) A well-understood semantics and a formal means of relating code to the Formal Design.
> d) Block-structured
> e) Strongly typed.

The purpose of this chapter is first to present a simple approach to reasoning about programs in a formal way closely related to the informal techniques many good programmers already practise, and second to show how this approach can be applied in C, answering the requirements for formal reasoning support stated in the safety standards above. *Note that an essential pre-requisite for formal proof support in* **any** *language is to purge the language of those features whose behaviour is not sufficiently consistently defined as to lend itself to formal reasoning.* This is the central purpose of this book with regard to C.

Of the many formal methodologies, the author has a preference for simple propositional and predicate calculus on the grounds that simplicity should infuse all aspects of good engineering. This preference is also shared by other workers in the field of safety-related systems, such as Leveson (1993). A detailed survey of formal methods in general has been carried out by Austin and Parkin (1993).

The value of even this simple approach was well illustrated in a BBC video on this subject in which the author took part some years ago (Saunders, 1986). In particular, the producer of the program during the screening spotted an inconsistency in the authors formal proof, even though he, the producer, had no idea of the application area, although he did have considerable mathematical training. Nothing could have made the point better. The application area in which the author and his team were practising a formal approach was seismic data processing in the earth sciences and a restricted version of the formal argument appears shortly to exemplify the technique. The full proof support for the particular functional component under treatment took some six weeks and the resulting heavily used FORTRAN component had no recorded failures in the subsequent three years, (Hatton, 1988). FORTRAN 77 is not known for its formal proof support and so this experience reinforces the important points that one programs *into* a language, not *in* it, and that any language with a well-defined subset is suitable for such treatment. Before embarking on a demonstration of the more accessible of these techniques, the author would like to reiterate that there is nothing mysterious about formal methods and many programmers will immediately identify with them once the smokescreen of hype and notational obscurity is penetrated. It is hoped that the following section will enable those unfamiliar with these techniques to make an immediate improvement in the way they think about program design and construction. In particular it illustrates an important principle very well indeed. If a program is developed hand in hand with its formal argument, the process is not inherently difficult. However, supplying a correctness proof for a program after the fact is considered impossible for all but the most trivial of programs.

5.4.1 A quick introduction to propositional and predicate calculi

Propositional calculus (also known as sentential logic), is likely to be familiar at least in part to many programmers in better known manifestations such as Boolean algebra. Although a restricted form of calculus, in that it cannot describe all algorithms, it is nevertheless extraordinarily useful. Propositional calculus is limited to two state values (true or false) and to logical conjunctions. Its laws are stated in full below.

Let A, B and C be expressions which are either true (T) or false (F).

- *Commutativity*

$$(A \wedge B) = (B \wedge A)$$
$$(A \vee B) = (B \vee A)$$
$$(A = B) = (B = A)$$

- *Associativity*

$$(A \wedge B) \wedge C = A \wedge (B \wedge C)$$
$$(A \vee B) \vee C = A \vee (B \vee C)$$

- *Distributivity*

$$A \vee (B \wedge C) = (A \vee B) \wedge (A \vee C)$$
$$A \wedge (B \vee C) = (A \wedge B) \vee (A \wedge C)$$

- *De Morgan's laws*

$$\neg(A \wedge B) = \neg A \vee \neg B$$
$$\neg(A \vee B) = \neg A \wedge \neg B$$

- *Law of negation*

$$\neg(\neg A) = A$$

- *Law of the excluded middle*

$$A \vee \neg A = T$$

- *Law of contradiction*

$$A \wedge \neg A = F$$

- *Law of implication (by agreement!)*

$$A \Rightarrow B = \neg A \vee B$$

- *Law of equality*

$$(A = B) = (A \Rightarrow B) \wedge (B \Rightarrow A)$$

- *Laws of or-simplification*

$$A \vee A = A$$
$$A \vee T = T$$
$$A \vee F = A$$
$$A \vee (A \wedge B) = A$$

- *Laws of and-simplification*

$$A \wedge A = A$$
$$A \wedge T = A$$
$$A \wedge F = F$$
$$A \wedge (A \vee B) = A$$

- *Law of identity*

$$A = A$$

It is interesting to note that the law of implication was arrived by consensus of agreement (cf. Hehner (1984) for an excellent discussion, as well as much practical advice). The laws can be verified by simply evaluating all legal possibilities, for example as:

A	A $\wedge$ F	F
T	F	F
F	F	F

Evaluating and dealing with all legal possibilities is at the heart of safe programming practice and the reader might like to verify a few of the above laws in this manner.

Propositional calculus is an excellent way of writing assertions in a compact and unambiguous way. Consider for example the following:

do	The distillery is open
mtwt	It is Monday, Tuesday, Wednesday or Thursday
aug	It is August
hdb	It is the head distiller's birthday

The proposition 'If it is not August and it is Monday, Tuesday, Wednesday or Thursday and it is not the head distiller's birthday, the distillery is open', can be rendered as

$$(\neg aug \wedge mtwt \wedge \neg hdb) \Rightarrow do$$

To widen the applicability of the propositional calculus to software development, some things have to be added. In essence, the *predicate calculus* is such a superset in which the following have been added

- *Identifiers* in a proposition may be replaced by any expression which has the value T or F, for example, $x > y$.
- The *existential* qualifier, $\exists$ ('there exists') is added. For example, $(\exists i : m \leq i < n : E_i)$ means that there exists an i such that one of E_i, $i \in [m, n)$, is true.
- The *universal* qualifier, $\forall$ ('for all') is added. For example, $(\forall i : m \leq i < n : E_i)$ means that for all i, $i \in [m, n)$, the E_i are true.
- The *numerical* qualifier, N ('number of') is added. For example, $(N i : m \leq i < n : E_i)$ means the number of i, $i \in [m, n)$, for which the E_i are true.

To evaluate a proposition in the predicate calculus, the appropriate values of T or F for the expressions are substituted and the resulting expression evaluated using the normal rules of propositional calculus. The reader is referred to Gries (1981) for more detail. It should be noted that the existential and universal qualifiers are not independent and both are included for notational convenience. To illustrate this fact and to illustrate how such expressions can be manipulated, a proof is now given.

$$(\forall i: m \leq i < n: E_i) = E_m \land E_{m+1} \land E_{m+2} \ldots \land E_{n-1}$$
$$= \neg\neg(E_m \land E_{m+1} \land E_{m+2} \ldots \land E_{n-1})$$
$$= \neg(\neg E_m \lor \neg E_{m+1} \ldots \lor \neg E_{n-1})$$
$$= \neg(\exists i: m \leq i < n: \neg E_i)$$

Similarly, it can be shown that $\neg\forall\neg$ (not for all not) is logically equivalent to $\exists$ (there exists).

In essence, as will be seen, the propositional calculus can be used to argue formally about program structure, whereas the additional power of the predicate calculus is necessary to argue about detailed manipulations.

5.4.2 An example of the practical use of propositional calculus

The following example is a reduced version of a full proof as discussed in Saunders (1986), but is in every sense a real example. It is noteworthy not only because it shows how a difficult specification can be reduced formally but also how it can then be manipulated consistently thereafter, according to various criteria, without any need to understand the application.

The application area is seismic data processing. The particular application is known as signature deconvolution, whereby a measurement of the time series (i.e. an amplitude versus time function) corresponding to an impulse applied to the Earth is used to decode the recorded echo time series (e.g. Hatton *et al.*, 1986). Each time an impulse is applied to the Earth, an echo time series is recorded by 'listening' instruments. The decoded form consists of events corresponding to key geological layers. The full written (or more usually spoken) specification might go something like this:

> The signature deconvolution function should operate as follows. There is a copy of the input impulse time series ('sweep') recorded with its corresponding echo time series. Unfortunately, it is sometimes no good, so a fixed simulated impulse time series can be used. However, if the last recorded impulse time series is good, use that instead, only there might not be a last good sweep. In fact, it might be known at the beginning that all the recorded impulse time series are no good, so the simulated impulse time series should be used on every echo time series.

It is not important that the reader understand the above gobbledygook. Suffice it to say that, in the author's experience, it is typical of the way specifications for algorithms are given to programmers in the computer applications industry in general. Producing a correct version of this program from specifications like this is, as can be appreciated, very difficult. In spite of the fact that the underlying deconvolution algorithm referenced in the above has been known for more than forty years (Wiener, 1949), it turns out to be one of the worst implemented of all algorithms in this application area (Hatton and Roberts, 1992). It is interesting to note that it is not the fundamental mathematics that the programmers get wrong, it is the logistical details involved in its use, as exemplified by the above idealised conversation. For reference, an up-to-date description of the underlying mathematics in this case is given in Robinson and Treitel (1980).

In its original form, the author and his colleagues spent some six weeks exhaustively rendering the specification into a complete set of *states* and *actions* associated with each of those states, which numbered seven giving $2^7 = 128$ possibilities to explore! The states are either true or false, as required by propositional calculus. The above restricted specification is rather simpler, involving only three states, as can now be seen.

Define the following three states:

S1   The recorded sweep is OK by some criterion.
S2   There exists a last good sweep.
S3   Simulate sweep use is mandatory.

and the following four actions:

A1   Use the recorded sweep.
A2   Use the last good sweep.
A3   Use the simulated sweep.
A4   Store this recorded sweep as good.

The next step then is systematically to consider all possible states and define an action for each. This guarantees the completeness of the specification and is at the heart of any safety argument. If a program is to be proved safe, *every* possible state must be evaluated and a suitable action defined. Anything less is inadequate unless it could be proved that those states not covered were only encountered with some acceptably low frequency. In practice, it would be as hard to prove this as to evaluate them. The practising programmer might argue that such completeness arguments are impracticable for all but a few independent states. If this is the case, how else can the programmer argue for completeness? This is completed by people expert in the application area and the equivalent table to the earlier informal specification is:

S1	S2	S3	A1	A2	A3	A4
F	F	F			√	
T	F	F	√			√
F	T	F		√		
T	T	F	√			√
F	F	T			√	
T	F	T			√	√
F	T	T			√	
T	T	T			√	√

The above table can now be turned into statements in the propositional calculus as follows:

$$A1 = (S1 \land \neg S2 \land \neg S3) \lor (S1 \land S2 \land \neg S3)$$

$$A2 = (\neg S1 \land S2 \land \neg S3)$$

$$A3 = S3 \lor (\neg S1 \land \neg S2 \land \neg S3)$$

$$A4 = (S1 \land \neg S2 \land \neg S3) \lor (S1 \land S2 \land \neg S3) \lor (S1 \land \neg S2 \land S3) \lor (S1 \land S2 \land S3)$$

For example, the first action A1 is constructed by ORing together rows 2 and 4 of the table. These statements can now be manipulated formally using the laws of propositional calculus stated earlier. Such laws allow an infinite number of transformations. The appropriate transformations will depend on the desired final form of the program, and some examples will now be given.

A canonical form—the most natural decomposition

First, the above statements will be simplified to see what kind of structure naturally emerges. Noting that the first three actions all contain S3 or its negation and also that the fourth action decomposes simply using the law of the excluded middle. The use of commutativity to move S3 to the left gives

$$A1 = (\neg S3 \wedge S1)$$

$$A2 = (\neg S3 \wedge \neg S1 \wedge S2)$$

$$A3 = S3 \vee (\neg S3 \wedge \neg S1 \wedge \neg S2)$$

$$= S3 \vee (\neg S1 \wedge \neg S2)$$

giving an equivalent C program

```
if    (S3)
{
      A3;
}
else
{
      if    (S1)
      {
            A1;
      }
      else
            if    (S2)
            {
                  A2;
            }
            else
            {
                  A3;
            }
      }
}
```

and A4 = S1, giving

```
if    (S1)
{
      A4;
}
```

In practice, the original predicates and their formal transformation would be left in the code so that the reviewer could understand how the structure had evolved from the formal specification. In this sense, C (or indeed any other language supporting fundamental language structures such as block if statements), can support a formal approach. Note in the above that there is a reused action A3. This is simple forewarning to the implementor that a function reference will be suitable here.

Combining into a single block if

Supposing now that it was required to combine all four actions into a single block if. This can be done by leaving the A1, A2 and A3 rules alone and rewriting the A4 rule using the law of the excluded middle and distributivity as:

$$A4 = S1 \wedge (S3 \vee \neg S3)$$

Expanding, the following tree results:

```
if    (S3)
{
      A3;
      if    (S1)
      {
            A4;
      }
}
else
{
      if    (S1)
      {
            A1,A4;
      }
      else
      {
            if    (S2)
            {
                  A2;
            }
            else
            }
                  A3;
            }
      }
}
```

Reducing to a single block if introduces greater redundancy, with action A4 now also affected, suggesting that this be implemented as a function also.

Removing redundancy

Such redundancy might be deemed inappropriate. If this is the case, the redundancy can be removed at the expense of more complicated predicates, as can be seen by implementing each action guarded by the appropriate predicate:

```
if    (!S3 && S1)
{
      A1;
}

if    (!S3 && !S1 && S2)
{
      A2;
}

if    (S3 || (!S3 && !S1 && !S2) )
{
      A3;
}

if    (S1)
{
      A4;
}
```

An advantageous side-effect of this is that since each action only appears once, it is easy to manipulate them if the order in which they are carried out is important. For example, initialization should precede use.

Changing the specification—adding actions and states

One of the central problems in the maintenance of software systems is analysing the effects of perfective change. To a harassed software development manager, the first reaction might be to give some suitably long period in the future off the top of his or her head. Such estimates are not estimates of when something will be completed but of the amount of time required to clear the decks to begin even thinking about the requested change. One of the main benefits of a formal argument constructed using the propositional calculus is that the effects of change are much more easy to predict.

For example, consider the effects of a perfective change which involves adding an action to the existing specification. In the above case this might be the addition of:

A5   Perform some analysis of the sweep.

Inspection of the table above shows that adding an action simply adds a column, in other words, the modifications are not great.

On the other hand, adding a state doubles the number of possibilities which must be considered for every action. This must be considered a major change.

If the reader is interested in other examples of the use of these techniques, the treatise by Warnier (1974) is highly recommended. Other authors who support such techniques include Leveson (1986, 1993), who stated that many problems in safety-related systems stemmed from incomplete specifications, and also Mead and Conway (1980), who use it to specify VLSI systems. In the author's experience, one of the most difficult parts of the above is determining a set of mutually independent states, but as with all things, the situation improves markedly with practice. The most important point is to resist the temptation to start coding until the above is completed with complete satisfaction.

5.4.3 Another example—errno

An example which naturally occurs in the formal static analysis of C programs is the treatment of errno. As the reader may be aware, the idea of errno is to return some error state to the user resulting from a failure inside a run-time library function. Unfortunately, through lack of precise specification, the concept has been abused to the point whereby a strict code of practice is necessary to use it correctly. The reader is referred to Plauger (1992) for a detailed discussion. Its proper use requires resetting it to zero immediately before use, and checking it immediately after use against a small number of values defined by Standard C. If it is not reset beforehand, it can be in any state and it will not be reset by functions in the run-time library. If it is not checked after, the running program may be continuing in error. If it is checked against values not defined in Standard C, it exhibits implementation-defined behaviour. So how should it be used? Again, it is a three state system.

Define the following three *states*:

S1   errno has been preset to zero immediately before use.
S2   errno has been checked immediately after use.
S3   Implementation-defined features of errno have been used.

and the following four *actions*:

A1   Accept.
A2   Flag implementation-defined behaviour.
A3   Flag unchecked use.
A4   Flag undefined use.

Again, the next step then is systematically to consider all possible states and define an action or actions for each. This leads to the following table:

S1	S2	S3	A1	A2	A3	A4
F	F	F			✓	
T	F	F			✓	
F	T	F				✓
T	T	F	✓			
F	F	T		✓	✓	
T	F	T		✓	✓	
F	T	T		✓		✓
T	T	T	✓	✓		

The final algorithm looks like:

```
if   (S3)
{
     A2;
}

if   (!S2)
{
     A3;
}

if  (S1 && S2)
{
     A1;    /*    PASS   */
}

else
{
     if (!S1 && S2)
     {
          A4;
     }

     /*    FAIL    */
}
```

Again, there are many different ways of expressing this, but its apparent complexity from a seemingly innocuous specification is worth noting.

To finish this section appropriately, if there are many complex states, which are difficult to organize hierarchically, the program can be designed to fail safe by setting a valid trigger for any combination of legal states and returning the trigger value at the end. The trigger is set by default to failure on entry, as shown below:

```
program_state
func( void )
{
     int   trigger = INVALID;

     if ( (... && ...) || ... )
     {
          trigger = VALID;

          ...
     }
     if (  ... && ... && ... )
     {
          trigger = VALID;
```

```
        . . .
    }
        return( trigger );
}
```

Of course, in a safety-related system, it can be very difficult to decide on the appropriate action when an invalid state is encountered. For example, in the fly-only-by-wire European Fighter Aircraft (EFA), which reputedly and quite deliberately has the aerodynamic properties of a refrigerator, the appropriate action presumably would not be to resort to manual control.[6]

Pre- and post-conditions and weakest precondition

As has been seen above, the propositional calculus can be an extraordinarily effective tool given its simplicity, and this can easily be rendered into a C program. However, the price for its simplicity is that its suitability is limited primarily to the control structure of a program. To argue convincingly about code not involving the control structure the use of several techniques can be considered, although such techniques are not so amenable as the propositional calculus.

Pre- and post-conditions

This technique is originally due to Hoare. In essence, each active statement of the program is preceded and followed by logical assertions as to the program state. This can be done in any language, but the presence of the `assert` macro in C makes the technique particularly amenable, as can be seen by the definitions for formal support in C given later in this section.

Weakest precondition

This concept is due to Dijkstra. It is defined as follows:

> The *weakest precondition* wp(S,R) is the set of all states such that execution of S in any one of them guarantees termination in a state R in a finite time.

W.P. has a number of properties:

- *Law of the excluded miracle*

$$wp(S, F) = F$$

- *Distributivity of conjunction*

$$wp(S, Q) \wedge wp(S, R) = wp(S, Q \wedge R)$$

- *Law of monotonicity*

$$\text{if } Q \Rightarrow R \text{ then } wp(S, Q) \Rightarrow wp(S, R)$$

- *Distributivity of disjunction*

$$wp(S, Q) \vee wp(S, R) \Rightarrow wp(S, Q \vee R)$$

---

[6] If the author was the test pilot, he would require the ejector seat to be manually controlled.

Note also the following definitions:

- *skip*

$$wp(skip, R) = R$$

- *abort*

$$wp(abort, R) = F(\text{Should never be executed!})$$

- *composition*

$$wp(\text{“S1; S2”}, R) = wp(S1, wp(S2, R))$$

As an example, consider the simple act of incrementing a variable in C.

$$wp(\text{“}i++\text{”}, i \leq 1) = (i \leq 0)$$

The close relationship between weakest pre-condition and pre- and post-conditions can be seen by writing the above in pre-/post-condition form as:

$$/* \; i \leq 0 \; */ \quad i++; \quad /* \; i \leq 1 \; */$$

Using the weakest pre-condition, Gries (1981) defines the complete semantics of a sophisticated language including such features as the infamous goto. In practice, the author has not used it anywhere near as much in practical situations as the other techniques discussed in this section, but it is a practical concept, as evidenced by Gries when he uses it to derive a difficult array bound. For reference, 'one-off' errors in array bounds are a notorious source of program problems in all languages.

Useful definitions to support formal reasoning in C

The following definitions can be used in a C program to provide effective support for the formal techniques described in this chapter. They should be taken as indicative rather than literal, but together they provide a satisfactory solution to the requirement of the draft and interim safety standards discussed in Chapter 1 for support for formal reasoning.

```
/*
 *    Support for propositional calculus to improve clarity
 */
#define    AND                    &&
#define    OR                     ||
#define    NOT                    !
/*
 *    Assertion support.
 */
#define    IMPOSSIBLE_STATE(x)    fprintf(stderr,x),\
                                  take_safety_action(),\
                                  abort()
#define    ILLEGAL_STATE(x)       fprintf(stderr,x),\
                                  recover_illegal_state()
```

```
/*
 *    Support for pre- and post-conditions.
 */
#define    PRE(p)                    assert(p)
#define    POST(r)                   assert(r)
/*
 *    Support for data flow analysis in interfaces.
 */
#define    IN
#define    OUT
#define    INOUT
```

Examples of code fragments using the above definitions follow:

```
if ( n == 0 )
{
       IMPOSSIBLE_STATE("n cannot be zero\n");
}
...
long
factorial(  IN    int n )
{
       ...
}
...
PRE( i >= 0 ); i++; POST( i >= 1 );
```

Note that `assert` only works with the desired effect if the parameter `NDEBUG` is *not* set.

Other formal techniques

Many other formal techniques have been proposed to assist in both specification and implementation of systems, including (but by no means limited to!) CSP (Hoare, 1985), VDM (Jones, 1986) and Z (Hayes, 1987), but it is outside the scope of this book to devote any more attention to them over and above that referenced already to support the notion of formal reasoning in C, and it is perhaps suitable to finish this section with two quotations from famous computer scientists.

> One cannot learn to write large programs effectively until one has learned to write small ones effectively. (Gries)

> Constructing a big program without ever writing a big program is the key to constructing correct big programs. (Parnas)

This advice has strong intuitive appeal, but the author is unclear as to how to reconcile the powerful empirical evidence reported in Section 3.3, showing that small modules are relatively more error-prone than large programs, with the above statements.

5.5 PROVISION FOR THE SAFETY ARGUMENT

The safety argument is a centrepiece of any engineering effort related to safety. Unfortunately, there is no standard nomenclature for this yet. It is also known as a safety case, and in some sources neither safety argument nor safety case explicitly appears (MOD, 1991). In this text, it will be referred to as the safety argument in line with its use in IEE (1992). The purpose of the safety argument is to present a case whereby the engineering solution is believed to be safe to be deployed. Safety arguments are usually very complex documents (Forder *et al.*, 1993). Here, only those aspects relating to the choice of programming language will be covered. Traditionally, such aspects have not even appeared in safety arguments, but when most programming languages contain inherently unsafe features it is only a matter of time before this omission is filled. The following indicates a way of rectifying this omission for the language C, although the issues are equally relevant to other programming languages.

In order to make a convincing case for the use of C, at least the following must be done:

- A detailed justification of the reasons for using C must be given. It is reasonable to include economic issues but unreasonable to exclude everything else. Standardization, compiler stability, tool support and availability of skilled programmers are good reasons, but an informed and balanced discussion is important. Given that there is very little guidance for any language as yet, the justification should be a separate document to draw attention to the fact that the decision was not taken without due care and consideration. The exposition should cover the following:
    - The environment, including the validation status of the compiler environment. If a validated compiler is available for the environment, it should be used; otherwise the reason for using an unvalidated compiler should be given. For example, in many cross-compiler environments, the compilers will currently be unvalidated. Deficiencies in the environment, for example, lack of test coverage support, should be discussed in depth.
    - A discussion of all relevant literature surveyed to show that the decision was not uninformed. Explicit working knowledge of the Standard C definition should be shown.
- Relevant unsafe areas of the language should be specifically recognized and formally rejected, along with a discussion of how such rejection would be achieved in practice. As has been seen, many unspecified and undefined features are statically detectable using existing technology. Such features should be recognized as prejudicial to safety and reliability and listed as such. It is also appropriate to refer to the relatively low number of interpretation requests outstanding against C in comparison with other languages used in safety-related systems as evidence of the quality of its definition.
- The portability of the application should be discussed. If a safety-related application is intended to work on more than one platform, implementation-defined features likely to be problematic should be listed and rejected.

6

COMPARISON WITH OTHER LANGUAGES

Just as with spoken language, the choice of programming language is an emotive issue. Throughout this book recourse has been made to more mature engineering disciplines such as architecture. However, even in architecture, similar conflicts arise with different practitioners advocating particular techniques. The common denominator which leads to high engineering performance is that the tools are used efficiently and consistently to solve a particular problem; their nature is largely irrelevant. One of the central problems in software engineering is that there are so many tools that their efficient use by a programmer is greatly inhibited. For example, at a recent software development trade show, the author was unable to work out what problem some of the tools and methodologies were attempting to solve. With this backcloth, it is perhaps not surprising that software engineering quality is so erratic.

The recurring theme of this book is quite simply that, *in safety-related systems, the intrinsic safety of the standard language is irrelevant, it is how safe the use of the language can be made that matters.* Hence to make the statement that C is an unsafe language compared to, for example, Ada, Modula-2 or Pascal is a very shallow appraisal. The object of assessment should be the language *plus* whatever tool support is available for that language to promote safe usage, including the quality of implementations.[1] As was seen in the previous chapter, C is particularly well-endowed with such tool support, and in this regard is almost certainly the best supported language known.

To develop this theme a little further, it is enough to realize that many recent compilers for languages other than C actually generate C as an output language to

---

[1] Pragmatic tool support is being referred to here, i.e. tool support to automate things we know how to do manually in principle, rather than some of the more exotic species.

take advantage of the portability and reliability of available C compilers which take the code the rest of the way to machine language. This latter fact is one of the reasons cited by safety-related developers to the author when adopting C as an implementation language. The fact that its implicit use is unavoidable in some contexts is seen to be one step away from its explicit use. C has always enjoyed this split personality of containing both high- and low-level features. For such compilers, therefore, it is quite reasonable to consider the act of programming in a language such as Ada as a constrained form of programming in C. As the reader might have spotted, there is, however, an intrinsic danger in such environments. Even though use of the source language might lead to a *conceptually* constrained version of C, it is quite possible that the C code generation part of the compiler could generate features of C known to be problematic as discussed in Chapter 2. The author's experience in analysing unsafe subset dependence of machine-generated C suggests that this is not at all uncommon and the original source code developer is unaware that it is going on.

The nature of the comparisons in this chapter will be a review of similar features in each language or supporting tool environment with safety-related intent. For example, the language Ada *requires* exceptions to be raised in a wide range of circumstances. These exceptions take several forms, including `Numeric_Error`, `End_Error` and `Constraint_Error`. The book by Watt *et al.* (1987) gives an excellent account of Ada and its use. Comparisons will be made with several languages which are specifically referenced in the IEC SC65A draft standard discussed in Chapter 1. Some of these, such as Ada and FORTRAN currently benefit from the existence of international standards, and others, such as C++ and assembly language, do not, although safety-related systems are already being implemented in these languages, or have already been. C++, however, should benefit from such a standard towards the end of this decade if current progress towards the standard continues.

This language comparison will be carried out a little differently to that carried out by Cullyer *et al.* (1991). They compared C, Coral 66, Pascal, Modula-2 and Ada. The paper has laudable motives, but unfortunately it suffered somewhat by appearing before the C standard was finalized and does not treat C++ at all. In addition, tool support is not addressed, and so the paper does not address the question considered so important in this book, i.e. how safe can the use of a language be *made*? As a result, C is treated rather heavy-handedly and somewhat incorrectly, and has consequently been deprecated for use in safe systems. In the author's experience, this has disturbed a number of developers who have been forced to use C in such systems, and who treat the fact that as such views have been aired in the public domain they represent best practice in this area. This is unhelpful given the amount of safety-related development known to be taking place, and is misleading given that tool support was completely absent from the comparisons and given also that there were errors in the assessment of C. These authors compared each language against a set of questions that are assumed to define the minimum set of acceptable properties of a language for use in safety-critical systems. These were:

- *Wild jumps*: Can the program jump to an arbitrary store location?
- *Overwrites*: Are there language features which prevent an arbitrary store location being overwritten?

Table 6.1 Comparison of Ada, Modula-2 and C by Cullyer *et al.* (1991). See text for explanation of symbols

Item	Ada	Idea Ada subset	Modula-2	Modula-2 subset	C
Wild jumps	*	*	?	*	?
Overwrites	?	*	?	*	X
Semantics	?	?	*	*	X
Model of maths	?	*	*	*	X
Operational arithmetic	?	*	?	?	X
Data typing	*	*	?	*	X
Exception handling	*	*	?	?	?
Safe subset	X	?	?	*	X
Exhaustion of memory	X	?	?	?	?
Separate compilation	*	*	*	*	X
Well understood	?	*	*	*	?

- *Semantics*: Are the semantics of the language defined sufficiently for the translation process needed for static code analysis to be feasible?
- *Model of maths*: Is there a rigorous model of both integer and floating-point arithmetic within the language standard?
- *Operational arithmetic*: Are there procedures for checking that the operational program obeys the model of the arithmetic when running on the target processor?
- *Data typing*: Are the means of data typing strong enough to prevent misuse of variables?
- *Exception handling*: If the software detects a malfunction at run-time, do mechanisms exist to facilitate recovery (e.g. global exception handlers which may in themselves introduce hazards if used unwisely)?
- *Safe subsets*: Does a subset of the language exist which is defined to have properties that satisfy these requirements more adequately than the full language?
- *Exhaustion of memory*: Are there facilities in the language to guard against running out of memory at run-time (e.g. to prevent stack or heap overflow)?
- *Separate compilation*: Does the language provide facilities for separate compilation of modules, with type checking across the module boundaries?
- *Well understood*: Will the designers and programmers understand the programming language sufficiently to write safety-critical software?

In addition, the authors used the following nomenclature:

X Facility is not provided, and this may result in equipment that is unsafe.
? The language provides some protection, but there remains a risk of malfunction.
* Sound protection is provided, and good design and verification should minimize the risk of serious incident.

Leaving aside a discussion of whether the above rather general features satisfactorily define the requirements of a safe language, Table 6.1 summarizes how C was marked against Ada and Modula-2. On analysing this table, it is easy to get the impression that the probability of writing a reliable program in C is vanishingly small, unless the dice have been rather loaded against it. For example, C is probably the *best* understood language of any given the huge amount of experience with it in many different contexts, from serious developments to the essentially cathartic

Table 6.2 Revised comparison of C and Modula-2

	C	*C re-marked*	*C + tool support*	*Modula-2 subset*
Wild jumps	?	?	*	*
Overwrites	X	X	*	*
Semantics	X	?	*	*
Model of maths	X	?	?	*
Operational arithmetic	X	X	?	?
Data typing	X	X	*	*
Exception handling	?	?	?	?
Safe subset	X	*	*	*
Exhaustion of memory	?	?	?	?
Separate compilation	X	?	*	*
Well understood	?	*	*	*

Obfuscated C competition described in Section 2.12. The existence of such excellent and wide-reaching journals as the *C User's Journal*, edited by P. J. Plauger, further promotes this view. In addition, the standard itself describes the notion of a safe subset under the name of a *strictly conforming program* and proceeds to define all those issues that must be absent. The semantics of this subset is essentially well defined (there are far fewer outstanding interpretation requests for C than Ada at the time of writing), and finally there is a separate compilation model which is well defined and easily (and frequently) enforced. As a result, if C is re-marked and then tool support included, Table 6.2 results.

In essence, the automatically enforced features which lead to the upgraded definition in Table 6.2 have been discussed in earlier chapters and are in place in numerous organizations, but these points are given specifically in Table 6.3. By these criteria, C should certainly not be deprecated if the required tool support is present, and there is indeed an argument that it should be included at the top level of safety use since it compares favourably with a Modula-2 subset (and indeed anything else) using this tool-guaranteed inhibition of potentially dangerous features.

Table 6.3 Automatically enforced restriction in C

Item	*Automatically enforceable restriction*
Wild jumps[2]	Enforce use of default clause in `switch` statement.
Overwrites	Enforce bound checking and pointer tracking
Semantics	Enforce strictly conforming program
Model of maths	Forbid mixed signed and unsigned arithmetic and undefined shifts.
Operational arithmetic	Floating-point model being studied by Numerical Extensions group.
Data typing	Enforce strong typing of defined types and also `typedefs`.
Exception handling	—
Safe subset	Enforce strictly conforming program
Exhaustion of memory	Forbid recursion and use of `malloc`, `realloc` and `calloc`. If dynamic objects necessary, enforce use of a standard allocator with defined error recovery when allocation denied.
Separate compilation	Enforce use of function prototypes and forbid implicit declarations.
Well understood	—

---

[2] Oddly, Cullyer *et al.* (1991) left out the justifiably infamous and potentially far more lethal `setjmp` and `longjmp`. These are treated later on.

Quite apart from this, the average quality of C compilers is typically very high indeed, with the AT&T portable C compiler, written in C, enjoying a considerable reputation as one of the most bug-free and reliable large programs ever written. Ada compilers do not yet enjoy such a reputation. This is of considerable importance, as there is a large effort going on in the Ada community (see for example Forsyth *et al.* (1993)) to prove the equivalence of high-level language to low-level generated language, as one of a number of initiatives to promote Ada as the language of high-integrity systems. Unfortunately, as is readily admitted in Forsyth *et al.* (1993), Hutcheon *et al.* (1993a, b), Ada is such a complex language that this is proving extremely difficult, and the ever more wonderful features being added to Ada 9X are just as quickly being removed by the safety-critical users. C has a massive advantage over many modern languages; it is fundamentally small and very simple.[3] Not surprisingly, this has manifested itself in generally very high-quality compilers. It is interesting to speculate how safe C would become if the effort equivalent to that put into Ada was expended on it.

Finally, it should be noted in passing that the existence of an international standard is not the end of the story, as standards must be updated every few years. Unfortunately, Ada is now under review in the form of Ada 9X, as indicated above, and a number of potentially dangerous features, including support for object-oriented development, are candidates for inclusion. The author is particularly wary of language updates, as the inevitable effect is to make the language concerned bigger and even more incomprehensible. Features are very rarely removed, however disastrous, and yet more new features of frequently unproven reliability are added to make the language more 'attractive'. The situation has strong similarities to the marketing of soap powders in that market share seems to be one of the main design goals and the 'need for FORTRAN 90 to compete with Ada', for example, was frequently voiced to the author in his days on FORTRAN 90 committees. This is simply not good enough when the safety of people and the environment is at stake. The author watched FORTRAN 77 grow from a relatively benign and controllable language into a programmer-eating monster whose language definition more than doubled in size in the form of FORTRAN 90, released in 1992, a mere eight years late. At the time of writing C++, although not an update of C, seems to be going the same way, to the extent that there are still syntax problems to be resolved. Furthermore, it appears to be extremely difficult to define a simple one-token lookahead resolvable grammar. This issue will be taken up later in Section 6.1. The common denominator is that few things ever get taken out. Things simply get added. It will take a stupendously brave effort by the Ada committee to stop the same thing happening in Ada 9X. For the reader's information, the phrase usually used to defend existing bad practice is that removing it 'will break existing code'. In the author's opinion, this is the most beneficial thing which could happen to it. For a pragmatic, enlightening, highly valuable, but ultimately depressing insight into the design politics of modern computer languages, the reader is referred to the ACM Turing award paper of Tony Hoare (Hoare, 1981), himself a veteran of Algol 68, PL/1

---

[3] No modern widely used language, to the author's knowledge, has successfully combined a high degree of expressive ability with simplicity and a low degree of irregularity.

and finally Ada committees.[4] As he concluded there, the two keys to success in language design are as follows:

> 'One way is to make it so simple that there are *obviously* no deficiencies and the other way is to make it so complicated that there are no *obvious* deficiencies.'

Before discussing the languages themselves, it is worth spending a little time discussing modern language trends and their potential impact on safety. Historically, of course, the widespread use of assembly language in safety-related systems has meant that high-level design constructs have been largely absent at the code level. Today, languages tend to have highly sophisticated constructs, such as overloading, support for object-orientated design and, rather less often, direct support for some form of formal reasoning. At least some of these constructs appear to have significant drawbacks for safety-related systems, although there is yet little real experience of their use.

6.1 LANGUAGE FEATURES AND SAFETY

Experience has shown over the years that certain language constructs lead to problematic behaviour. Aspects of this have already been discussed in Chapter 2 as well as in the discussion of the paper by Cullyer *et al.* (1991), but this discussion will concentrate on those features that draft standards such as IEC SC65A explicitly restrict, along with some other features of modern languages that are likely to lead to similar problematic behaviour. These features all fall into the category of being well-defined, but whose use tends to lead to unreliability. The discussion has been delayed until this point in the book as it includes features not present in C, but present in C++ and in other languages which might otherwise be considered as preferable replacements for C in a safety-related application.

6.1.1 Use of dynamic objects

The use of dynamic objects is considered to be a dangerous feature by safety standards such as IEC SC65A. There are two principal problems with them:

- *Unreliable use.* In the case of C, this has been comprehensively addressed by the discussion and toolset given in Section 5.3.
- *Memory leakage.* This simply means that memory which is allocated is not subsequently freed. Memory allocation using `malloc`, `calloc` and `realloc` and memory freeing using `free` are generally well-defined, but a net imbalance between them means the application will gradually increase in size as it runs (it is a terrible mistake to release memory which has not been allocated, but this can be prevented by the tools discussed earlier). Unfortunately, there are limits to the size which a running program can reach. On UNIX systems, this is determined by the size of

---

[4] The author is sure that Tony would not be surprised to hear that C++ and Ada 9X seem to be following exactly the same path as Algol 68, PL/1, the original Ada and now FORTRAN 90—each a massively complex language full of anachronisms and exceptions.

the *swap space*. When swap space is exhausted, a request for more memory is refused. This should be handled correctly as:

```
if ( (mp = malloc(sizeof(object))) == NULL )
{
        /*    Request denied, attempt recovery    */
        ...
}
```

Frequently the possibility of denial is ignored, with catastrophic results. Even when correctly handled, the application may not be able to continue, which should lead to appropriate close-down.

The problems associated with such growth should not be underestimated. The author has come across many graphical applications that have to be restarted every few hours as they have exhausted all available swap space through gradual memory leakage. For example, the widely used graphical interface Motif has an unenviable reputation for such software obesity. This would hardly be considered appropriate behaviour in a safety-critical environment. On the other hand, so much of the modern theory of data structuring is built around dynamic objects and their manipulation that attempting to develop software using static entities only is likely to lead to a great deal of re-invention of existing wheels and loss of notational elegance, with potentially serious implications for a safety-related system. This author therefore believes that provided leakage and misuse can be guaranteed to have been avoided by appropriate tools, as already described, the use of dynamic objects is appropriate in the interests of using proven data structuring technology. Otherwise there is a distinct danger of throwing the baby out with the bathwater. Dynamic store allocation and the equivalent of pointers is also disallowed by Ada subsets such as the SPARK subset (Carré, 1990), but Forsyth *et al.* (1993) make the same points as above: that the language may be less safe as a result because of the unnatural way in which many well-known algorithms would have to be re-coded.

6.1.2 Recursion

The principle reason why recursion, which in essence is the ability of a function to call itself, either directly or indirectly, is not recommended in safety-related software is because it relies on dynamic memory for its action. When a function calls itself, as is allowable in C, it must store the current values of local variables somewhere so that they can be retrieved in the correct order as the recursion 'unwinds'. Of course the problems occur if there is no dynamic memory left to allow this to be done. Since there is no error mechanism for handling recursion failure in C, things simply fail catastrophically. This is the pessimistic view.

The optimistic view recognizes that recursion is a natural and therefore more reliable way of expressing certain classes of algorithm. For example, as Kernighan and Ritchie (1988), who need no introduction, note on p. 88:

> Recursion may provide no saving in storage, since somewhere a stack of the values being processed must be maintained. Nor will it be faster, but recursive code is more compact, and often much easier to write and understand than the non-recursive equivalent. Recursion is especially convenient for recursively defined data structures like trees...

Perhaps a better course of action in a safety-related environment is to assess what the dynamic memory requirements of recursion are likely to be and if the memory can be guaranteed to be provided, allow recursion. At least this uses a central feature of safety engineering, that of seeking the most natural and comprehensible solution and analysing any constraints that might impose. Trying to write a naturally recursive algorithm in a non-recursive way is more likely to cause problems than in analysing and providing for the likely maximum storage needs of the recursive equivalent.[5] This point is also made by Forsyth *et al.* (1993) in discussing high-integrity Ada.

6.1.3 Multiple entrance/multiple exit

This tends to be a contentious issue among programmers. The concept originates in structured programming and is quite simple: every functional component should have only one way in and one way out, to facilitate reasoned argument. However, in some circumstances, this requires setting numerous state variables to test on program exit, and in other circumstances can also lead to deeply nested code to avoid a perhaps more natural separate `return`. It is related to the `goto` debate which raged in the 1970s and 1980s. The author has not personally found this a problem when functional components are complexity limited using the techniques described in Section 7.3.1, and is unaware of any studies showing that such programs are unequivocally worse as a result. As such, no recommendations will be made here, *provided* complexity limiting is in operation.

6.1.4 Overloading and reloading

Overloading is one of those concepts that appears terribly attractive on first inspection but whose implications for problematic behaviour only sink in after some experience. In a nutshell, overloading occurs when the same item, for example an operator, is used for more than one kind of operation, and the actual operation carried out depends on the context in which the operator is encountered. *Reloading* is the author's nomenclature when an item, such as an operator, is used for other than its more usual meaning but has essentially only one meaning within the language. An example in C and FORTRAN, among other languages, is the assignment operator, '='. Although C and FORTRAN have expressions built on mathematical notation, both use the mathematical equality operator '=' for assignment. This fact confused the author terribly during his early days as a mathematician trying to get to grips with digital computation as he simply could not come to grips with statements such as a = a + 1. Eventually, to the author's relief, a kindly passing guru explained that it didn't actually mean what it said. There followed a period of enlightenment where the author could proudly explain what this strange expression meant, until he started working on formal systems in the early 1980s when he realized that his first reactions were correct and he really didn't understand this kind of thing. Such confusion is at the heart of the problem with overloading and reloading.

---

[5] It may be alright for Brian and Dennis, but this author at least feels as though his brain has been turned inside out after analysing some pieces of recursive code.

Most languages inherently use overloading. For example, the + operator is used to add together integer-valued components as well as floating-point components in many languages. In each case, the compiler must generate different code. The degree of overloading varies of course, as in the following example, whereby the C assignment operator is extended for structures:

```
...
struct s_t a,b;
...
a = b;
```

In this case, the assignment operator assigns each corresponding component of the structure a to its equivalent component in b. Since the nature of the structure is arbitrary, this assignment can do many sub-assignments, and as such is overloaded. Overloading of the assignment operator rarely causes confusion, and is a natural thing to overload. Unfortunately, some languages have taken this concept to extremes. In C++, for example, overloading is allowed to such an extent that the consequent effect on readability and therefore understandability must certainly prejudice the ability to write safe code. For example, the fact that the comma operator can be overloaded means that the issue of sequence points in C, i.e. points in the execution flow at which it can be guaranteed that all side-effects have been completed, is not yet resolved and may be extremely difficult to resolve satisfactorily in C++, prejudicing an important contribution to safe programming in C. Among the very few operators that cannot be overloaded currently is the '.' connective operator, and proposals were processed to overload even this! If this were not enough, a suggestion to overload white space was also apparently considered at one stage, but not formally proposed.[6] Perhaps the language designers might as well overload all the keywords as well, moving C++ to the very pinnacle of the Tower of Babel.

The following example was constructed by Sean Corfield to illustrate just how opaque code can become with indiscriminate overloading:

```
class C
{
public:
        operator int ();
};
class B
{
public:
        operator char* ();
};
class A
{
```

---

[6] It was actually suggested on 1 April—a lovely joke taken seriously in some quarters. There is a nice phrase in German for this: '*Man weiss nie wo der witz ist*'.

```
public:
        int operator[] (int);
};
main()
{
        A          a;
        B          b;
        C          c;
        int        i;
        char *     p;

        i = a[0];   // a.operator[] (0)
        i = b[0];   // b.operator char * () [0]
        i = i[p];   // reversed operands, i.e. p[i]
        i = c[p];   // c.operator int () [p]
                    // i.e., p[c.operator int ()]
        i = b[c];   // b.operator char* () [c.operator int ()]
        i = c[b];   // c.operator int () [b.operator char* ()]
                    // i.e. b.operator char* () [c.operator int () ]
```

The last two examples are particularly obscure! Other examples, also from Sean Corfield, show that it is quite simple to overload standard arithmetic operators, such as '+' , so that they are no longer even commutative. This, unfortunately, is also possible in C if either operand has a side-effect. While there are mathematical entities for which this is the case, the author can imagine the havoc that casual use could wreak.

The author has always believed that it should not be necessary to write a compiler in order to understand a language, but the current progress of C++ certainly gives cause for concern if its rapid growth continues into the safety-related development area, with features such as the above legally available to the applications programmer.

To the author's knowledge, overloading is not addressed by any of the draft safety standards at the moment, but examples such as the above suggest rather strongly that it should be. In this regard, C is quite simple in that no overloading beyond that described already is allowed. Other existing standardized languages, such as Ada and FORTRAN 90, already allow some degree of overloading of operators, although in the case of Ada, assignment overloading is somewhat constrained. Overloading is a classic example of a linguistic feature which is an excellent idea for a certain class of problem and infinitely abusable for all other classes.[7] Features of this kind should be explicitly banned in safety-related development unless there are strong, independent and highly experienced auditing bodies who can confirm

---

[7] For example, overloading arithmetic operators to include higher-order objects such as vectors and matrices is highly laudable and has a formal basis in mathematics provided the overloading is defined sensibly (unlike an early version of FORTRAN 90 whereby matrices of different rank and dimension could be assigned without requiring the compiler to complain).

that use is indeed suitable for the problem at hand and who are prepared to officially condone their use.

6.1.5 Inheritance

Inheritance in terms of computer languages means that one object derives properties from another and is a key feature of object-oriented development. In C++, such properties can be derived from base classes by the mechanism of inheritance. Provided that inheritance is hierarchical, i.e. each inheriting object has only one parent object, things remain simple, just as in database design. However, if an inheriting object has more than one parent object, the resulting structure is complex. In database design jargon, it has become a *network* or *plex* structure (Martin, 1977). In C++, this concept is known as *multiple inheritance*. Unfortunately, the complexity of plex structures means that if you design the objects incorrectly or you wish to change them to incorporate new functionality, exactly the same maintenance problems occur as arise in database manipulation, when the underlying data schema become inappropriate with respect to new requirements. Much was written in the database world on this subject in the 1970s and 1980s and the C++ community is beginning to learn the same painful lessons. As a result, most C++ standards in the author's experience explicitly forbid multiple inheritance. The situation does not directly affect C users as yet, so no recommendations can be made and the matter will be left here.

6.1.6 The influence of grammar

The grammar of a language has an enormous effect on its readability. Consider for example the problems of moving between French, German and English. In French and English, verbs generally separate the subjects and the objects of the sentence, whereas in German the verb conventionally appears at the end of the sentence. This does not cause a problem for the German reader reading German or the English reader reading English, but it certainly causes a problem for the English reader reading German and vice versa. This is akin to the problems caused by variable programming style, although with spoken and written languages, the enormous natural redundancy, as hinted at in Section 3.1, allows unambiguous communication to be carried out if required, although this seems to be increasingly rare in the worlds of diplomacy and so on.

Although the average C programmer need not generally be familiar with the intricacies of programming language grammar in general, a minor digression will be made at this point to illustrate some of the most important points. The reason for this is that *a human programmer reads a programming language just as a compiler does*. Therefore, languages that are difficult to write compilers for are likely to be difficult to read if those features that cause the difficulty are used. Languages that are difficult to read and write encourage mistakes and are therefore intrinsically unsafe. Three features essentially determine how simple, and therefore safe, it is to express algorithms in a programming language:

- The *context sensitivity* of the language.

- The number of *semantic irregularities*.
- *Notational complexity*.

Context sensitivity

Programming languages are easy to read if, at any point, the next word uniquely determines the sentence construction. This is called a *one-token lookahead grammar*. Computer scientists have nice formal ways of describing the *syntax* of grammars known as Backus–Naur Form (BNF) (Naur, 1963). Consider a grammar for which the basic structure is a noun followed by a verb followed by either an adverb or a noun. This grammar could be written in BNF form as:

```
sentence:   noun verb noun
          | noun verb adverb

noun:       DOG  | CAT
verb:       ATE
adverb:     WELL | BADLY
```

Here, the upper case words are called *terminals*. They are atomic in the sense that they cannot be split up. The lower case words are *non-terminal* in that they can be split up and must therefore appear on the left-hand side of a *rule*. A rule is simply a non-terminal separated from its decomposition(s) by a colon. Terminals must, by definition, only appear on the right-hand side of a rule. The '|' character is used to indicate 'or'.

Now consider a typical sentence using this grammar:

```
dog ate well
       ^
```

Assume a language parser (machine or human) has just absorbed the word ate as indicated by the ^. (The parser has been fed the word 'ate' by the earlier *lexical analysis* stage, which glued together the 'a', 't' and 'e' into a *token*.) The structure of the grammar is such that looking at the next word alone uniquely determines the structure of the sentence. It can only be a noun or an adverb.

Intrinsically simple languages can always be written in this form. For example, with the single exception that typedef needs special treatment, the C language can be written in this form (Kernighan and Ritchie, 1988). The advantage of this is that parsers for such grammars can be automatically generated using tools such as the admirable UNIX utility yacc, or its cousin, GNU bison. This obeys one of the central rules of safe software development, whereby use is made of existing exceedingly robust technology, quite apart from the speed advantages (which are frequently considerable).

Some languages, such as FORTRAN 77, do not appear at first hand to be one-token lookahead grammars because of such features as the i/o implied do loop:

```
write(*,*) (a(i),b(j),i=1,10,j=1,10)
                 1    2
```

The problem here is that there are essentially two types of comma, indicated by the 1 and 2 above. If they are simply passed through as commas to the grammar parser, the parser cannot tell which is which and cannot resolve the grammatical construct uniquely (called a shift-reduce conflict in parsing-speak). However, this problem can be resolved by introducing more intelligence into the lexical analysis stage, such that the lexical analyser recognizes the two different types of comma and passes this distinction to the grammar parser. The parser can then be written using one-token lookahead parsing technology.

Unfortunately, the grammar for some languages is such that this can be extremely difficult, if not impossible, and for which front-ends have to be hand-crafted using *recursive descent*, which inevitably involves a considerable degree of recreating the wheel, with potential implications for unreliability. This seems to be the case with C++ at the time of writing, where as far as is known, it is very difficult to write a one-token lookahead grammar for the full language, owing essentially to ambiguities in the grammar, such as that involving expression statements and declarations.[8] In this case, it may be necessary to inspect the whole statement to determine which one it is.

It is from small features such as this that big problems grow. Here, the similarity between expression statements and declarations in some circumstances, as well as a couple of other subtle issues, is forcing at least some C++ compiler writers to hand-craft a large part of the grammar analyser, which could otherwise make use of a large body of extremely robust parsing technology based around one-token lookahead grammars. In other words, a small apparently innocuous addition to the grammar could be responsible, via a long chain of events, for a failure in a nuclear reactor control software component in the future, demonstrating again that software development is essentially *chaotic*. Other engineering disciplines have learned to their cost to avoid such casual increase in system complexity, and software engineering should follow suit as quickly as possible. From a safety-related viewpoint, a notable reduction in complexity could be achieved by mandating the use of languages for which one-token lookahead grammars existed, at least until such time as hand-crafted parsers could be proved correct. The author understands that this would be a highly controversial requirement!

The growth of semantic irregularity

The second issue of semantic irregularity is of particular importance in the safe use of programming language. The grammar syntax defined in the previous section generates the following sentences:

```
DOG ATE CAT
CAT ATE DOG
DOG ATE DOG
CAT ATE CAT
DOG ATE WELL
DOG ATE BADLY
CAT ATE WELL
CAT ATE BADLY
```

---

[8] The ambiguity arises if an expression statement with a function-style explicit type conversion as its leftmost sub-expression is encountered. This could be confused with a declaration in which the first declarator begins with a '(' unless the whole statement is inspected (Stroustrup 1991).

All these sentences are legal syntactically and furthermore make sense (the cat could have been a panther). This grammar therefore has well-defined syntax and semantics, with no irregularities. If however, the meaning of cat was restricted to be a household cat, the second sentence (and possibly the fourth) would be nonsensical. The general syntax would remain the same, but the semantics would become irregular in that there would be *exceptions*. From these simple beginnings, real programming languages, while remaining well-defined syntactically, can degenerate quickly in a combinatorial explosion of irregularities. Consider for example adding the terminal IGNORED to the possible verbs. The number of syntactically legal sentences would be doubled, but only half of the new ones would make any real sense. Hence the addition of one new terminal would degrade the semantic integrity of the language, i.e. the proportion of sentences making sense, from a notional 100 per cent to $12/16 = 75$ per cent. To see this explosion of irregularity in real life, the reader should consult the FORTRAN 90 programming standard, for example, where even a simple declaration has many exceptions.

The problem with exceptions is quite simply that they significantly affect the programmer's ability to construct sensible sentences. By definition, therefore, they prejudice the ability to write safely. It takes many years for a child to learn a spoken language so as to avoid the nonsensical irregularities. If the same is required of programming staff, it is not surprising that software is so unreliable, given the author's observation that the average amount of relevant experience a programmer might have is still relatively low.

Notational complexity

C has a poor reputation in this regard due to its highly compact syntax, but when this is assimilated, C is not a complex language, as might be expected from its essentially one-token lookahead parsing nature. There remain, however, some areas that definitely require some thought to dissect. An example of this is provided by the existence of pointers to functions. These can be so difficult to read for the inexperienced programmer that Kernighan and Ritchie (1988) actually include a simple programming tool which parses them and translates them into plain English. For example:

```
void * (*PFV)(char *, int *);
```

declares a pointer to a function taking two arguments, a pointer to char and a pointer to int, and returning a pointer to void. As Kernighan and Ritchie (1988) point out, this mechanism is best used with the typedef mechanism to declare types of direct relevance to objects of interest to the programmer, as in the following:

```
typedef    void * (*PFV)(char *, int *);
...
PFV        funky;
```

However, when used indiscriminately, they can rapidly obscure the simplest of code and feature frequently in the entries for the annual Obfuscated C competition (Libes, 1993). From a safety-related viewpoint, the simple answer is that they should never be allowed outside the typedef mechanism.

C++ currently has a formidable notational complexity, which does not bode well, but in view of the evolutionary nature of the language, nothing more will be said until the language is comparatively discussed below, although the author confesses to mild nausea faced with certain C++ constructs.

Readers who wish to know more about language grammars in general and those for C in particular should consult the excellent texts of Kernighan and Pike (1984) and Schreiner and Friedman (1985).

6.1.7 Problems with pointers

Pointers have a shaky reputation in any language. They can be simultaneously responsible for the most elegant, stable algorithm and the most appalling abuse imaginable. Experienced users might not go so far as the eminent computer scientist C. A. R. Hoare, who is quoted as saying that 'pointers are the goto of the '80s',[9] but many attempts have been made to tame this beast with very variable and generally limited success. In C, unfortunately, the use of pointers is almost completely uninhibited by the language definition itself, although some of the worst abuses, such as illegally dereferencing a pointer (i.e. accessing an uninitialized or illegal part of memory to which it currently points), are at least formally undefined behaviour. It has also been seen in Section 5.3.5 that such abuse can be detected by various dynamic reliability tools.

Current draft safety standards skirt around the problem. While they might specifically address dynamic objects, which are intimately associated with pointers, they do not guide the programmer in how to deal with this attractive but potentially lethal feature.

It can be expected that pointers might prove difficult to deal with by considering the following two points:

- Gries (1981), in discussing formal proof arguments for various language features, mentions the difficulty in dealing with indexed arrays, before settling on an elegant way of handling them as function references. Other authors have gone further and banned them directly from their axiomatic approach.
- Indexed arrays are no more than disguised pointers, as is evidenced for example by the fact that in C, indexed arrays are immediately converted to pointers by the compiler, so that:

```
a[i] is synonymous with *(a+i)
```

It is worthwhile discussing briefly just a few typical abuses, which, nevertheless, might surprise even the relatively experienced user.

Alignment and byte order

The C language allows casting between different data types using a labyrinthine and

---

[9] Leaping on the bandwagon, an anonymous contributor has already made the quotation that 'Polymorphism is the goto of the '90s'. Note that each succeeding generation needs a more complex word to express its collective mistake. This may be because other users keep trade-marking all the normal words, leading[TM] to[TM] many[TM] potential[TM] complications[TM] in[TM] the[TM] future[TM].

largely misunderstood set of rules.[10] This itself can be a dangerous practice, but a potentially far worse abuse concerns the ability explicitly to cast pointers to different types.[11] This is discussed in detail by Czeck and Feldman (1993), for example, and can be summarized by the following code fragment:

```
int     i, *ip;
char    c, *cp;
char    memblock[] ={ 'abcdefghijk'};
...                      /*    Assume to be aligned    */
cp      = memblock;
cp++;                    /*    Point at b in memblock  */
ip      = (int *) cp;    /*    Cast the pointer         */
i       = *ip;           /*    What goes into i?        */
```

The contents of i vary dramatically from machine to machine. On some widely used machines the code simply crashes, because int addresses are supposed to be aligned on a word boundary, whereas on others with no such requirement, it works systematically. The author has seen such code with the reason given that the programmer wanted to operate on blocks of four characters at a time, but it is very easy for a relatively inexperienced programmer to use this kind of feature quite innocently without realizing the effects. In safety-related code, it should of course be forbidden, and is detectable by a number of the tools discussed earlier. Czeck and Feldman (1993) argue that because its use is allowed by the standard, it should be defined so as to behave portably, which is very reasonable, although the author would prefer it to be banned altogether rather than elevated from its currently undefined behaviour.

Multiple indirection

In essence, multiple indirection allows the ability to define pointers to pointers to pointers.... Two levels of indirection, i.e. a pointer to a pointer, is sometimes called a *handle*. However, anybody who has used multiple indirection will agree on how difficult it is to think about, let alone to reason about. More than two levels should not be considered in a safety-related application, unless it arises implicitly through the use of a multi-dimensional array.

To summarize, it would be counter-productive to ban pointers in safety-related software, as many fundamental data structures, such as linked lists and trees, rely on their existence for elegant and therefore comprehensible and more reliable implementation. Special care must be taken to guarantee their valid use, such as the use of assertions and dynamic analysis tools as discussed in Chapter 5.

---

[10] The reader ought to go away and read about *compatible types* and *assignment compatibility* in the standard or one of the numerous translations into the vernacular, for example Jaeschke (1991) or Plum (1989). To give a feel for this vital but impenetrable area, the standard itself states 'Two types have compatible type if their types are the same'. It then promptly footnotes this with the statement that 'Two types need not be identical to be compatible'. To close this particular logical nightmare, the author's *Oxford English Dictionary* defines 'identical' as 'the same'. Faced with this, either a stiff gin and tonic is recommended or, alternatively, the reader could lie down until the need to understand it goes away.

[11] For example, it is a potentially fatal mistake to assume that pointers and int are the same size.

6.2 C vs. Ada

Ada, as is well-known, was sponsored by the US Department of Defense both to reduce the vast number of implementation languages in which its projects were realized and also to improve the reliability of the resultant software. Ada has many good points, but also a considerable number of flaws. The paper by Hoare (1981) casts an interesting, largely negative, but highly entertaining light on the development of this language. For whatever reasons, it has not been as widely adopted as was hoped, and at the time of writing, C and C++ were the languages with the most rapidly growing user base, with the use of Ada perhaps even slightly diminishing, although it is probably used in the majority of the really big software projects. The response of the standards committee is to move Ada 83 to object orientation with Ada 9X. Given that the standard is already enormous, the move to object orientation may lead to gravitational distortion in the immediate vicinity of a copy and perhaps little else. In 50 years' time, computer scientists will look back and ask themselves why the computer scientists of the 20th century had to keep *adding* things. It is interesting to note that in Forsyth *et al.* (1993) and Hutcheon *et al.* (1993a, b), great efforts are made to make Ada safe by removing many of the features which the committee keeps adding.

The requirement to use Ada in some form, as is mandatory for certain developments, has led to extraordinary contortions in certain projects, and the author has personally come across the following:

- Writing projects in C and machine-converting them to Ada. Perhaps the only thing that can be said about this practice is that the requirements of machine conversion might place some desirable restrictions on the otherwise uninhibited use of C. This practice seems surprisingly widespread.
- Proposing both Ada and C solutions for the same project and allowing the generally much cheaper C development to win out on strictly economic grounds. Little, too, can be said about this. Even safety-related projects have budgets and deadlines, but the author feels passionately that a decision made purely on economic grounds for a development with large-scale implications for human or environmental safety is simply negligent.
- Writing C with an elaborate set of `#define` statements such that the resulting code looks like Ada. The author has audited such packages in the aerospace industry. The main problem with this is that the programs don't look like either Ada or C, with potentially serious implications for readability and therefore maintainability. Perhaps more seriously, from a reliability point of view, the effectiveness of code inspections, which are known to detect many problems, may be damaged because of the stylistic unfamiliarity.

The first reaction of many Ada supporters is to argue that it is a much better specified language than C and therefore far more suitable than C. One of the aims of this book is to emphasize the point that the real object is to determine *how safe the language can be made* rather than the intrinsic safety of its basic definition. It is therefore probably worthwhile again pointing out to the purists that whereas the C language standard is currently subject to only around 50 interpretations (cf. Chapter 2), the Ada language standard has over 2000 such items outstanding and even the extended Pascal standard has 85 (although the original Pascal standard has only 1). This amply justifies the emphasis that the draft safety standard IEC SC65A, discussed at some length in Chapter 1, places on the use of subsets of languages in its higher integrity levels.

As one of the design goals of Ada was safety, many potentially dangerous situations in Ada are marked as such. In essence there are five kinds:

- `Constraint_Error`
  This exception error is raised when there is a *constraint violation*. (This nomenclature is also used for C.)
- `Numeric_Error`
  If an arithmetic operation evaluates to a value outside the range defined for the output, this exception is raised.
- `Storage_Error`
  Ada implementations can allocate a fixed amount of storage to run a program, so that if this storage is exceeded for any reason this exception is raised.
- `Program_Error`
  These exceptions *may* be raised by an Ada implementation when dependence on undefined behaviour is detected, which in Ada parlance is known as an erroneous program, but this is not mandated and is a terrible loophole in the Ada language.
- `Tasking_Error`
  These are raised in certain abnormal tasking conditions.

Although not simple, Table 6.4, attempts to compare various features in the Ada and C languages for safe use. The table is not complete and the author is certainly not familiar with all the tools available for both languages, but it is representative of many concerns in safety-related development and it gives an idea of comparative treatment of unsafe features. The author welcomes any feedback on absent or incomplete items. The list was loosely extracted from the comprehensive Ada text by Watt *et al.* (1987), and consequently differs from the discourse given in Cullyer *et al.* (1991) and described earlier. Constraint errors for features in Ada that have no equivalent in C, such as the selected wait mechanism, have been omitted. It should be pointed out that there are a number of Ada subsets that broadly attempt to inhibit the weak areas, but the subsets are rather different, which casts a little doubt on the process. Forsyth *et al.* (1993) is recommended for further reading.

Note that in the case of qualified expressions in Ada, whereby the safe programmer will qualify an expression allowing a compiler check to be made, a similar mechanism is available in C. In both cases the feature is optional, so its use is dependent on training.

In the case of `Unchecked_Conversion`, the Ada community may feel unfairly treated by its appearance in the above table, but the fact of the matter is that it is often used on the grounds of efficiency and it is notoriously error-prone and its effects are, by definition, unchecked.[12] The feature is present in C without such a conspicuous name but with excellent tool support which can detect its abuse.

---

[12] The author interviewed a major developer for Ada defence systems in February 1994, whose safety-related systems had developed serious problems because of the use of this feature. It was argued that its use was necessary because of deficiencies in Ada and no tools existed to support its use. Numerous other examples were cited by the same developer.

Table 6.4 Comparison of various Constraint (C) and Program (P) errors in Ada with equivalent Undefined (U), Unspecified (S), Implementation-defined (I) or Constraint Violation (C) features of C, and their detection

Feature	Ada type	Check	C type	Check	Where
Violation of a range constraint	C	√	—	—	—
Violation of an index constraint	C	√	U	√	Tool
Violation of length restriction	C	√	—	—	—
Arithmetic overflow	C	√	U	√	Tool
Use of undefined value	P	X	U	√	Tool
Dependence on evaluation order	P	X	S	√	Tool
Dependence on mechanism for passing parameters	P	X	U/I	√	Tool
Directional restriction on parameter passing	C	√	C/—	√	Compiler/Tool
Actual and formal parameters must match by type and number	C	√	C/U	√	Compiler/Tool
Qualified expressions	C	√	—	√	assert
Dereferencing a null pointer	C	√	U	√	Tool
Miscalling of library functions	C	√	U	√	Tool
Use of Unchecked_Conversion	—	X	—	√	Tool

To summarize this section, Table 6.4 may certainly help to adjust a generally held belief that Ada is *much* safer than C. C is a very simple language, and in many of the notorious areas for error-prone behaviour the tool support for C is so good that it can match and in some cases exceed the equivalent security in Ada. Of course, there remain areas not represented in the above table in which Ada is fundamentally more secure and also in some areas of exception handling in which Ada is very *insecure*, but which C does not even attempt to address (although C++ intends to). Be that as it may, it should be obvious that if C is used with the available tool support, many common classes of error can be detected statically or dynamically and a highly reliable implementation produced. *The important thing in safety-related development in C is the guarantee that the tools were actually used and used in a suitably restrictive manner.* The Ada community could reasonably argue that the above comparison concerns a subset of C and the full Ada. In defence, it is a naturally defined subset (cf. the concept of a strictly conforming program) and there are a number of safe subsets of Ada, unfortunately partially disjoint (Hutcheon *et al.*, 1993b), so the area is somewhat confusing.

One aspect in which C enjoys a massive and incontrovertible advantage is in implementation costs. According to current figures, a validated C compiler, complete with all the third-party tools mentioned in Chapter 5, comes out significantly cheaper than a single copy of an Ada compiler.[13] Cost is an important issue in safety-related systems. Cheaper tools and more widely available skills, mean that a greater percentage of the overall budget can be spent on manual inspections, better design and other safety-enhancing activities.

[13] The author has recently been informed of the release of a GNU Ada compiler. Whether this widens the use of the language or narrows it by putting the Ada compiler developers under pressure remains to be seen. The GNU C compiler did not affect the C market when it was first introduced as C compilers were normally free, and C++ compilers are pretty cheap anyway (at least on PCs!). The author can strongly recommend the GNU C and C++ compilers.

Finally, it is a matter for very considerable concern that Ada is such a massively complex language in which even compiler validation is a major problem (Forsyth *et al.*, 1993). For example, there is a strong perceived need to prove the equivalence of the generated object code to the source code. In contrast, the simplicity of C and its relationship to the underlying machine makes this rather more realistic, quite apart from the legendary reliability quoted for C compilers, certainly in comparison with their Ada counterparts.[14] Ada 9X appears regrettably to be following in the dishonourable tradition of Algol 68, FORTRAN 90 and C++ in the race to provide poorly defined new features, such as object orientation, which the safety-related community by and large cannot handle with sufficient confidence. As has been noted already elsewhere, it is in the face of no empirical evidence that these features actually improve matters.

This section has not sought to elevate C over Ada in safety-related systems. Rather, it seeks to make a strong argument that a tool-constrained C environment is at least comparable to a tool-constrained Ada environment.[15]

6.3 C vs. C++

It is a little difficult to describe the safety-related implications of the differences between these two languages, for the following reasons:

- C++ is not yet a standardized language nor is it likely to be until at least 1997. In addition, its definition is still changing.
- The author has as yet few statistics to perform direct comparisons between the languages, and a detailed comparison will have to wait.

Be that as it may, C++ applications for safety-related work are already being produced, and so a brief attempt will be made here to address the differences.

Opinions vary alarmingly on the benefits of C++ and indeed its relationship with C. For example, in the same conference Bailey (1993) notes that C++, if anything, is more prone to run-time errors leading to corruption than C, while O'Carroll (1993) concentrates almost entirely on eulogies. Simultaneously, Whitehead (1993) incorrectly states that 'Migrating from C to C++ is made more simple by the fact that C is a subset of C++', while Jones (1993b) carefully points out the truth. If the experts disagree so alarmingly, the programmer in the trenches can certainly be forgiven for being confused.

---

[14] The author talked to numerous Ada developers in the period of writing this book (March 1993–February 1994). Each one confirmed that it was only the last year or so in which reasonably reliable compilers had become available, some eleven years after the standard appeared. To contrast the relative complexity, the author knows of a remarkably sophisticated C interpreter, developed from scratch over a period of a few weeks by Mark Russell at the University of Kent in the UK, to embed within ups, his formidable public domain graphical C source debugger. This considerable intellectual feat led to the temporary reputation of being the least sun-tanned person in Southern England.

[15] David Blyth, in a personal communication to the author, makes the point that, in a safety-related environment, the language and the compiler should be treated simultaneously. A good language for which there exists only average compilers is no better than an average language for which compilers are good.

Bailey's paper (Bailey, 1993) is worth closer attention on the subject of run-time errors. He states that C++ inherits all of C's sources of corruption but adds references, which, although a powerful part of the C++ language, may end up referencing objects that no longer exist, just as with conventional C pointers. He then goes on to state that a characteristic of C++ programs is that so much of the action is buried away in constructors and destructors, for example, which can hide mistakes in otherwise innocuous places. The author entirely concurs with this and has seen a number of C++ systems whose class system was so forbiddingly complex that many such problems were experienced. This style of hiding vast amounts of complexity in the class system appears to be a C++ programming paradigm. From a safety-related view, any language which puts more strain on the run-time system's ability to detect errors while hiding complexity in new ways is cause for some concern, especially when the language is not yet stable.

Points in favour of the way C++ is currently developing include:

- It is essentially a strongly typed language.
- It mandates function prototypes, guaranteeing interface consistency.
- It has a more natural and explicit way of providing initialization within the mechanism of constructors.

Although beyond the scope of the present book, the author's experience in implementing safety-related systems in C++, although limited, suggests that very considerable restrictions are currently necessary to promote a safe style. A simple example would be the explicit banning of multiple inheritance, which figures in a number of C++ programming standards that the author has seen.[16]

6.4 C vs. FORTRAN

Historically, FORTRAN has been used in many safety-related areas in the last 20 years or so as a result of its central position in scientific computing. These areas include aerospace modelling, chemical modelling for drugs and nuclear reactor control, each at the heart of safety-related computing. Most of the safety-related FORTRAN software in use today has been updated from the original FORTRAN 66 standard, to the FORTRAN 77 standard (ANSI X3.9-1978). In 1992, the very long-awaited FORTRAN 90 appeared at last. Unfortunately, this latest standardization attempt took so long to appear that many FORTRAN users appear to have deserted the language in favour of C or C++, and most FORTRAN organizations in the author's experience are only maintaining their FORTRAN applications. New developments are being carried out in C or C++, and hybrid systems of mixed C/C++ and FORTRAN seem to be increasingly common. If the interface consistency can be appropriately guaranteed, this seems a reasonable step forward given the existence of large, very widely used and presumably tested FORTRAN libraries. It also seems to be an essentially portable practice, even though outside the remit of either the C, C++ or FORTRAN standards. It can be noted in passing

---

[16] Note that, unfortunately, the C++ `iostream` library makes extensive use of this feature.

Table 6.5 Comparison of similar fault statistics on large FORTRAN 77 and C populations. In this case, faults were all statically detected

Type	FORTRAN 77	C
Number of executable lines per fault	86	41
Number of calls per fault	6.8	8.9
Number of arguments per fault	27.8	57
Interface faults as percentage of total faults	96%	26%
Total lines analysed so far in populations	3 305 628	1 583 104

that, as a block-structured language, C is more closely related to Ada, PL/1 and Pascal than to FORTRAN.

FORTRAN appears in this book because it is specifically mentioned in the IEC SC65A draft standard document. FORTRAN 66 and 77 are weakly typed languages with a static memory model. FORTRAN 90 provides *inter alia* several mechanisms for dynamic memory allocation.[17] As FORTRAN 90 is very recent and very little software has yet appeared in this dialect, attention will be focused on FORTRAN 77. One thing at least is certain. The FORTRAN 90 standard is monumentally complex, rendering the production of reliable compilers a difficult process. A mere glance at this standard can induce a catatonic state. For example, Rider (1993) quotes one of their compiler developers as saying, 'If something seems simple, you probably need to re-read the standard'. This is worrying to say the least, as the author believes that if a standard is sufficiently complex through irregularity to make writing a compiler difficult, it will be similarly complex to use. After all, the user and the compiler writer start from the same basic document. Linguistic complexity to *hide* complexity from the user is a different matter.

The author has performed large-scale experiments on FORTRAN 77 analogous to those described in Chapter 4 (Hatton, 1993b). Table 6.5 summarizes his findings.

As can be seen, in terms of inline fault rates, FORTRAN 77 is considerably superior to C, essentially due to the static memory model of the language and the absence of pointers. However, in terms of interface fault rates it is considerably worse, due most likely to the presence of function prototypes in C, which although used intermittently in C development generally, are used sufficiently to lower the static interface fault rate dramatically. The table also re-emphasizes the point that the initial safety of the language is irrelevant: it is how safe it can be made that matters. C has initially more potential problem areas, but static analysis can find them. The author cannot yet claim knowledge of which one finishes up the safest, but his experience with portability and compiler reliability strongly suggests that this may be C.

In the light of the above, the requirement of IEC SC65A to minimize the use of dynamic memory at the highest safety integrity levels seems justified, although, as discussed earlier, this perhaps should be reviewed in the case of C, given the presence of considerable tool support to detect abuse of this otherwise easily abusable feature. This appears to be the view of numerous developers, and dynamic memory and

---

[17] Recall, as was seen in Chapter 1, that the highest safety integrity levels consider dynamic memory to be a bad thing.

pointers frequently feature in safety-related developments *even though the tool support is not present*. This is very definitely unsafe practice.

To summarize, the tool support for avoidance of unsafe C features considerably exceeds that for FORTRAN, so a reasonable conclusion is that *provided such support is in place*, the move from FORTRAN to C in safety-related environments should be viewed as appropriate.

6.5 C vs. MODULA-2

Although Modula-2 is included in the comparison made by Cullyer *et al.* (1991), a more detailed and ultimately more useful one appears in Angele and Küpper (1992), although these authors too ignore the tool support for C. In this latter paper, the authors compare C and Modula-2 using the following criteria:

(a) *Separate vs. independent compilation*
   The authors distinguish between these by defining separate compilation as being compilation of a distinct component in isolation, but in such a way that the compiler is allowed to check the interface with its definition elsewhere. Independent compilation is compilation in isolation without any such checks. Modula-2 is a language supporting separate compilation, whereas in its standard definition, C is a language supporting separate compilation via the function prototype, but not mandating it, effectively providing independent compilation only. However, tool support such as QA C or PC-lint/Flexelint can enforce the consistent use of function prototypes by forbidding any old-style or implicit declarations or old-style definitions or by simply checking them.

(b) *Information hiding*
   Again Modula-2 naturally supports this concept better than C, but tool support such as QA C and PC-lint allows dangerous or illegal use of objects of unnecessarily wide scope to be detected.

(c) *Administration of modules*
   Modula-2 includes a mechanism that allows dependencies between modules to be described. C does not, but the UNIX make tool can be used instead, cf. Oram and Talbott (1991). Indeed, the standard C compiler on many UNIX platforms allows dependencies to be built in a form suitable for direct inclusion in make. On the author's Sparc, the command is essentially:

```
% cc -M *.c | grep -v '/usr/include' >> makefile
```

   This builds all the user-defined dependencies automatically and *appends* them to the existing makefile. (The earlier part of the makefile will contain the usual definitions, lists of object files, include file directories, compiler options and so on.) Note that here the grep is removing standard dependencies by deleting any lines containing references to /usr/include.

(d) *Mechanisms for passing parameters*
   Modula-2 provides more flexibility than C for passing parameters, but ultimately this is not a reliability issue. However they are passed, *consistency* is the most important thing, and this has been dealt with already. The authors of the

comparison make the incorrect observation here that every C subroutine is a function and therefore returns a value. This of course is not the case for a function declared to have a return type void.

(e) *Locality*

Modula-2 supports true block structuring, whereby functions can, for example, be nested. C does not. Like item (d), this is not of relevance to a safety argument.

(f) *Strong typing*

Modula-2 supports strong typing, although it allows it to be broken explicitly, which is unfortunate. C allows implicit casting as well as explicit casting, therefore breaking strong typing. However, this can be prevented by tool support, such as QA C and PC-lint. PC-lint even allows the enforced consistency of types derived from the built-in types using the typedef construct.

(g) *Detection of run-time errors*

Modula-2 compilers provide some support for the detection of run-time errors, although it can usually be switched off. C has at least a comparable level of run-time detection via a whole suite of tools, as was discussed in Section 5.3.5.

The languages are also compared for terseness, optimization and portability, with rather less forthright conclusions. In particular, there appear to be some problems with porting Modula-2. As has been reiterated at length, more is known about porting C between different platforms than any other language as a result of the huge amount of experience gained by porting UNIX, which is written almost entirely in C. If the guidelines in this book are followed, porting C amounts simply to re-compilation and linkage, as noted in Section 5.1.1.

Overall, this comparison is very valuable, and were the tool support not available this author would have no hesitation in recommending Modula-2 over C (and Ada for that matter). However, this book is not about the relative superiority of different programming languages. It is about the recognition that C is already being used without explicit guidance in many safety-related systems, and that provided the developers are mandated to use the kind of tool support described herein, thereby eliminating many of the dangerous coding practices described in this book, then C is at least as safe and well-defined as any of the other languages commonly used in safety-related systems. For something as complicated as a modern programming language, experience is the precursor to theory, and not the other way round.

7

PUTTING IT ALL TOGETHER:
EXAMPLE STANDARDS AND ENVIRONMENTS

In this section, all the results and advice documented in the previous chapters will be pulled together to provide examples of standards and environments embodying a current 'best practice' for safety-related C development.

7.1 THE STRUCTURE OF A SAFETY-RELATED PROGRAMMING STANDARD

There must be a programming standard and a set of stylistic guidelines, preferably in separate documents. The role of the programming standard is to define rules of linguistic use which *must* not be broken. The role of the style guide is to promote a common look to assist readability and therefore maintainability; however, the nature of style guides is such that they are not an enforceable document.

7.1.1 The programming standard

The programming standard is a crucial document in safety-related development, as it mirrors the background and expertise of the development staff. If a standard is sloppy, the code is likely to be sloppy. Its structure should address a number of issues that are considered to be of importance in safety-related systems and which were discussed in Section 1.2. These include:

- *Language justification* With any language, even a supposedly safe one, a justification for its use should be given. With C, which needs particularly careful treatment, a justification is of paramount importance. Such a justification

195

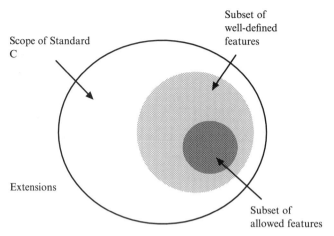

Figure 7.1 Explicit recognition of the subsetting approach which must form part of safety-related language use. The diagram is not to scale, although the author wonders sometimes, given the way modern programming languages swell so alarmingly.

should contain the precise reasons why the language was chosen—economic, efficiency, skill availability, compiler availability, status of validation of compiler and tool support and so on. For safety-related work, *everything* must be carefully considered. Decisions do not make themselves.

- *Scope and base standard*   It is important to define the developments to which the standard is to apply. In addition, the base document should be specifically defined to be the underlying internationally recognized standard, a theme which runs through all the current draft safety standards. *No extensions must be allowed.*

From this standard, safe subsetting can then follow to a level commensurate with the level of safety integrity required and budget available. Knowledge of the unspecified and undefined features should be exhibited, as discussed shortly, and developers should have access to the Standard C document. Figure 7.1 shows a subsetting approach like the layers of an onion. Note that not all well-defined features should be used: for example, `switch` statements without a `default` clause giving logical incompleteness, as discussed earlier.

- *Escalation policy*   It is vitally important that the programming standard should not be seen as static. Periodically, say every six months, the standard should be reviewed for its effectiveness by its authors and users, simultaneously taking into account any further developments in safe use of the base language, and perhaps tightening the standard further. It may in some circumstances even be relaxed, as features previously thought to be of concern turn out to be benign in practice. Either way, the standard is subject to the same pressures for change as the software itself. All such changes, and the reasons for them, should be formally documented as addenda to the initial language justification.
- *Nomenclature*   The standard should define all the terms it uses. This may sound obvious, but it is frequently missing from standards the author has seen. Defining the terms makes clear the intention that the standard is an instrument of quality to be read by any potential third-party auditors as well as the developers.

- *Automatically enforceable rules, manually enforceable rules and guidelines* By definition, rules are enforceable by some means. An audit for standards conformance is an audit against the rules governing the development. On the other hand, guidelines are recommendations, but which are not enforced. The standard *should clearly distinguish between these three categories.* If a rule is automatically enforceable, it is possible for the developer to *guarantee* the absence of transgressing items. If the rule cannot be automatically enforced but is considered important enough to be a rule, it is impossible to guarantee that all offending issues are detected, although manual inspections should be present to monitor such things. However, no manual inspection is perfect. *The ideal standard is 100 per cent automatically enforceable.* For safety's sake, however, if an issue is not automatically enforceable it is better to leave it as a rule and commit best endeavours to its detection than to downgrade it to a guideline and hope nobody notices. An example of such a feature would be an illegal pointer dereference, which, although tool-detectable, is detectable only dynamically and might therefore not be detected due to inadequacies in test coverage when the tool is active.

  When standards can, in the main, be enforced automatically, manual inspections can concentrate on algorithmic considerations and equivalence to requirements, which are difficult if not impossible to automate with today's level of understanding. *It is of vital importance not to squander manual inspection time in safety-related systems on items that can be automated.*

- *Complexity and coverage standards* These might appear in a separate document, although they are directly relevant to the code itself and can reasonably be included in the programming standard.

- *Portability* A safety-related application needs to address whether or not it is intended to run on multiple platforms. In the author's experience, many development groups would like to think that they are developing platform-independent code, but have not formally considered the implications and requirements. C has a formally defined set of features, which, although sufficiently well-defined to construct reasoned arguments, are implementation-defined, as was discussed in Section 2.4. Hence any reasoned argument may become invalid immediately the platform (and in some cases simply the compiler) changed. The standard should carefully state whether portability is a design goal and, if so, should state clearly what extra checks have been incorporated to facilitate this. In practice, this means analysing the list of implementation-defined features of the C standard for potential risk and, if migration to C++ is contemplated when that language is standardized, the known incompatibilities, as discussed in Section 2.10, should be addressed. In any case, application-compliant environments must be stated as discussed next.

Finally, the programming standard should clearly state the allowable conditions of compilation by providing an equivalent to Tables 7.1 and 7.2.

7.1.2 The style guide

As was stated above, the style guide is not intended to be an enforceable document, and in contrast to the programming standard, style guides would be expected to vary

Table 7.1 Compilation compliance table for a safety-related application. Ideally, it should be filled out as follows

Compliance item	Yes	No
Compilable on a Standard C platform	√	
Compilable on a K&R C platform		√
Contains implementation-defined features		√
Compilable by a C++ compiler	√	

Table 7.2 List of compliant compilers, i.e. compilers and platforms on which the application has been successfully compiled *and* has successfully completed its regression and other tests. The nature of safety-related applications suggests that it would be prudent that this list should have at least *two* members, even if it is only to be run on one. If a safety-related application uses floating-point arithmetic, the more the merrier. Note that it would be reasonable to include any compiler options in use

Compiler	Version	Platform
Compiler X	1.1.1Y	Whatever
...		

considerably from site to site. The style guide would typically address the following:

- *Indentation standards* This crusty item is responsible for more acrimony on standards committees than any other. The three main types are K&R, indented and exdented, as documented, for example, by Plum (1989). In truth, it is far more important that a file is consistent in its use of one type than which type is used. Consistency at least should be strongly encouraged. (The author stubbornly refuses to be drawn into commenting on the number of character positions per indent, although he would note that 100 is probably too many.)
- *Identifier naming conventions* This also proves controversial, and again the actual convention is probably less important than achieving a reasonable mnemonic level, bearing in mind the restrictions of Standard C of 6 characters for identifiers of external visibility. Given that most environments allow more, it is entirely reasonable to use more, but *marking this as a requirement for the product.*
- *Layout of comment* Yet again, the content is more important than the style. For example, each file should have a standard comment header containing information such as:
  —Keywords for an automated revision control system such as sccs or rcs. A manual revision control system with lots of version information in the header will almost certainly fail under the weight of change which affects most software systems.
  —Copyright notice.
  The authors experience has been that nearly everything else that goes in comment headers is impossible to keep up to date, and may in fact be dangerously misleading.[1]

---

[1] The author can recall a FORTRAN component he audited some years ago in the aerospace industry with a comment header in excess of 14 000 lines, i.e. about half as big as this book. By the time he got to the code, which consisted of a couple of hundred lines, his forehead was slumped against the screen and he was gibbering quietly.

7.2 CODE RESTRICTIONS FOR SAFETY-RELATED C

Much has been said throughout this book about the need to limit the use of language in safety-related systems, a view strongly supported by the draft safety standards discussed in Chapter 1, which refer to well-defined subsets, as well as by individual authors, for example Jackson (1993). Here specific recommendations will be made, making reference to more detailed discussions earlier in this book for justification.

In theory, as a minimum then, a safety-related program should contain no unspecified or undefined behaviour and a *portable* safety-related program should be strictly conforming, thereby making it well-defined. However, this can reasonably be weakened in one sense, but should be strengthened in another. It can be weakened in the sense that a number of the features leading to unspecified, undefined or implementation-defined behaviour are sufficiently obscure or irrelevant that they can safely be ignored. It should be strengthened by specifically excluding well-defined items that can lead to problematic behaviour, going beyond the stated requirements of the draft standards discussed in Chapter 1. This was illustrated in Fig. 7.1.

In practice, it has proved a little awkward to arrange the items hierarchically. They could be arranged in a similar order to Sections 2.2–2.11; however, the difference between static and dynamic detection is a complicating factor in that static detection can be guaranteed if tool-supported, whereas dynamic detection cannot be guaranteed, even if tool-supported. In the end, the author decided that static/dynamic was a more natural split.

7.2.1 Static restrictions

All of the items which follow are detectable by one or other of the tools discussed in Section 5.3.4 and should *not* form part of a safety-related application unless any hazard associated with their presence has been quantified as acceptable.

(a) *Unspecified behaviour.* On the face of it, the very definition of unspecified behaviour suggests that it is of lesser importance than undefined behaviour because it refers to the behaviour of certain *legal* constructs; however, this is misleading, and items 7, 8 and 9 from Section 2.2 have all caused very serious problems in practice, although only when compilation environments have changed. Item 12 is not as serious but should be forbidden. Items 10, 14–18 and 20–22 can be avoided quite simply by wrapping functions or banning items, as described in (c) below. The rest are not of direct interest and are therefore omitted.

(b) *Undefined behaviour.* Items 1, 2, 4–14, 16–18, 21–25, 28–29, 35, 36, 42–54, 56–58, 61 and 62 of Section 2.3 could reasonably be excluded by static screening using the tools described in Section 5.3.4, although some are more important than others, and the degree of exclusion may be environment- or safety level-sensitive.

Forbidding the use of `setjmp/longjmp`, `offsetof` and `signal` statically avoids items 59 and 64–69. The many practical problems in the use of these features suggest that they are far too loosely defined to be safe (Plauger, 1992). Another candidate for exclusion on the grounds of incomplete definition is the concept of *bit-fields*, which takes out items 37 and 38. It is far safer to use masked integral types in practice. Item 93 can be avoided by wrapping functions, as described in (c) below. Finally, and perhaps regrettably, in spite of its unique capabilities, the use of variable number of arguments also falls into the same category of having numerous potential pitfalls, and should also be excluded, avoiding items 70–76. Banning multibyte characters avoids item 3. Exceptional cases will always arise justifying the use of `setjmp`, `longjmp`, `signal` and variable number of arguments, *but every occurrence should have a written justification and be highly localized.*

(c) Function wrappers should be provided for potentially problematic standard functions. A number of functions do not define their interfaces sufficiently unambiguously and should be wrapped by consistent functions and direct use of the raw functions banned. These functions are `ungetc`, `fopen`, `fgetpos`, `ftell`, `remove`, `rename`, `bsearch`, `qsort`, `time`, `date`, `clock`, `isalnum`, `isalpha`, `iscntrl`, `islower`, `isprint`, `isupper`, `perror`, `strerror`, `calloc`, `malloc`, `realloc`, `exit`, `fmod`, and, for floating-point arithmetic, all the mathematics functions. Actions can be anything from simply returning an agreed value for a successful call to `fgetpos` (unspecified behaviour) to always checking `malloc` for a returned null pointer or for a request to allocate zero bytes, with a defined response. The use of `system` probably ought to be banned completely as it is exceptionally difficult to wrap portably.

Banning the use of `#pragma`, `volatile` and `register`, takes out three implementation-defined behaviours.

It is interesting to note that the simple act of wrapping some functions for consistency and banning other items avoids no fewer than 9 unspecified behaviours, 18 undefined behaviours and 28 implementation-defined behaviours, accounting for 55/195 of the items in Appendix F or over 28 per cent, a significant achievement.

(d) *Interface consistency. Either* function prototypes should be enforced and implicit declarations banned if use can be made of a validated compiler, *or* none of the items mentioned in Table 4.5 should be allowed.

(e) *Stronger typing.* Implicit casting should be forbidden (Section 2.1.2). This overlaps some of the earlier undefined behaviour, but forces a strongly typed nature. Explicit casts should be formally justified.

(f) Any of the items in Table 2.5. These are either sloppy or likely to lead to problematic behaviour.

(g) Indirection of greater than two levels is definitely not recommended as discussed in Section 6.1.7.

(h) Function pointers should not be allowed, other than in a formally approved `typedef`.

(i) Recursion should be allowed only if accompanied by an analysis of the maximum additional memory necessary.

(j) Only ASCII-based character set implementations[2] should be used in a safety-related application at the moment, as the handling of other character sets,

---

[2] There is a reasonable argument to allow EBCDIC of course. In practice, the author has come across portability problems between this and ASCII-based systems, and the recommendation relates to the overwhelming preponderance of ASCII-based systems. A safety-related system should not be moved between the two with impunity.

multibyte characters and so on is too poorly defined and in a state of flux, as indicated in Section 2.1.3.

(k) Objects local to a file should be declared as static. In addition, it could be argued that the use of const (to protect objects from change) and volatile (to warn compilers of potentially invisible access) are safety-enhancing, where relevant, but the reader should be aware that when access is attempted to either volatile or const qualified objects through an lvalue which is not thus qualified the result is formally undefined.

7.2.2 Dynamic restrictions

No safety related program should be released with any of the following dynamically-detectable defects occurring during testing:

- Memory leakage.
- Array bound violations.
- Illegally dereferenced pointers.
- Arithmetic exceptions such as divide by zero.
- Illegally freed memory.
- Actual reliance on uninitialized memory (some potential dependencies are statically detectable).

These and other dynamically-detectable items allow the undefined items 12, 15, 19, 20, 26, 27, 29–34, 39–41, 55, 60, 63, 77–94, 96 and 97 of Section 2.3 to be avoided. Again, a number of these are extremely obscure and could reasonably be ignored with appropriate argument.

This means that, wherever possible, all unit testing should be run with the tools described in Section 5.3.5 active, while the test coverage targets described in Section 7.3.2 are achieved. In cross-compilation environments and time-critical applications, such detectability is greatly inhibited and other techniques must be considered.

7.2.3 Rationale

The recommendations in this book devolve directly from the author's observations that linguistic inconsistency is rife in real systems, as was proved in Chapter 4. However, although the nature of statically- and dynamically-detectable inconsistency is such that no reasonable person could argue against its removal once detected, it is important in safety-related work to estimate just how much protection this is likely to give. Unfortunately, a direct relationship between this and an improvement in mean time between failure is impossible to draw with current understanding; however, the following argument, due to Corfield (1993), suggests that a significant percentage of errors occurring in real systems are detectable by the techniques described in this book and therefore are capable of eradication.

The analysis centres around the taxonomy of bugs described in the Appendix of Beizer (1990). In essence, Beizer has divided up the various classes of bugs and their percentage of occurrence as in Table 7.3. Each category is further subdivided into detailed failures (indicated by the xxx). On the face of it, static and dynamic feature inhibition will not impact requirement or system-related issues, but should

Table 7.3 Beizer's classes of bugs

System, software/architecture	Beizer's category	Percentage
Functional requirements	1xxx	8.12
Functionality as implemented	2xxx	16.19
Structural bugs	3xxx	25.18
Data	4xxx	22.44
Implementation	5xxx	9.88
Integration	6xxx	8.98
System, software/architecture	7xxx	1.74
Test definition/execution	8xxx	2.76
Other	9xxx	4.71

impact data, implementation, structural and integration issues. Corfield found by systematically going through Beizer's comprehensive taxonomy and error occurrence rates that the static toolset he analysed, QA C, could in its then current form detect somewhere between 17 and 27 per cent of all bugs. The uncertainty relates to tying some of Beizer's more general concepts, for example, scoping, to a specific language such as C. Given that this and other similar toolsets have yet to achieve their full potential and are also somewhat disjoint, it seems quite reasonable to expect that around 40 per cent of all errors or bugs cited in Beizer's terminology can be eliminated statically. There is some empirical evidence for this but no definitive case-histories were available at the time of writing.

In contrast, analysing the dynamically-detectable issues against one of the most sophisticated of such analysers, Safe-C, revealed that only 1.6 per cent of all bugs could be detected (i.e. around 20 times less than static issues). However, these were bugs that could not by definition be detected statically (or indeed any other way). This supports findings by Grady and Caswell (1987), for example, who found that inspections, which static screening seeks at least in part to automate, were considerably more efficient at eliminating errors than dynamic analysis.

This is really very good news, and the combination of automatable static and dynamic screening described in the first part of this section should contribute significantly to improving the safety of safety-related C systems, allowing the inspection time thus saved to be applied to improving the requirements side.

Finally, it should be noted that static screening tools find *faults* whereas dynamic screening tools find *errors*, by definition. Because of this, static tools typically find many things that are inconsistent but which are very unlikely to fail. This strongly supports the findings of Adams (1984), and Table 7.3 reflects this. Adams showed that a third of all errors only occurred about once every 5000 executable years on average. The author has always believed, however, that if something is statically detectable and therefore easily removable, but likely to fail only once in the lifetime of the galaxy, it should be removed, because that occurrence might be next week and might kill someone. If its presence is known and its implications understood, it may well be negligent in the eyes of the law to leave it (see discussion in Section 8.4.2). The reader might like to reflect on the fact that in 1987, there were two 'once in a hundred years' storms in the North Sea within three months of each other (one of which was described in more colourful detail in Chapter 1).

7.3 COMPLEXITY AND COVERAGE RESTRICTIONS FOR SAFETY-RELATED C

As was pointed out in Section 3.2, it is difficult to give concrete guidelines with the current state of metrics research for many metrics, but some studies provide workable solutions. The class of metrics most amenable to these appears to be the structural metrics rather than the token-based metrics such as those of Halstead, so recommendations for this former set only will be given.

7.3.1 Structural complexity restrictions

The two main structural metrics for which there appear to be appropriate guidelines relevant to C development are cyclomatic complexity and static path count (Section 3.2). As was pointed out earlier, demographic comparisons make the most sense, but there seems to be good evidence for limiting the absolute values as follows.

Cyclomatic complexity

Functions with a cyclomatic complexity greater than 10 should have mandatory manual inspection to determine the reason for so many decisions, unless the decisions correspond largely to the presence of case statements. Components with a cyclomatic complexity greater than around 30 should only be allowed with explicit sign-off by the development manager responsible, as such components are strongly associated with unreliability in the life cycle. Again, the presence of case statements should be taken into account.

Static path count

Functions with a static path count of more than 1000 should be subject to manual inspection, and again, only allowed with explicit sign-off.

7.3.2 Test coverage

In the absence of sufficient case history, this book currently falls short of detailed recommendations as to test strategy, for which the reader is referred to the evergreen Myers (1979) and the more modern Beizer (1990). However, it is inconceivable that a safety-related system could be released without 100 per cent statement coverage in the sense defined in Section 5.1.2. Given that many important safety-critical systems fail to achieve this, for example the Sizewell B nuclear power station control software discussed at length in Chapter 1, at least it represents a step forward, although documents such as Def Stan 00–55 go considerably further and arguably too far to achieve in one step. However, test coverage is basically an issue of budget. If a developer quoted the real cost of achieving the test coverage required of Def Stan 00–55, for example, it could reasonably be asked if the project would ever go ahead.

Perhaps the most important thing is to make sure that an adequate *test plan* exists with minimum fixed goals such as 100 per cent statement coverage, and *which mandates error frequency monitoring at all stages of testing*, to allow reliability growth models to be built to predict the likely reliability of the final product. Note that ultra-high reliability is likely only to be met by combining different kinds of measurement (Littlewood and Strigini, 1993; Littlewood, 1993). If other more stringent fixed goals cannot be met within budget (such as 75 per cent branch coverage instead of 100 per cent), this should at least be acknowledged with an estimate of risk. Perfection cannot be reached, but estimates of imperfection are good engineering practice.

7.3.3 Rationale

The discussion and reported measurements shown in Section 3.2 show that a cyclomatic complexity of around 30 and a static path count of more than around 1000 both correspond to approximately their individual 20th percentile in the demographic analyses shown in Chapter 4. Furthermore, such components can be expected to contribute a disproportionately high share of the bugs. The evidence is such that any safety-related development must have a mechanism for the detection of such modules and a formal policy for dealing with transgressors.

A plan for test coverage is an essential component of the draft safety-related standards.

7.4 ENVIRONMENTAL CONSIDERATIONS FOR SAFETY-RELATED C

The following points should be addressed:

- A validated environment should be used (Section 2.13.1). This of course may not always be possible. If it is not possible, the justification described in Section 7.1 must reflect this and *the developer should take active steps if possible to assess the quality of the implementation*, for example by running some of the tests published by Plauger (1992). If a validated environment is available and is not used in preference to a non-validated environment, this would surely not impress an auditor, much less a jury.
- If floating-point operations are allowed in the code, the floating-point behaviour of the machine should be assessed if possible, using, for example, paranoia, and zero failures reported (Section 2.13.2). In addition, safety-related development groups using floating point should exhibit understanding of the restrictions of floating-point computation from such basics as comparing numbers for equality to the more erudite problems of pathological loss of precision in certain classes of algorithm. Such a loss of precision (in that case statically detectable) was responsible for an expensive NASA shuttle problem, as referenced in Table 2.5.

7.5 THE SOFTWARE PROCESS FOR SAFETY-RELATED DEVELOPMENT

The importance of a defined and efficient process for safety-related development has been discussed at length and is at the heart of the draft safety standards discussed in

Chapter 1. It goes without saying that stringent change and configuration control, as outlined briefly in section 5.2, should be in place. From the point of view of the intrinsic quality of the code, it is of vital importance that the programming standard is maintained and seen to be maintained, and that a formalized framework for the use of dynamic reliability tools, as discussed in Section 5.1.2, is inbuilt into the test plan to guarantee the absence of the defects reported above.

7.5.1 Miscellaneous procedures

This chapter closes with a few miscellaneous procedures which suggested themselves during the text, but which did not seem to fit in anywhere else.

- The occurrence of a fault in a function should trigger a procedure to search the package for clone functions in which the same fault may have occurred, (Section 1.6.4). Clones can often be detected by studying the distributions of combinations of disparate metrics such as (cyclomatic complexity, number of extern variables, total operand count) triplets, plotted using exploratory data analysis tools such as xgobi (Swayne *et al.* 1991). In the author's experience, half an hour with this tool studying various such combinations reveals an awful lot about similar components within a package (as well as a lot of other things).
- Reusable components should be marked and made subject to more stringent quality checks given the wider implications of any failure.
- If third-party libraries are utilized for which the source code is not available, they should be included in dynamic checking using object code monitoring tools such as described in Section 5.3.5.
- All testing should be done with and without optimization turned on in the compiler and the results tested for agreement. Any disagreement should be resolved.

8

LEGAL ISSUES[1]

Anthony Garrod (with software contributions from Les Hatton)

Clyde & Co.

The reader might find it a little unusual to find a whole chapter of a book on C devoted to a discussion of the legal implications of developing software, with particular reference to the safety-related application. Its relevance is illustrated by noting that BSI (1990) includes the statement that 'Compliance with a British Standard does not of itself confer immunity from legal obligations'. It should also be recorded that the Rationale in the ANSI version of Standard C notes that legal considerations were one of the reasons that code was not produced for the run-time library. There is very little in the way of existing case law on this subject to provide guidance. However, the rapid proliferation of software in many walks of life affecting the ordinary man or woman means that this situation is unlikely to continue for much longer. Many domestic appliances, such as televisions, video recorders and even washing machines, now contain significant amounts of software. In addition, important functions in a car are now software-controlled, for example, engine ignition and braking systems, not to mention the fly-by-wire nature of modern airplanes. An extreme form of this is the European Fighter Aircraft, which can only be flown by software, such are its aerodynamics. These grant huge benefits in manoeuvrability, but with an obvious attendant risk. To this can be added the fact that the significant number of homes which have a computer is leading to a growing awareness that software fails quite often: games freeze, word processors lose words or crash and

---

[1] It is informal legal practice that case studies are known by name only if they are unique names and dates are not included.

so on, quite apart from the catalogue of typical problems discussed in Chapter 1. If the average home computer user were aware that their word processor, which has just crashed again, is likely to have been tested more thoroughly than some pieces of safety-related software,[2] they would be rightly concerned, not to say terrified.

8.1 THE NATURE OF SOFTWARE FROM A LEGAL PERSPECTIVE

There are difficulties in fitting software into traditional legal categories. One area where there has been some recent development in the law generally is in the area of intellectual property. Although software has been in use for a number of decades, it was only in 1985 that it became clear in English law, for example, that computer software was protected by the law of copyright in the same way as other literary work. This has at least one implication which tends to take people by surprise. The rights of ownership in software written by an employee vest in his or her employer, as would reasonably be expected. *However, if software is written by subcontractors (which it is in many cases) the principal does not own the software and in the absence of a formal written assignment, all the principal has is an implied licence to use the software.*

Having established that software is protected by copyright, however, it is still far from clear as to whether it is goods or a service. Note that English contract law distinguishes between *goods* and *services*, whereas the Consumer Protection Act 1987, which implements EC (European Commission) legislation, considers whether software is a *product* or not.[3] This latter issue was considered at length by Triaille (1993) in the context of whether or not software was excluded from the scope of the 25 July 1985 EC directive on liability for defective products and its application to computer programs. Of course, if software were declared a pure *service* it would be exempt. His conclusions were that although software may sometimes be the object of a service, as such it is not a service and therefore is not excluded from the scope of the EC directive. This will be expanded upon further in the discussion of contract.

So far then, it has been established that software comes under the scope of copyright law (at least in English law); it comes within the scope of the EC directive and it is sometimes a product and sometimes a service.

At this point, it is useful to define the possible points of contact between software and the law. There are basically two forms of liability, criminal and civil.

8.1.1 Criminal liability

As Lloyd and Simpson (1993) point out, criminal liability may arise through either the Trade Descriptions Act of 1968, which makes it a criminal offence to supply a false description of goods, or the Health and Safety at Work Act of 1974 and the Consumer Protection Act of 1987. Of these latter two, those parts of the Health

---

[2] Some of the larger producers of business software have literally thousands of test sites, far more than some pieces of safety-related software ever see.

[3] There is no distinction to be made between goods and product in this sense. It simply depends on which piece of legislation is being considered.

and Safety at Work Act perhaps of most relevance relate to the enactment of EC legislation concerning the ergonomics of computer equipment, although the connection is somewhat amorphous. The Consumer Protection Act 1987 relates specifically to the need for products to be safe. Lloyd and Simpson (1993) argue that this is likely to have only limited relevance to software suppliers, as, for example, if a robot arm causes damage in the event of malfunction, it is the object which causes the damage, and not its controlling software. This may seem rather bizarre to the reader, and is analogous to saying that 'I didn't hit that person, my fist did . . .'.

8.1.2 Civil liability

It is through the mechanism of civil liability that software development is most likely to be affected by the law. There are essentially three ways in which such liability can manifest itself: Contract, Negligence (Tort) and Statutory Liability. Although perhaps the most immediate concern to the safety-related developer might be liability through non-contractual means, it is useful to discuss contract first. Note also that although the discussion is based on English law,[4] mention will be made of other countries at appropriate points. For example, the points of contact with English law may well be of relevance to the USA, although, unlike English law, US law has both Federal and State laws. The paper by Lloyd and Simpson (1993) gives an excellent overview of the issues and the discussion here will reiterate some of the points made in that paper and add further supporting information, cross-referencing it with specific points made elsewhere in this book. In the absence of much related case law, the discussion will centre on how liability might arise by analogy.

8.2 CONTRACT

A contract relating to software will, in law, be classified as a contract for the supply of either goods or services. It is clear that a contract for bespoke software is a contract for services and that a contract for a system (including software) is a contract for goods. It is not clear where the line should be drawn between the two, although it is likely that packaged software, on a disk and with a manual, will be goods.

The law implies certain *conditions* and *warranties* into contracts. The implied conditions cannot be varied. Warranties can generally be varied between businessmen and women, where it is reasonable to do so (the law actually talks only about businessmen, but the policy of this book is to treat all such references equally). The implied warranties differ depending on whether what are being provided are goods or services:

- In contracts for the sale of *goods,* implied warranties relate to merchantable quality or fitness for purpose, and sale by sample, whereby a sample of the software is used to demonstrate capability.

---

[4] Even in the UK, English law is the law of England and Wales. Scotland has its own legal system, broadly similar to many of the statutes enacted. In particular, case law may be highly persuasive.

- In a contract for *services*, it is implied that the person providing the service will use reasonable skill and care.

These implied terms are easier to apply to more traditional goods and services, such as having a car repaired, than to the far more complex computer services and equipment. If the software was supplied as a bespoke service, it could reasonably be expected that the programmer would have the reasonable skill of programmers experienced in the language, writing software for the particular application and on the intended operating system and platform. One issue of interest in English legal circles at the time of writing is that of *Salvage Association vs. CAP Financial Services Ltd* (Small and Allan, 1994). In essence, CAP Financial Services Ltd contracted to supply to the Salvage Association an accounting system based on an existing relational database which would be appropriately customized. To cut a long, sad story short, the evidence showed that there was no realistic prospect that CAP would supply the required system in the time-frame required. The judge found that CAP's lack of familiarity with the proposed relational database was the key factor in failing to deliver the required system. In other words, CAP had taken on a project it was ill-equipped to perform, and by any standards the resulting system was not fit for its intended purpose. CAP had attempted to restrict liability in their contract to a nominal £25 000 and exclude all consequential losses. Applying the Unfair Contract Terms Act 1977, the judge ruled, among other things, that this limit did not apply and the plaintiff was entitled to recover most of the loss and damage it had suffered in attempting to have an accounting system installed, in this case amounting to several hundreds of thousands of pounds. The limitation of liability clause might have been enforceable if it had been more carefully worded, but only of course if the Salvage Association had agreed. CAP simply seem to have made a mess of things by virtue of insufficient experience, and no contractual shenanigans should detract from this basic fact. It is an unfortunate but frequently occurring mistake that company management generally underestimates the skill factor necessary to complete a software project successfully, often believing that the relevant skills can readily be acquired 'off the street'.

To return to the argument, when is software of merchantable quality? If a potato is rotten it is palpably not of merchantable quality, but any software user will be aware of software packages which don't work on the chosen operating system or platform, but which have operated in accordance with their published specifications on another. Such packages will be of merchantable quality, although not of use for their intended purpose. So when is software fit for its intended purpose? For this implied term to apply the purpose must be made known to the seller, either express or implied; that is:

- He or she is told and this is relied upon, or
- The purpose to which it is to be put is implied, for example if accounting software is to be sold.

Further, in any contract, the buyer places reliance upon the seller's skill and judgement. It is therefore important in the contract to state the specific requirements for the software and to provide for testing software against those agreed specifications before being obliged to pay for it.

It has already been mentioned that these implied terms may be excluded to the extent that it is reasonable. As is well known, it is most common in software contracts to purport to replace statutory implied warranties, in particular, fitness for purpose and merchantable quality, with a contractual warranty such as 'The software will operate substantially in accordance with its published specification for a period of 90 days and that if it fails to do so, the customer will receive free maintenance and support'. It is also equally common to exclude or limit liability, e.g. limit liability for 'direct' losses to the amount that has been paid or a fixed sum and to exclude liability for indirect or consequential losses.

The Unfair Contract Terms Act 1977 provides that, between businessmen or women dealing on standard terms, these implied warranties may be excluded, and liability limited, to the extent that it is reasonable. What is reasonable depends on a number of factors, including the parties' respective bargaining power, whether the exclusions were brought to the other's attention, and whether any consideration was given for the lesser liability.

Although non-lawyers think of damages in terms of direct and indirect losses, this may be misleading. Courts will award damages for losses which were foreseeable by the parties at the time the contract was entered into and will, for instance, award damages for loss of profit (which are often considered as indirect or consequential losses) where these have been suffered, and where foreseeable. Therefore, if it is desired to exclude specific sorts of loss or damage the contract should say so. It should not be forgotten that exclusion and limitation clauses are construed against the person seeking to rely upon them, and if they are in any way ambiguous or unclear, reliance cannot be placed upon them.

8.2.1 Acceptance/rejection

It is in both parties' interests that they should discuss the levels of skill and expertise that are expected and required, and that the parties agree criteria against which the function and performance of the software can be measured leading to acceptance tests, the passing of which will trigger payment. In law, the purchaser has a right to reject goods not in conformity with the contract until he or she has accepted them. The purchaser is only deemed to accept goods:

- When he or she says so, or
- When he or she does some act in relation to the goods which is inconsistent with the seller's ownership—whatever that means. For example, if software is supplied and run for the purpose of testing, is this an act that is inconsistent with the owner's rights?

It is equally important to agree on the consequences of passing or failing the acceptance tests. One consequence of passing a test is usually that it triggers payment. However, it should be made clear that the purchaser has a right to reject software at any time until it has passed acceptance tests. In the case of Salvage Association vs. CAP Financial Services reported above, one of the key issues was the fact that the software had never got as far as acceptance testing, and on a strict interpretation of the limitation of liability clause, liability was not limited. In yet another case, that of *Saphena Computing vs. Allied Collection Agencies Ltd*, it was held that

> Just as no software developer can reasonably expect a buyer to tell him what is required without a process of feedback and reassessment, so no buyer should expect a supplier to get his programs right first time.

In other words, it is not of itself a breach of contract to deliver software in the first instance with a defect in it.

8.2.2 Licensing issues

Because intellectual property rights remain vested in the supplier in general, all that the purchaser actually acquires is a right to use it. There are particular contractual problems to be overcome in protecting the purchaser's rights, which have considerable commercial importance:

- Who has the right to use the software? Most large companies have many associated companies: is only the one company or is the whole group permitted to use the software?
- Is the purpose for which the software can be used restricted?
- It is common for software to be licensed for use on a particular machine. Circumstances such as if that machine goes down or if it is desired to migrate the software on to another machine, either of the same make and type or on to a completely different machine, must be addressed.
- At a time when all vendors are selling 'open systems', whether or not the application software works on a range of open systems must be considered. If so, is this warranted in the contract?

A recent amendment to the English Copyright, Designs and Patents Act 1988 permits a lawful user of software to copy or adapt it. This includes arranging, altering or translating a program where it is necessary for its lawful use, and such adaptation may include error correction. However, the vendor has the right to exclude the user's right to modify the software and, in any event, if the software is modified without such agreement, the vendor is unlikely to maintain the software within the warranty or within the maintenance terms. The same modification to the English Copyright, Designs and Patents Act also, to a limited extent, permits the user to reverse compile software and to be able to create an interface to another independent program.

8.2.3 Escrow

Where the user has spent a significant amount of money on acquiring software, particularly bespoke software, he or she should require the source code. It is understandable that the supplier be reluctant to release source code to software, and an increasingly frequently taken route is for the source code to be held by a third party in *escrow*. Under the escrow agreement, the source code is usually only released to the user upon the occurrence of certain events, such as the insolvency or failure of the supplier to maintain the software. Unfortunately, in the authors' experience, this is unlikely to be of any use, for the following frequently encountered reasons:

- As was intimated in the discussion of the Carnegie-Mellon software maturity model in Section 1.2.1, owing to deficiencies in change and configuration control procedures, many developers are unable, at least at the first attempt, to actually supply all the source code necessary to remake an application.[5] Hence the source code supplied under escrow could be inadvertently useless.
- One of the central points of this book is that rather strict rules must be adhered to in order to make an application truly portable. Not everybody succeeds in this endeavour and so, at the very least, a complete history of the compiler and system versions and examples of making the system from the source should be registered along with the source code.

The supplier should be under an obligation to demonstrate that the escrow version can indeed be used to remake the executable code when the escrow facility is first set up and also to keep it up to date, preferably annually if the purchaser so wishes, demonstrating the continuing ability to remake the executable correctly. There should be a further obligation to provide documentation and notes to the source code, and most importantly regression testing suites, such that a reasonably competent programmer, familiar with the language, would be able to remake the executable *and demonstrate that it passed its test suites*. Before suppliers start complaining about this to the publisher, it is in everybody's interests for escrow source to be fit for its purpose, and if this costs a little more to provide, then the purchaser should be prepared to contribute for peace of mind. Note that escrow agreements are specifically referenced by Section 4.4.7 of the Supplier's Guide of ISO 9001.

8.2.4 Reducing risks

In many respects, waiting until acceptance testing to see if software is in accordance with the contract is leaving matters too late. If the software passes the tests, it is not necessarily any guarantee that it will be easy to maintain, expand or modify as needs and requirements develop. If it fails the acceptance test, the purchaser may well be in a position where he or she cannot afford to reject the software because there is no other practical solution. It is frequently too late to go elsewhere.

Many purchasers are addressing these problems by moving towards quality certification.[6] The point has already been made that it is cheapest to correct faults in software at the development stage—it is 10 times more costly to fix an error when the software is compiled, and 100 times more costly when the software has been released. You can't test quality into software. As a result, it is now more common to require suppliers to be accredited to BS 5750 (ISO 9000). This, however,

---

[5] LH has frequently encountered this when doing source code audits in which the code is sent *off site*. On one particular occasion, after three separate unsuccessful attempts to send all the required source code, the audit had to be done *on site*. It is rare to get all that is required at the first attempt, and on the rare occasions when it happens, it creates an excellent impression with the auditor!

[6] The jargon is that the purchaser is *certified* by an *accredited* body. Getting this mixed up may invite a certain amount of grumpiness from the auditor.

is only a step towards quality software, in that these requirements address how the supplier operates its business—they do not address the process of developing software or the quality of the software itself. There are, however, moves to remedy this, from initiatives such as that described in Section 1.2, whereby software shall be free of statically-detectable faults, to producing strict validation suites for appropriate software, such as accounting packages.

The inevitable effect of this move towards quality will be to narrow the field of potential suppliers. If a supplier is unable to meet the standards, it probably will not get past the initial stages of tendering. Since the big spenders on information technology are public bodies and large corporations and it is these groups who are most likely to develop the requirements for quality assurance, it is in the interest of all suppliers to ensure that they keep abreast of these developments, simply to be able to compete in the future. One initiative, which has already started in some companies is to have software audited during development by an independent body to check for potential problems, even when the software developer has already successfully been certified to ISO 9001.

8.3 NEGLIGENCE (TORT)

Negligence is 'conduct falling below the requisite standard to protect others against unreasonable risks of harm'.

Everybody has obligations to third parties. In England, in common with other countries, the law of *tort* deals with those relationships which fall outside the law of contract, and the area of tort most relevant to software is negligence. This does not mean to say that in either business or private lives people are strictly liable, i.e. liable without fault, for the consequences of all of their actions. This is covered by the area of statutory liability, to be discussed shortly. On the other hand, it would be expected that manufacturers of defective products, including defective software, have some liability for damage caused to consumers.

Tests have been developed by the courts to achieve a sensible balance. These are:

- Is there a duty to take care?
- What is the standard of care?
- Did the defect cause the damage?
- Could the ordinary person have foreseen that this damage might result from this cause?

8.3.1 Duty of care

First and foremost, a duty of care is owed to the subject's *neighbour in law*. The 'neighbour in law' is:

> Those persons who are so closely and directly affected by the subject's act that the subject ought reasonably to have them in contemplation as being so affected when directing his or her mind to the acts or omissions which are called into question.

In English, this means those people who the subject could reasonably have foreseen being adversely affected. In 1932, the courts in England first held a manufacturer liable in negligence for a defective *product*. In the case of *Donohue vs. Stephenson*, a woman drank ginger beer from an opaque bottle which she subsequently discovered contained a decomposing snail. She was later ill, and since the court found that decomposing snails had no place in ginger beer bottles, and that the manufacturer had a duty of care to somebody who might drink its ginger beer, the unfortunate lady was awarded damages.

8.3.2 Standard of care

In tort, the standard of care will probably be that expected of a reasonably competent programmer. In areas of greater risk, the standard imposed by the court is likely to be higher. However, given that standards are currently not very high in software development, there will be an inevitable development in the law requiring higher, more professional, standards to be exercised by producers. This cannot be addressed by tort, however, and should be addressed by contract. If a higher standard is desired, it should be contractually required. To see that standards change, for example, would the reader expect the same standard of care from a doctor at the beginning of the century as now? In the UK, the British Computer Society has recently become a member of the Engineering Council, which governs standards in various engineering disciplines, and suitably qualified software developers can, as a result, be granted the Chartered Engineer[7] qualification (C. Eng.). Among other things, this has recently enabled developers to get professional indemnity insurance for probably the first time, so evidently the insurance companies believe in the screening process! This is in stark contrast to the USA, where the principle of professional malpractice requires the observance of a higher duty of care from members of recognized professions, and to which software engineering does not yet belong. As a result, a number of cases have been dismissed by the courts on the basis of a refusal to accept the concept of computer malpractice. No doubt this will be reviewed as similar initiatives to the C. Eng. qualification spread to the USA.

Another example illustrating, by way of analogy, how the law develops with respect to changing views of acceptable practice, concerns the attitude to the wearing of safety belts. If drivers or passengers were involved in an accident and suffered damage as a result of another road user's negligence, then they would be awarded damages. However, Lord Denning, in the English Court of Appeal, found that an occupant of a car involved in an accident caused by somebody else's negligence *contributed towards their own injuries by failing to wear a safety belt and the damages awarded were reduced by 20 per cent* from what they would otherwise have been. Now it is a criminal offence not to wear a safety belt in the UK. The same holds true in many other countries.

---

[7] The British Computer Society now recommend that the quality of every safety-related computer system be the responsibility of a named engineer holding this qualification or its equivalent, as was discussed in Chapter 1. The equivalent European qualification is the Eur. Ing., which is available to those British holders of the C. Eng. who have spurned a centuries-old tradition of not being able to speak any language other than English.

Table 8.1 Standard of care in maritime law and comparison with software

Case	Result	Software Analogy
T. J. Hooper (USA)	Failure to provide radio led to a storm sinking two barges, which could have been avoided.	Failure to supply tools or process preventing a known class of defect.
Lady Gwendolen (UK)	Radar was provided but no steps were taken by the employer to ensure its proper use, *even* though the employer was aware of regular transgressions from the evidence of logs which showed that ships were charging about in fog, leading to a collision.	Tools are provided to avoid well-known problems, but their use is not mandated even though evidence exists to show that they are not being used. The developers are charging around in a software fog.
Marion (UK)	Ship's anchor hit pipeline unmarked on out-of-date charts. The court ruled that it is the *owner's* duty to ensure that up-to-date charts are available and used for navigation.	Senior Management's duty is to make sure standards and other guiding documentation is up to date before the project starts and that they are used throughout the project.
	Out-of-date charts should not be edited because of the danger of giving a false impression of their being up to date.	This is directly relevant to the notion of forbidding parallel updates, as discussed in Section 5.2.2.

It is enlightening to compare the concept of standard of care as it has arisen in well-known and apparently highly relevant cases in maritime law. Three important cases have occurred: the US case of the *T. J. Hooper*, and the cases of the *Lady Gwendolen* and the *Marion*, heard in the English courts. Each case concerns the failure of process in the sense of that defined in Chapter 1, and the issues are summarized in Table 8.1 to avoid going into too much detail.

To conclude, in software development, if a regular agreed set of checks is verifiably used, the developer would be in a far better position to demonstrate it had discharged its duty of care than if not. This certainly helps justify the presence of formal quality systems, such as those based around ISO 9001.

8.3.3 Defect and damage caused

It is normally a question of fact whether or not the defect caused damage, although the development of artificial intelligence which either directly or indirectly causes damage, will further complicate the issue. If there is no factual link between the defect and the damage, there will be no liability in tort.

8.3.4 Foreseeability

This revolves around whether the reasonable man or woman could have foreseen that the particular fault could have caused the damage. There is a famous case which helps delineate this. Some years ago, there was an oil spillage in Sydney Harbour and some workmen were operating an oxyacetylene torch on a pier. The foreman, on hearing of the spillage, first instructed them to stop work but after a brief inspection told them to continue. Molten metal from the oxyacetylene torch then dripped from the pier and instead of falling into the water, landed on a piece of driftwood covered in cotton waste, which ignited and then set fire to the oil. This fire in turn destroyed the pier and ships. Not surprisingly, the Privy Council held that the ordinary man or woman would not have foreseen that that particular damage could have been caused!

This may well turn out to be an important defence in any software case, as the connection between a software fault and the failure it causes is frequently very tenuous and would have been very difficult indeed to foresee.

8.3.5 Physical loss vs. economic loss

The examples of negligence that have been discussed so far relate to physical loss or damage. However, it is likely that loss caused by defective software will be economic loss. Where economic loss, such as loss of profit, is consequent upon physical loss or damage, then the courts may award this. The case of *Martin vs. Spartan Steel Alloys* illustrates this point well. Workmen hit an electricity cable while digging the road. The local electricity board disconnected the cable, as a result of which Spartan Steel had to close down their electrical furnace, in which they were smelting stainless steel around the clock. To save the furnace they injected oxygen into the metal to enable it to be poured out and were successful in claiming damages for the metal and the loss of profit on that smelt, but were not allowed loss of profit on four other smelts which they could have carried out before the electricity was turned back on again. Lord Denning and Lord Wilberforce both said that the loss of profit on the lost smelts were equally as foreseeable as the loss of profit on the damaged metal, *but, as a matter of policy, they drew the line on economic loss consequent upon physical damage.*

The courts have awarded damages for pure economic loss caused by negligence where there has been a special relationship between the person causing the loss and the person suffering it, or where it can be demonstrated that the person suffering loss relied upon the person causing it exercising a particular skill.

There were a number of cases in England in the 1960s and 1970s which indicated that where a professional man or woman gives advice which affects the safety of buildings, machines or materials, his or her duty is to all who may suffer loss. However, in a recent case in the House of Lords, *Murphy vs. Brentwood District Council*, these cases have been largely overturned. Lord Harwich made the following points in relation to the difference between dangerous defects and defects of quality:

- When a manufacturer negligently puts into circulation a product containing a latent defect that renders it dangerous to persons or property, he or she will be liable in tort for injury to persons or damage to property which that product causes. This is particularly relevant to safety-related development, where, by definition, failures in product may be dangerous to persons or property.
- If a manufacturer produces and sells a product which is merely defective in quality, i.e. it does not cause loss or damage—even if it is valueless for the purpose for which it is intended—the manufacturer is only liable at common law under contract—the common law does not impose any such liability in tort except where there is a special relationship or proximity (as in *Headley Byrne vs.*

Heller) imposing on the manufacturer a duty of care to safeguard the user from economic loss.

- No such special relationship exists between a manufacturer and a remote user. Therefore, if you discover a defect in software which would render it unusable, e.g. because it could cause personal injury or damage, this is a defect merely in quality and no liability lies in tort.

In many respects the treatment of software in law will be similar to the treatment of information. So far, both physical loss and damage and consequential economic loss caused by software have been considered. However, the situation when software corrupts data which is used or relied upon by a third party, who as a result suffers loss, has not yet been considered.

Consider, for example, the position of accountants or auditors who negligently produce accounts. They would clearly have liability both in contract and in negligence to their client if they suffer loss. It is reasonable to ask if they are also liable to shareholders or third parties who rely upon the accounts for valuing shares in the company which they purchased. This of course is an example of economic loss.

In *Comparo Industries vs. Dickman* the court added to the list of tests for negligence that of the reasonableness or otherwise of imposing a duty of care.

In this particular case, the financial accounts were in more or less general circulation and may foreseeably have been relied upon by strangers for one of a number of different purposes which the auditors had no specific reason to anticipate. There was not sufficient proximity in the relationship between them and the person relying on the statement unless it could be shown that the auditors knew that the accounts would be communicated to the person relying on it, either as an individual or as a member of an identifiable class, specifically in connection with the particular transaction or transactions of a particular kind, and that the person would be very likely to rely on the accounts for the purposes of deciding whether to enter into a transaction. In this case, it was ruled that the auditors had no duty of care to the public at large who relied on the accounts to buy shares in the company.

Therefore, apart from the immediate client, if software is written with the knowledge that it is going to be used by another person or a group of people, e.g. a trade association, and it is known that they are going to rely upon the software for the particular purpose for which it has been developed, then there may well be liability to those third parties for economic loss. On the other hand, if software is written to be issued generally to the public at large, then, outside of the contractual liability, unless it can be shown that there is a special relationship or close proximity with the customer, the software developer is unlikely to be liable for economic loss caused by the software.

8.4 STATUTORY LIABILITY

This is liability under Act of Parliament, and in many cases has evolved from the laws of contract and tort. Many of the relevant acts in the UK arise out of its implementation of European Community legislation, for instance the Consumer

Protection Act 1987. This act creates strict liability, that is *liability without fault*, and to this extent it differs from negligence.

In essence, the act implies a statutory partnership of producer/supplier/retailer, all of whom are jointly and severally liable for damage (which means death, personal injury or damage to private property caused by a defect, i.e. a fault rendering a product less safe than it could reasonably be expected to be). Product covers most goods and materials sold, and, as was discussed earlier, software is certainly not excluded from its scope (Triaille, 1993).

8.4.1 Defences

There are a number of defences available under the Consumer Protection Act 1987. One of particular interest to software developers is that relating to state-of-the-art knowledge, also known as the *development risks defence* (Lloyd and Simpson, 1993). In essence, this states:

> ...the state of scientific and technical knowledge at the relevant time was not such that a producer of products of the same description as the product in question might be expected to have discovered the defect if it had existed in his [or her] products while they were under his [or her] control.

In essence, this means that the onus is on the producer to prove that no producer of the same products could have avoided a particular defect. So, as Lloyd and Simpson (1993) point out, such a defence would *not* cover failures in a quality system which led to a software producer releasing software containing, say, some known frequency of defects. In other words, the producer is knowingly releasing a defective product, but without negligence. It appears that this defence is applicable only if:

- The defect arises from something unforeseen at the time of production, or
- The defects are foreseeable, but that current technology does not allow the elimination of risk, for example on economic grounds.

8.4.2 Implications for software

Given the contents of this book and all the related work it references, it would be unlikely for a producer of a safety-related system to succeed in a claim that faults, statically detectable by a number of tools described here, could not economically be removed. It is equally unlikely that the producer could argue that a non-zero occurrence rate of faults during unit testing, dynamically detectable by the tools described here, was reasonable. *The state of the art is quite clear, and it seems therefore that the presence of such faults could not reasonably be argued to fall within the development risks defence.*

This[8] is a natural concomitant of the techniques described in this book and other places and also of the nature of the initiatives like the BSI debate which moved that ISO 9001 certified companies should not release products with statically-detectable

---

[8] At this point, in spite of its thousands of test sites, Microsoft Word 5.1 fell with the impenetrable message 'Bad F-line instruction' taking about one hour of corrections with it.

faults, as was described in Section 1.2.2. Even if a particular software package had a much lower than average, but nevertheless non-zero, frequency of such a fault, this would not be a defence, as was proven in the *Smedleys vs. Breed* case, which involved the presence of a caterpillar in a can of peas. A defence to the extent that only four complaints had arisen in an annual production of 3.5 million cans was rejected on the grounds that an inspection *could have found even those, if it had looked in the right place.* A further nail in the coffin of invoking the development risks defence for software is that *any defects in software are of human origin.* Software is not subject to the laws of the natural world.

One final point is worth making. Since much software is produced outside the EU and is distributed within the EU, it should be noted that *the first importer into the EU may end up with residual liability for defective products which it distributes,* and should therefore in its agreements with principals outside the EU have appropriate indemnity provision in its contract.

8.5 CONCLUSIONS

In contractual relationships, many lawyers now believe that much of the effort currently expended in drafting exclusion clauses might more profitably be spent on attempting to allocate risks reasonably, as a clause which acknowledges liability, but seeks to limit it in some reasonable fashion, is much more likely to be acceptable to a court than one which seeks totally to exclude liability, or to restrict it to derisory levels.

In considering negligence, legal precedents, notably from marine law, clearly imply that *an employer must supply proper tools, lay down proper procedures for their use, and ensure that these procedures are followed.* In this regard, many software developers today would be decisively inadequate.

For statutory liability, at least in Europe, the development risks defence is not likely to provide software developers with much protection. There remains therefore a strong incentive, especially in safety-related systems, to do the very best that the budget will allow, recognize risk explicitly in the system, and keep careful records as to exactly what was done and why. In this regard, the law, used wisely, can lead developers to much higher levels of quality in safety-related systems, to everybody's benefit.

REFERENCES

Adams, N. E. (1984), 'Optimizing preventive service of software products', *IBM J. Res. Dev.*, 28(1): 2–14.

Angele, J. and Küpper, D. (1992), 'Modula-2: an alternative to C?', *ACM SIGPLAN Notices*, 27(4): 17–26.

Austin, S. and Parkin, G. I. (1993), *Formal Methods: A Survey*, National Physical Laboratory, UK.

Bailey, D. (1993), 'Debugging C and C++ programs', in *Fortran and C in Scientific Computing*, Brunel Conference Centre, Unicom, London.

Beizer, B. (1990), *Software Testing Techniques*, 2nd edn, Van Nostrand Reinhold, New York.

Bornat, R. (1974), *Understanding and Writing Compilers*, Macmillan, Basingstoke.

BSI (1990), *Specification for a total quality assurance programme for nuclear installations*, BSI, Milton Keynes.

Bush, M. (1990), 'Improving software quality: the use of formal inspections at the Jet Propulsion Laboratory', in *Proc. 12th IEEE Int. Conf. Software Engineering*, pp. 196–9, Nice, France.

Business Week (1992), Special issue titled *Business Week/Quality 1991*, published in January 1992.

Canning, A. (1993), 'Software engineering methods for industrial safety-related applications', in F. Redmill and T. Anderson (eds.), *Directions in Safety-critical Systems*, Springer-Verlag, London.

Carré, B. A. e. a. (1990), *SPARK – The SPADE Ada Kernel*, Program Validation Ltd, April 1990.

Coleman, T. (1968), *The Railway Navvies*, Penguin Books, London.

Connolly, B. (1993), 'A Process for Preventing Software Hazards', *Hewlett-Packard J.*, June: 47–52.

Corfield, S. (1993), 'An analysis of Beizer's taxonomy of bugs against QA C', January. Private communication.

Crosby, P. (1979), *Quality is Free*, McGraw-Hill, New York.

Cullyer, W. J., Goodenough, S. J. and Wichmann, B. A. (1991), 'The choice of computer languages for use in safety-critical systems', *Software Eng. J.* March: 51–8.

Czeck, E. W. and Feldman, J. M. (1993), 'On defusing a small landmine in the type casting of pointers in the C language', *ACM SIGPLAN Notices*, 28(8): 53–6.

Darwin, I. F. (1990), *Checking C programs with lint*, O'Reilly & Associates, Sebastopol, CA.

Davey, S., Huxford, D., Liddiard, J., Powley, M. and Smith, A. (1993), 'Metrics collection in code and unit test as part of continuous quality improvement', in *EuroStar '93*, BCS, London.

DRA (1988), apply to the Defence Research Agency (DRA), a part of the Ministry of Defence (MOD), for details.

Feldman, S. I., Gay, D. M., Maimone, M. W. and Schryer, N. L. (1990), 'A Fortran-to-C converter', *Computing Science Technical Report No. 149*, AT&T Bell Labs, Murray Hill NJ.

Fenton, N. E. (1991), *Software Metrics: A Rigorous Approach*, Chapman & Hall, London.

Feuer, A. R. (1985), *Introduction to the Safe C Runtime Analyzer*, Catalytix Corporation, Boston, Mass.

Finkelstein, A. (1992), 'A software process immaturity model', *ACM Software Eng. Notes*, 17(4): 22–3.

Flynn, S. (1993), 'Code verification for TickIT', *EuroStar '93*, 438pp. London.

Forder, J., Higgins, C., McDermid, J. and Storrs, G. (1993), 'SAM – a tool to support the construction, review and evolution of safety arguments', in F. Redmill and T. Anderson (eds.), *Directions in Safety-critical Systems*, Springer-Verlag, London.

Forsyth, C., Jordan, D. and Wand, I. (1993), *A Study of High Integrity Ada: Trusted Ada Compilation*. MOD reference No. SLS31c/73-3-D, York Software Engineering and British Aerospace.

Genuchten, M. v. (1991), 'Towards a Software Factory', *Ph.D. Thesis*, Eindhoven.

Ghezzi, C. and Jazayeri, M. (1982), *Programming Language Concepts*, John Wiley & Sons, New York.

Gleick, J. (1988), *Chaos: Making a New Science*, Penguin, New York.

Grady, R. B. and Caswell, D. L. (1987), *Software Metrics: Establishing a Company Wide Program*, Prentice-Hall, Englewood Cliffs NJ.

Greeno, J. G. (1972), *The Structure of Memory and the Process of Problem Solving*, No. 37, Human Performance Centre, University of Michigan.

Gries, D. (1981), *The Science of Programming*, Springer-Verlag, New York.

Halstead, M. H. (1977), *Elements of Software Science*, Elsevier/North-Holland, New York.

Hatton, L. (1988), 'The seismic kernel system – a large-scale exercise in Fortran 77 portability', *Software Practice and Experience*, 18(4): 301–29.

—— (1993a), 'The automation of software process and product quality', in M. Ross, C. A. Brebbia, G. Staples and J. Stapleton (eds.), *Software Quality Management*, pp. 727–44, Computation Mechanics Publications/Elsevier, Southampton.

—— (1993b), 'The quality and reliability of scientific software', in M. Ross, C. A. Brebbia, G. Staples and J. Stapleton (eds.), *Software Quality Management*, pp. 519–26, Computation Mechanics Publications/Elsevier, Southampton.

—— (1994a), 'Population studies of C and Fortran using automated inspection – complexity metric distributions', in press.

—— (1994b), 'Population studies of C and Fortran using automated inspection – non-conformance and static fault rates', in press.

—— and Hopkins, T. R. (1989), 'Experiences with Flint, a software metrication tool for Fortran 77', in *Symposium on Software Tools*, Napier Polytechnic, Edinburgh.

—— and Roberts, A. (1992), 'Analysing the agreement between seismic software packages: a seismic software calibration experiment', in *62nd SEG*, Society of Exploration Geophysicists, New Orleans.

—— —— (1994), 'How accurate is scientific software?', *IEEE Trans. Software Eng.*, in press.

—— Worthington, M. H. and Makin, J. (1986), *Seismic Data Processing: Theory and Practice*, Blackwell Scientific, Oxford.

Hayes, I. (ed.) (1987), *Specification Case Studies*, Prentice-Hall, Englewood Cliffs NJ.

Hehner, E. R. C. (1984), *The Logic of Programming*, Prentice-Hall, Englewood Cliffs NJ.

Hetzel, W. (1993), 'The sorry state of software practice measurement and evaluation', in *CSR '93*, Chapman & Hall, Amsterdam.

Hewson, M. (1993), 'A sustainable TQM programme', in M. Ross, C. A. Brebbia, G. Staples and J. Stapleton', (eds.), *Software Quality Management*, pp. 85–93, Computation Mechanics Publications/Elsevier, Southampton.

Hilgard, E. R., Atkinson, R. C. and Atkinson, R. L. (1971), *Introduction to Psychology*, 5th edn, Harcourt Brace Jovanovich, New York.

Hoare, C. A. R. (1981), 'The Emperor's Old Clothes: 1980 Association of Computing Machinery Turing Award Lecture', *Comm ACM*, 24(2): 75–83.

—— (1982), *Programming is an Engineering Profession* (Notes No. PRG-27), Oxford University Programming Research Group.

—— (1985), *Communicating Sequential Processes*, Prentice-Hall, Englewood Cliffs NJ.

Humphrey, W. S. (1990), *Managing the Software Process*, Addison-Wesley, Reading MA.

—— (1993), personal communication.

—— and Sweet, W. L. (1987), 'A method for assessing the software engineering capability of contractors', SEI Technical Report, SEI-87-TR-23, September 1987.

Hunt, N. (1993), 'Testing techniques for timely delivery of reliable software', in *Software Testing, Analysis and Review '93*, Software Quality Engineering in conjunction with the British Computer Society, Jacksonville Florida.

Hutcheon, A., Jepson, B., Jordan, D., McDermid, J. and Wand, I. (1993a), *A Study of High Integrity Ada: Analysis of Ada Programs*, MOD reference No. SLS31c/73-2-D, York Software Engineering and British Aerospace.

—— —— and McDermid, J. (1993b), *A Study of High Integrity Ada: Tool Support*, MOD reference No. SLS31c/73-4-D, York Software Engineering and British Aerospace.

IEC (1986), *Software for Computers in the Safety Systems of Nuclear Power Stations*, No. 880, International Electrotechnical Commission.

—— (1991), *Software for Computers in the Application of Industrial Safety-related Systems*, No. IEC 65A WG9, International Electrotechnical Commission (drafts only: cannot yet be referenced).

IEE (1992), *Safety-related Systems*, Professional brief of the Institution of Electrical Engineers.

IEEE (1989), *Software Engineering Standards*, 3rd edn, Institute of Electrical and Electronics Engineers, New York.

—— (1992), *Standard for Software Quality Metrics Methodology*, Institute of Electrical and Electronics Engineers, New York.

Ince, D. C. (1991), 'History and industrial applications', in *Software Metrics*, pp. 277–95, Chapman & Hall, London.

—— and Tully, C. (1993), 'Software process modelling in practice', *Information and Software Technol.*, 35: 322–424.

—— Pearce, A. and Levene, A. (1993), 'Implementing quality management', in M. Ross, C. A. Brebbia, G. Staples and J. Stapleton (eds.), *Software Quality Management*, pp. 271–82, Computation Mechanics Publications/Elsevier, Southampton.

Jackson, D. (1993), 'New developments in quality management as a pre-requisite to safety', in F. Redmill and T. Anderson (eds.), *Directions in Safety-critical Systems*, pp. 257–69, Springer-Verlag, Bristol.

Jaeschke, R. (1988), *Portability and the C Language*, Hayden Books, Indianapolis.

—— (1991), *The Dictionary of Standard C*, McGraw-Hill, London.

Jones, C. B. (1986), *Systematic Software Development using VDM*, Prentice-Hall, Englewood Cliffs NJ.

Jones, D. (1993a), 'Bugs in the C Standard', *.EXE*, November: 12–15.

—— (1993b). 'The C Standard and its continuing evolution', in *Fortran and C in Scientific Computing*, pp. 214–20, Unicom, Brunel Conference Centre, London.

Kanasewich, E. R. (1981), *Time Sequence Analysis in Geophysics*, 3rd edn, The University of Alberta Press, Alberta.

Kaufer, S., Lopez, R. and Pratap, S. (1988), 'Saber-C, an interpreter-based programming environment for the C language', in *Summer USENIX Conference*, June, pp. 161–71.

Keller, T. W. (1993), 'Achieving error-free man-rated software', in *2nd International Software Testing, Analysis and Review Conference*, Monterey CA.

Kernighan, B. and Ritchie, D. (1988), *The C Programming Language*, 2nd edn, Prentice-Hall, Englewood Cliffs NJ.

—— and Pike, R. (1984), *The UNIX Programming Environment*, Prentice-Hall, Englewood Cliffs NJ.

Koenig, A. (1988), *C Traps and Pitfalls*, Addison-Wesley, Reading MA.

Lehman, M. M. (1993), 'Models in software development and evolution', in *Software Process Modelling in Practice*, Butterworth-Heinemann, London.

Leveson, N. (1986), 'Software safety: what, why and how', *ACM Computing Surveys*, **18**, (2), pp. 125–63.

—— (1993), 'Software system safety', in *STAR '93*, Monterey CA.

Libes, D. (1993), *Obfuscated C and Other Mysteries*, John Wiley & Sons, New York.

Lientz, B. P. and Swanson, E. B. (1980), *Software Maintenance Management*, Addison-Wesley, Reading MA.

Littlewood, B. (1993), 'The need for evidence from disparate sources to evaluate software safety', in F. Redmill and T. Anderson (eds.), *Directions in Safety-critical Systems*, Springer-Verlag, London.

—— and Strigini, L. (1993), 'Validation of ultra-high dependability for software-based systems', *Comm ACM*, 36(11): 69–80.

—— and Strigini, L. (1992a), 'The risks of software', *Scientific American*, November: 38–43.

Lloyd, I. J. and Simpson, M. J. (1993), 'Legal aspects of software quality', in M. Ross, C. A. Brebbia, G. Staples and J. Stapleton (eds.), *Software Quality Management*, pp. 247–67, Computation Mechanics Publications/Elsevier, Southampton.

McCabe, T. A. (1976), 'A complexity measure', *IEEE Trans. Software Eng.*, SE-2(4): 308–20.

McIlroy, M. D. and Hunt, J. W. (1976), 'An algorithm for differential file comparison', *Computing Science Technical Report, No. 41*, Bell Labs.

Martin, J. (1977), *Computer Data-Base Organization*, 2nd edn, Prentice-Hall, Englewood Cliffs NJ.

Mathews, J. (1993), 'Totaled Quality Management', *Washington Post*, 6 June, pp. H1, H16.

Mead, C. and Conway, L. (1980), *Introduction to VLSI Systems*, Addison-Wesley, Reading MA.

Miller, G. A. (1957), The magical number 7 plus or minus two: some limits on our capacity for processing information, *Psychological Rev.*, 63: 81–97.

MOD (1991), *The procurement of safety-critical software in defence equipment: Part 1 requirements*, Ministry of Defence, Glasgow.

Mody, R. P. (1992), 'Is Programming an Art?', *ACM Software Eng. Notes*, 17(4): 19–20.

Moller, K.-H. (1993), 'An empirical investigation of software fault distribution', in *CSR '93*, Chapman & Hall, Amsterdam.

Myers, G. J. (1979), *The Art of Software Testing*, John Wiley & Sons, New York.

Naur, P. (ed.) (1963), 'Report on the Algorithmic Language ALGOL 60', *J. ACM*, 6(1): 1–17.

Nejmeh, B. A. (1988), 'NPATH: a measure of execution path complexity and its applications', *Comm. ACM*, 31(2): 188–200.

Neumann, P. G. (1993), 'Risks to the public in computers and related systems', *Comm. ACM Software Eng. Notes*, a regular column appearing in each issue.

O'Carroll, M. (1993), 'C++ language overview', in *Fortran and C in Scientific Computing*, Unicom, Brunel Conference Centre, London.

Oram, A. and Talbott, S. (1991), *Managing Projects with make*, O'Reilly & Associates, Sebastopol CA.

Plauger, P. J. (1992), *The Standard C Library*, Prentice-Hall, Englewood Cliffs NJ.

—— (1993), 'Standard C: Floating Point Extensions', *The C User's Journal*, September: 10–19.

Plum, T. (1989), *C Programming Guidelines*, 2nd edn, Plum Hall, Cardiff NJ.

Pylyshyn, Z. W., Bledsoe, W. W., Feigenbaum, E. A., Newell, A., Nilsson, N., Reddy, D. R., Rosenfeld, A., Winograd, T. and Winston, P. (1983), 'Artificial intelligence', in B. W. Arden (ed.), *What can be Automated? The COSERS Study*, MIT Press, Cambridge MA.

Rackham, N. (1988), *SPIN Selling*, McGraw-Hill, New York.

RIA (1991), *Safety-related Software for Railway Signalling (Consultative Document)*. BRB/LU Ltd./RIA Technical Specification No. 23:91, Railway Industry Association.

Rider, G. (1993), 'Fortran 90/HPF Components For Sale', *Fortran Source – Lahey Computer Systems Inc.*, May: 8.

Robinson, E. A. and Treitel, S. (1980), *Geophysical Signal Analysis*, Prentice-Hall, Englewood Cliffs NJ.

RSRE (1988), apply to the Defence Research Agency (DRA), a part of the Ministry of Defence (MOD), for details.

SAE (1967), *Design Analysis Procedure for Failure Modes, Effects and Criticality Analysis (FMECA)*, No. ARP 926, Society of Automotive Engineers, USA.

Saunders, D. (producer) (1986), *Formal methods in Software Engineering*, No. CP91. BBC video.

Schneidewind, N. F. (1993), 'New software quality metrics methodology standard fills measurement need', *Computer*, April: 105–6.

Schreiner, A. T. and Friedman Jr, H. G. (1985), *Introduction to Compiler Construction with Unix*, Prentice-Hall, Englewood Cliffs NJ.

Sexton, C. (1993), *C++ Pocket Book*, Butterworth-Heinemann, Oxford.

Shinskey, F. G. (1988), *Process Control Systems*, 3rd edn, McGraw-Hill, New York.

Shneiderman, B. (1980), *Software Psychology*, Winthrop Publishers, Cambridge MA.

Small, H. and Allan, G. (1994), 'Salvage Association v. CAP Financial Services Ltd', *IT Law Today*, February: 1–5.

Sommerville, I. (1984), *Software Engineering*, 2nd edn, Addison-Wesley, Wokingham.

Stiles, D. (1992), 'New improved lint', *.EXE*, May.

Stravinsky, I. (1970), *The Poetics of Music in the Form of Six Lessons*, Harvard University Press.

Stroustrup, B. (1991), *The C++ Programming Language*, 2nd edn, Addison-Wesley, Reading MA.

Swayne, D. F., Cook, D. and Buja, A. (1991), *User's Manual for XGobi, a Dynamic Graphics Program for Data Analysis implemented in the X Window System*, Technical Memorandum, Bellcore.

Thom, R. (1975), *Structural Stability and Morphogenesis*, Benjamin Cummings, Reading MA.

Thompson, K. (1991), *A Method for Assessing Organisational Software Development Capability*, Institute of Software Engineering, Belfast.

TickIT (1992), *Guide to Software Quality Management System Construction and Certification, UK.* Department of Trade and Industry, **2.0**, 28 Feb., 1992.

Triaille, J.-P. (1993), 'The EEC directive of July 25, 1985 on liability for defective products and its application to computer programs', *The Computer Law and Security Report*, 9: 214–26.

Unigram (1992), *Unix Users in the U.K.*, Unigram Products, London.

Vesely, W. E. (1981), *Fault Tree Handbook*, No. NUREG-0942, Division of System Safety Office of Nuclear Reactor Regulation, US Nuclear Regulatory Commission, Washington DC.

Wallis, P. J. L. (1982), *Portable Programming*, Macmillan, London.

Warnier, J. D. (1974), *Precis de logique informatique: les procedures de traitement et leurs données*, H.E. Stenfert Kroesse, Leiden.

Watt, D. A., Wichmann, B. A. and Findlay, W. (1987), *Ada Language and Methodology*, Prentice-Hall, Englewood Cliffs NJ.

Whitehead, N. (1993), 'Using CASE to maintain Fortran code and move forward to C & C++', in *Fortran and C in Scientific Computing*, Unicom: Brunel Conference Centre, London.

Whitgift, D. (1991), *Methods and Tools for Software Configuration Management*, John Wiley & Sons, Chichester.

Wiener, N. (1949), *Extrapolation, Interpolation and Smoothing of Stationary Time Series*, MIT Press, Cambridge MA.

Yourdon, E. (1992), *Decline and Fall of the American Programmer*, Prentice-Hall, Englewood Cliffs NJ.

INDEX

a = a + 1, 178
absolute standard, 126, 130
acceptance testing, 210, 212
accidental transposition, 6
actions (truth-table), 161, 165
actual complexity, 86, 105
Ada, 5, 45, 67, 73, 78, 127, 171, 172, 173, 175, 177, 180, 187
adaptive maintenance, 107
Algol, 68, 190
ANSI, 42, 78, 206
ANSI X3.159-1989, 39
ANSI-compliant, 82
Appendix F, 44, 45, 146
arithmetic overflow, 151
array bound violation, 150, 151
array notation, 74
array subscripts, 73
assembly language, 172
assert, 66
Australian Commonwealth Bank, 5
automated code audit, 20
automatic speech perception, 104

Backus-Naur Form, 182
Bank of America, 5
bit-fields, 199
Boolean algebra, 157
British Standards Institute (BSI), 27, 82
build control, 139
butterfly effect, 6

C user's journal, 174
C++, 38, 43, 73, 77, 79, 98, 116, 127, 129, 154, 172, 175, 179, 183, 189, 190
calibration package, 102, 120
cancellation, 85
Capability Maturity Model (CMM), 19, 20, 22, 23, 24, 25, 30, 127, 128, 135, 141
case law, 10
casting, 40, 186, 200

causal analysis, 7
Chartered Engineer (C.Eng.), 214
chunking, 103
CICS, 156
civil liability, 208
class system, 98, 191
clones, 37, 205
COBOL, 5
code inspections, 18, 141, 187
Communicating Sequential Processes (CSP), 92, 169
commutativity, 72
compiler stability, 170
completeness, 161, 196
complex instruction set computer (CISC), 10
complexity, 9, 31, 58, 87, 98, 124, 129, 131, 147, 183, 191
complexity limiting, 103, 119, 122, 178
complexity screening, 109
compound literals, 43
concurrent systems, 92
conditions (legal definition), 208
configuration management, 20, 29, 137, 138, 139, 212
constraint, 41
constraint violation, 45, 128, 129
constructors, 191
contract (law of), 11, 214
Control Data, 6
conversions, 41
core dump, 149
corrective maintenance, 107
correctness proof, 157
criminal liability, 207
cross-compiler, 83
cubit, 13
cyclomatic complexity, 93, 96, 97, 119, 121, 122, 148, 203, 204

Danish proposal, 42
Darlington Nuclear Reactor, 18
data flow, 106

Further titles in this Series

Related titles are available in McGraw-Hill's International Software Quality Assurance Series